ISBN 0-8373-1930-7

C-1930   CAREER EXAMINATION SERIES

*This is your
PASSBOOK® for...*

Senior Library Clerk

Test Preparation Study Guide

Questions & Answers

Clifton Park - Halfmoon Public Library
475 Moe Road
Clifton Park, New York 12065

NLC

NATIONAL LEARNING CORPORATION

Copyright © 2013 by

National Learning Corporation

212 Michael Drive, Syosset, New York 11791

All rights reserved, including the right of reproduction in whole or in part, in any form or by any means, electronic or mechanical, including photocopying, recording, or by any information storage and retrieval system, without permission in writing from the Publisher.

(516) 921-8888
(800) 645-6337
FAX: (516) 921-8743
www.passbooks.com
sales @ passbooks.com
info @ passbooks.com

PRINTED IN THE UNITED STATES OF AMERICA

PASSBOOK®
NOTICE

This book is SOLELY intended for, is sold ONLY to, and its use is RESTRICTED to *individual*, bona fide applicants or candidates who qualify by virtue of having seriously filed applications for appropriate license, certificate, professional and/or promotional advancement, higher school matriculation, scholarship, or other legitimate requirements of educational and/or governmental authorities.

This book is NOT intended for use, class instruction, tutoring, training, duplication, copying, reprinting, excerption, or adaptation, etc., by:

(1) Other publishers

(2) Proprietors and/or Instructors of "Coaching" and/or Preparatory Courses

(3) Personnel and/or Training Divisions of commercial, industrial, and governmental organizations

(4) Schools, colleges, or universities and/or their departments and staffs, including teachers and other personnel

(5) Testing Agencies or Bureaus

(6) Study groups which seek by the purchase of a single volume to copy and/or duplicate and/or adapt this material for use by the group as a whole without having purchased individual volumes for each of the members of the group

(7) Et al.

Such persons would be in violation of appropriate Federal and State statutes.

PROVISION OF LICENSING AGREEMENTS. — Recognized educational commercial, industrial, and governmental institutions and organizations, and others legitimately engaged in educational pursuits, including training, testing, and measurement activities, may address a request for a licensing agreement to the copyright owners, who will determine whether, and under what conditions, including fees and charges, the materials in this book may be used by them. In other words, a licensing facility exists for the legitimate use of the material in this book on other than an individual basis. However, it is asseverated and affirmed here that the material in this book *CANNOT* be used without the receipt of the express permission of such a licensing agreement from the Publishers.

NATIONAL LEARNING CORPORATION
212 Michael Drive
Syosset, New York 11791

Inquiries re licensing agreements should be addressed to:
The President
National Learning Corporation
212 Michael Drive
Syosset, New York 11791

PASSBOOK® SERIES

THE *PASSBOOK® SERIES* has been created to prepare applicants and candidates for the ultimate academic battlefield — the examination room.

At some time in our lives, each and every one of us may be required to take an examination — for validation, matriculation, admission, qualification, registration, certification, or licensure.

Based on the assumption that every applicant or candidate has met the basic formal educational standards, has taken the required number of courses, and read the necessary texts, the *PASSBOOK® SERIES* furnishes the one special preparation which may assure passing with confidence, instead of failing with insecurity. Examination questions — together with answers — are furnished as the basic vehicle for study so that the mysteries of the examination and its compounding difficulties may be eliminated or diminished by a sure method.

This book is meant to help you pass your examination provided that you qualify and are serious in your objective.

The entire field is reviewed through the huge store of content information which is succinctly presented through a provocative and challenging approach — the question-and-answer method.

A climate of success is established by furnishing the correct answers at the end of each test.

You soon learn to recognize types of questions, forms of questions, and patterns of questioning. You may even begin to anticipate expected outcomes.

You perceive that many questions are repeated or adapted so that you can gain acute insights, which may enable you to score many sure points.

You learn how to confront new questions, or types of questions, and to attack them confidently and work out the correct answers.

You note objectives and emphases, and recognize pitfalls and dangers, so that you may make positive educational adjustments.

Moreover, you are kept fully informed in relation to new concepts, methods, practices, and directions in the field.

You discover that you are actually taking the examination all the time: you are preparing for the examination by "taking" an examination, not by reading extraneous and/or supererogatory textbooks.

In short, this PASSBOOK®, used directedly, should be an important factor in helping you to pass your test.

SENIOR LIBRARY CLERK

DUTIES

Supervises or independently performs difficult clerical work in the circulation, reference, cataloging or administrative department of a library. Assists a librarian in charging and discharging books, registering borrowers, collecting fines, reserving books and answering routine questions concerning the library's collections and services while working at the circulation and reference desks. Prepares overdue notices and catalog cards; files shelf list cards; oversees and revises the pasting and lettering of new books; prepares books and magazines for the bindery. Maintains records and assists in the preparation of bills, purchase orders, payrolls and statistical reports for the main and branch libraries. Performs related work as required.

SCOPE OF THE EXAMINATION

The written test will be designed to test for knowledge, skills, and/or abilities in such areas as:
1. Library terminology and practices;
2. Office practices;
3. Understanding and interpreting written material;
4. Supervision;
5. English usage; and
6. Record keeping and data interpretation.

HOW TO TAKE A TEST

I. YOU MUST PASS AN EXAMINATION

A. *WHAT EVERY CANDIDATE SHOULD KNOW*

Examination applicants often ask us for help in preparing for the written test. What can I study in advance? What kinds of questions will be asked? How will the test be given? How will the papers be graded?

As an applicant for a civil service examination, you may be wondering about some of these things. Our purpose here is to suggest effective methods of advance study and to describe civil service examinations.

Your chances for success on this examination can be increased if you know how to prepare. Those "pre-examination jitters" can be reduced if you know what to expect. You can even experience an adventure in good citizenship if you know why civil service exams are given.

B. *WHY ARE CIVIL SERVICE EXAMINATIONS GIVEN?*

Civil service examinations are important to you in two ways. As a citizen, you want public jobs filled by employees who know how to do their work. As a job seeker, you want a fair chance to compete for that job on an equal footing with other candidates. The best-known means of accomplishing this two-fold goal is the competitive examination.

Exams are widely publicized throughout the nation. They may be administered for jobs in federal, state, city, municipal, town or village governments or agencies.

Any citizen may apply, with some limitations, such as the age or residence of applicants. Your experience and education may be reviewed to see whether you meet the requirements for the particular examination. When these requirements exist, they are reasonable and applied consistently to all applicants. Thus, a competitive examination may cause you some uneasiness now, but it is your privilege and safeguard.

C. *HOW ARE CIVIL SERVICE EXAMS DEVELOPED?*

Examinations are carefully written by trained technicians who are specialists in the field known as "psychological measurement," in consultation with recognized authorities in the field of work that the test will cover. These experts recommend the subject matter areas or skills to be tested; only those knowledges or skills important to your success on the job are included. The most reliable books and source materials available are used as references. Together, the experts and technicians judge the difficulty level of the questions.

Test technicians know how to phrase questions so that the problem is clearly stated. Their ethics do not permit "trick" or "catch" questions. Questions may have been tried out on sample groups, or subjected to statistical analysis, to determine their usefulness.

Written tests are often used in combination with performance tests, ratings of training and experience, and oral interviews. All of these measures combine to form the best-known means of finding the right person for the right job.

II. HOW TO PASS THE WRITTEN TEST

A. NATURE OF THE EXAMINATION

To prepare intelligently for civil service examinations, you should know how they differ from school examinations you have taken. In school you were assigned certain definite pages to read or subjects to cover. The examination questions were quite detailed and usually emphasized memory. Civil service exams, on the other hand, try to discover your present ability to perform the duties of a position, plus your potentiality to learn these duties. In other words, a civil service exam attempts to predict how successful you will be. Questions cover such a broad area that they cannot be as minute and detailed as school exam questions.

In the public service similar kinds of work, or positions, are grouped together in one "class." This process is known as *position-classification*. All the positions in a class are paid according to the salary range for that class. One class title covers all of these positions, and they are all tested by the same examination.

B. FOUR BASIC STEPS

1) Study the announcement

How, then, can you know what subjects to study? Our best answer is: "Learn as much as possible about the class of positions for which you've applied." The exam will test the knowledge, skills and abilities needed to do the work.

Your most valuable source of information about the position you want is the official exam announcement. This announcement lists the training and experience qualifications. Check these standards and apply only if you come reasonably close to meeting them.

The brief description of the position in the examination announcement offers some clues to the subjects which will be tested. Think about the job itself. Review the duties in your mind. Can you perform them, or are there some in which you are rusty? Fill in the blank spots in your preparation.

Many jurisdictions preview the written test in the exam announcement by including a section called "Knowledge and Abilities Required," "Scope of the Examination," or some similar heading. Here you will find out specifically what fields will be tested.

2) Review your own background

Once you learn in general what the position is all about, and what you need to know to do the work, ask yourself which subjects you already know fairly well and which need improvement. You may wonder whether to concentrate on improving your strong areas or on building some background in your fields of weakness. When the announcement has specified "some knowledge" or "considerable knowledge," or has used adjectives like "beginning principles of..." or "advanced ... methods," you can get a clue as to the number and difficulty of questions to be asked in any given field. More questions, and hence broader coverage, would be included for those subjects which are more important in the work. Now weigh your strengths and weaknesses against the job requirements and prepare accordingly.

3) Determine the level of the position

Another way to tell how intensively you should prepare is to understand the level of the job for which you are applying. Is it the entering level? In other words, is this the position in which beginners in a field of work are hired? Or is it an intermediate or advanced level? Sometimes this is indicated by such words as "Junior" or "Senior" in the class title. Other jurisdictions use Roman numerals to designate the level – Clerk I, Clerk II, for example. The word "Supervisor" sometimes appears in the title. If the level is not indicated by the title, check the description of duties. Will you be working under very close supervision, or will you have responsibility for independent decisions in this work?

4) Choose appropriate study materials

Now that you know the subjects to be examined and the relative amount of each subject to be covered, you can choose suitable study materials. For beginning level jobs, or even advanced ones, if you have a pronounced weakness in some aspect of your training, read a modern, standard textbook in that field. Be sure it is up to date and has general coverage. Such books are normally available at your library, and the librarian will be glad to help you locate one. For entry-level positions, questions of appropriate difficulty are chosen – neither highly advanced questions, nor those too simple. Such questions require careful thought but not advanced training.

If the position for which you are applying is technical or advanced, you will read more advanced, specialized material. If you are already familiar with the basic principles of your field, elementary textbooks would waste your time. Concentrate on advanced textbooks and technical periodicals. Think through the concepts and review difficult problems in your field.

These are all general sources. You can get more ideas on your own initiative, following these leads. For example, training manuals and publications of the government agency which employs workers in your field can be useful, particularly for technical and professional positions. A letter or visit to the government department involved may result in more specific study suggestions, and certainly will provide you with a more definite idea of the exact nature of the position you are seeking.

III. KINDS OF TESTS

Tests are used for purposes other than measuring knowledge and ability to perform specified duties. For some positions, it is equally important to test ability to make adjustments to new situations or to profit from training. In others, basic mental abilities not dependent on information are essential. Questions which test these things may not appear as pertinent to the duties of the position as those which test for knowledge and information. Yet they are often highly important parts of a fair examination. For very general questions, it is almost impossible to help you direct your study efforts. What we can do is to point out some of the more common of these general abilities needed in public service positions and describe some typical questions.

1) General information

Broad, general information has been found useful for predicting job success in some kinds of work. This is tested in a variety of ways, from vocabulary lists to questions about current events. Basic background in some field of work, such as sociology or economics, may be sampled in a group of questions. Often these are principles which have become familiar to most persons through exposure rather than through formal training. It is difficult to advise you how to study for these questions; being alert to the world around you is our best suggestion.

2) Verbal ability

An example of an ability needed in many positions is verbal or language ability. Verbal ability is, in brief, the ability to use and understand words. Vocabulary and grammar tests are typical measures of this ability. Reading comprehension or paragraph interpretation questions are common in many kinds of civil service tests. You are given a paragraph of written material and asked to find its central meaning.

3) Numerical ability

Number skills can be tested by the familiar arithmetic problem, by checking paired lists of numbers to see which are alike and which are different, or by interpreting charts and graphs. In the latter test, a graph may be printed in the test booklet which you are asked to use as the basis for answering questions.

4) Observation

A popular test for law-enforcement positions is the observation test. A picture is shown to you for several minutes, then taken away. Questions about the picture test your ability to observe both details and larger elements.

5) Following directions

In many positions in the public service, the employee must be able to carry out written instructions dependably and accurately. You may be given a chart with several columns, each column listing a variety of information. The questions require you to carry out directions involving the information given in the chart.

6) Skills and aptitudes

Performance tests effectively measure some manual skills and aptitudes. When the skill is one in which you are trained, such as typing or shorthand, you can practice. These tests are often very much like those given in business school or high school courses. For many of the other skills and aptitudes, however, no short-time preparation can be made. Skills and abilities natural to you or that you have developed throughout your lifetime are being tested.

Many of the general questions just described provide all the data needed to answer the questions and ask you to use your reasoning ability to find the answers. Your best preparation for these tests, as well as for tests of facts and ideas, is to be at your physical and mental best. You, no doubt, have your own methods of getting into an exam-taking mood and keeping "in shape." The next section lists some ideas on this subject.

IV. KINDS OF QUESTIONS

Only rarely is the "essay" question, which you answer in narrative form, used in civil service tests. Civil service tests are usually of the short-answer type. Full instructions for answering these questions will be given to you at the examination. But in case this is your first experience with short-answer questions and separate answer sheets, here is what you need to know:

1) Multiple-choice Questions

Most popular of the short-answer questions is the "multiple choice" or "best answer" question. It can be used, for example, to test for factual knowledge, ability to solve problems or judgment in meeting situations found at work.

A multiple-choice question is normally one of three types—

- It can begin with an incomplete statement followed by several possible endings. You are to find the one ending which *best* completes the statement, although some of the others may not be entirely wrong.
- It can also be a complete statement in the form of a question which is answered by choosing one of the statements listed.
- It can be in the form of a problem – again you select the best answer.

Here is an example of a multiple-choice question with a discussion which should give you some clues as to the method for choosing the right answer:

When an employee has a complaint about his assignment, the action which will *best* help him overcome his difficulty is to
- A. discuss his difficulty with his coworkers
- B. take the problem to the head of the organization
- C. take the problem to the person who gave him the assignment
- D. say nothing to anyone about his complaint

In answering this question, you should study each of the choices to find which is best. Consider choice "A" – Certainly an employee may discuss his complaint with fellow employees, but no change or improvement can result, and the complaint remains unresolved. Choice "B" is a poor choice since the head of the organization probably does not know what assignment you have been given, and taking your problem to him is known as "going over the head" of the supervisor. The supervisor, or person who made the assignment, is the person who can clarify it or correct any injustice. Choice "C" is, therefore, correct. To say nothing, as in choice "D," is unwise. Supervisors have and interest in knowing the problems employees are facing, and the employee is seeking a solution to his problem.

2) True/False Questions

The "true/false" or "right/wrong" form of question is sometimes used. Here a complete statement is given. Your job is to decide whether the statement is right or wrong.

SAMPLE: A person-to-person long-distance telephone call costs less than a station-to-station call to the same city.

This statement is wrong, or false, since person-to-person calls are more expensive.

This is not a complete list of all possible question forms, although most of the others are variations of these common types. You will always get complete directions for answering questions. Be sure you understand *how* to mark your answers – ask questions until you do.

V. RECORDING YOUR ANSWERS

For an examination with very few applicants, you may be told to record your answers in the test booklet itself. Separate answer sheets are much more common. If this separate answer sheet is to be scored by machine – and this is often the case – it is highly important that you mark your answers correctly in order to get credit.

An electric scoring machine is often used in civil service offices because of the speed with which papers can be scored. Machine-scored answer sheets must be marked with a pencil, which will be given to you. This pencil has a high graphite content which responds to the electric scoring machine. As a matter of fact, stray dots may register as answers, so do not let your pencil rest on the answer sheet while you are pondering the correct answer. Also, if your pencil lead breaks or is otherwise defective, ask for another.

Since the answer sheet will be dropped in a slot in the scoring machine, be careful not to bend the corners or get the paper crumpled.

The answer sheet normally has five vertical columns of numbers, with 30 numbers to a column. These numbers correspond to the question numbers in your test booklet. After each number, going across the page are four or five pairs of dotted lines. These short dotted lines have small letters or numbers above them. The first two pairs may also have a "T" or "F" above the letters. This indicates that the first two pairs only are to be used if the questions are of the true-false type. If the questions are multiple choice, disregard the "T" and "F" and pay attention only to the small letters or numbers.

Answer your questions in the manner of the sample that follows:

32. The largest city in the United States is
   A. Washington, D.C.
   B. New York City
   C. Chicago
   D. Detroit
   E. San Francisco

1) Choose the answer you think is best. (New York City is the largest, so "B" is correct.)
2) Find the row of dotted lines numbered the same as the question you are answering. (Find row number 32)
3) Find the pair of dotted lines corresponding to the answer. (Find the pair of lines under the mark "B.")
4) Make a solid black mark between the dotted lines.

VI. BEFORE THE TEST

Common sense will help you find procedures to follow to get ready for an examination. Too many of us, however, overlook these sensible measures. Indeed, nervousness and fatigue have been found to be the most serious reasons why applicants fail to do their best on civil service tests. Here is a list of reminders:

- Begin your preparation early – Don't wait until the last minute to go scurrying around for books and materials or to find out what the position is all about.
- Prepare continuously – An hour a night for a week is better than an all-night cram session. This has been definitely established. What is more, a night a

week for a month will return better dividends than crowding your study into a shorter period of time.
- Locate the place of the exam – You have been sent a notice telling you when and where to report for the examination. If the location is in a different town or otherwise unfamiliar to you, it would be well to inquire the best route and learn something about the building.
- Relax the night before the test – Allow your mind to rest. Do not study at all that night. Plan some mild recreation or diversion; then go to bed early and get a good night's sleep.
- Get up early enough to make a leisurely trip to the place for the test – This way unforeseen events, traffic snarls, unfamiliar buildings, etc. will not upset you.
- Dress comfortably – A written test is not a fashion show. You will be known by number and not by name, so wear something comfortable.
- Leave excess paraphernalia at home – Shopping bags and odd bundles will get in your way. You need bring only the items mentioned in the official notice you received; usually everything you need is provided. Do not bring reference books to the exam. They will only confuse those last minutes and be taken away from you when in the test room.
- Arrive somewhat ahead of time – If because of transportation schedules you must get there very early, bring a newspaper or magazine to take your mind off yourself while waiting.
- Locate the examination room – When you have found the proper room, you will be directed to the seat or part of the room where you will sit. Sometimes you are given a sheet of instructions to read while you are waiting. Do not fill out any forms until you are told to do so; just read them and be prepared.
- Relax and prepare to listen to the instructions
- If you have any physical problem that may keep you from doing your best, be sure to tell the test administrator. If you are sick or in poor health, you really cannot do your best on the exam. You can come back and take the test some other time.

VII. AT THE TEST

The day of the test is here and you have the test booklet in your hand. The temptation to get going is very strong. Caution! There is more to success than knowing the right answers. You must know how to identify your papers and understand variations in the type of short-answer question used in this particular examination. Follow these suggestions for maximum results from your efforts:

1) Cooperate with the monitor

The test administrator has a duty to create a situation in which you can be as much at ease as possible. He will give instructions, tell you when to begin, check to see that you are marking your answer sheet correctly, and so on. He is not there to guard you, although he will see that your competitors do not take unfair advantage. He wants to help you do your best.

2) Listen to all instructions

Don't jump the gun! Wait until you understand all directions. In most civil service tests you get more time than you need to answer the questions. So don't be in a hurry.

Read each word of instructions until you clearly understand the meaning. Study the examples, listen to all announcements and follow directions. Ask questions if you do not understand what to do.

3) Identify your papers

Civil service exams are usually identified by number only. You will be assigned a number; you must not put your name on your test papers. Be sure to copy your number correctly. Since more than one exam may be given, copy your exact examination title.

4) Plan your time

Unless you are told that a test is a "speed" or "rate of work" test, speed itself is usually not important. Time enough to answer all the questions will be provided, but this does not mean that you have all day. An overall time limit has been set. Divide the total time (in minutes) by the number of questions to determine the approximate time you have for each question.

5) Do not linger over difficult questions

If you come across a difficult question, mark it with a paper clip (useful to have along) and come back to it when you have been through the booklet. One caution if you do this – be sure to skip a number on your answer sheet as well. Check often to be sure that you have not lost your place and that you are marking in the row numbered the same as the question you are answering.

6) Read the questions

Be sure you know what the question asks! Many capable people are unsuccessful because they failed to *read* the questions correctly.

7) Answer all questions

Unless you have been instructed that a penalty will be deducted for incorrect answers, it is better to guess than to omit a question.

8) Speed tests

It is often better NOT to guess on speed tests. It has been found that on timed tests people are tempted to spend the last few seconds before time is called in marking answers at random – without even reading them – in the hope of picking up a few extra points. To discourage this practice, the instructions may warn you that your score will be "corrected" for guessing. That is, a penalty will be applied. The incorrect answers will be deducted from the correct ones, or some other penalty formula will be used.

9) Review your answers

If you finish before time is called, go back to the questions you guessed or omitted to give them further thought. Review other answers if you have time.

10) Return your test materials

If you are ready to leave before others have finished or time is called, take ALL your materials to the monitor and leave quietly. Never take any test material with you. The monitor can discover whose papers are not complete, and taking a test booklet may be grounds for disqualification.

VIII. EXAMINATION TECHNIQUES

1) Read the general instructions carefully. These are usually printed on the first page of the exam booklet. As a rule, these instructions refer to the timing of the examination; the fact that you should not start work until the signal and must stop work at a signal, etc. If there are any *special* instructions, such as a choice of questions to be answered, make sure that you note this instruction carefully.

2) When you are ready to start work on the examination, that is as soon as the signal has been given, read the instructions to each question booklet, underline any key words or phrases, such as *least, best, outline, describe* and the like. In this way you will tend to answer as requested rather than discover on reviewing your paper that you *listed without describing*, that you selected the *worst* choice rather than the *best* choice, etc.

3) If the examination is of the objective or multiple-choice type – that is, each question will also give a series of possible answers: A, B, C or D, and you are called upon to select the best answer and write the letter next to that answer on your answer paper – it is advisable to start answering each question in turn. There may be anywhere from 50 to 100 such questions in the three or four hours allotted and you can see how much time would be taken if you read through all the questions before beginning to answer any. Furthermore, if you come across a question or group of questions which you know would be difficult to answer, it would undoubtedly affect your handling of all the other questions.

4) If the examination is of the essay type and contains but a few questions, it is a moot point as to whether you should read all the questions before starting to answer any one. Of course, if you are given a choice – say five out of seven and the like – then it is essential to read all the questions so you can eliminate the two that are most difficult. If, however, you are asked to answer all the questions, there may be danger in trying to answer the easiest one first because you may find that you will spend too much time on it. The best technique is to answer the first question, then proceed to the second, etc.

5) Time your answers. Before the exam begins, write down the time it started, then add the time allowed for the examination and write down the time it must be completed, then divide the time available somewhat as follows:
   - If 3-1/2 hours are allowed, that would be 210 minutes. If you have 80 objective-type questions, that would be an average of 2-1/2 minutes per question. Allow yourself no more than 2 minutes per question, or a total of 160 minutes, which will permit about 50 minutes to review.
   - If for the time allotment of 210 minutes there are 7 essay questions to answer, that would average about 30 minutes a question. Give yourself only 25 minutes per question so that you have about 35 minutes to review.

6) The most important instruction is to *read each question* and make sure you know what is wanted. The second most important instruction is to *time yourself properly* so that you answer every question. The third most

important instruction is to *answer every question*. Guess if you have to but include something for each question. Remember that you will receive no credit for a blank and will probably receive some credit if you write something in answer to an essay question. If you guess a letter – say "B" for a multiple-choice question – you may have guessed right. If you leave a blank as an answer to a multiple-choice question, the examiners may respect your feelings but it will not add a point to your score. Some exams may penalize you for wrong answers, so in such cases *only*, you may not want to guess unless you have some basis for your answer.

7) Suggestions
   a. Objective-type questions
      1. Examine the question booklet for proper sequence of pages and questions
      2. Read all instructions carefully
      3. Skip any question which seems too difficult; return to it after all other questions have been answered
      4. Apportion your time properly; do not spend too much time on any single question or group of questions
      5. Note and underline key words – *all, most, fewest, least, best, worst, same, opposite,* etc.
      6. Pay particular attention to negatives
      7. Note unusual option, e.g., unduly long, short, complex, different or similar in content to the body of the question
      8. Observe the use of "hedging" words – *probably, may, most likely,* etc.
      9. Make sure that your answer is put next to the same number as the question
      10. Do not second-guess unless you have good reason to believe the second answer is definitely more correct
      11. Cross out original answer if you decide another answer is more accurate; do not erase until you are ready to hand your paper in
      12. Answer all questions; guess unless instructed otherwise
      13. Leave time for review

   b. Essay questions
      1. Read each question carefully
      2. Determine exactly what is wanted. Underline key words or phrases.
      3. Decide on outline or paragraph answer
      4. Include many different points and elements unless asked to develop any one or two points or elements
      5. Show impartiality by giving pros and cons unless directed to select one side only
      6. Make and write down any assumptions you find necessary to answer the questions
      7. Watch your English, grammar, punctuation and choice of words
      8. Time your answers; don't crowd material

8) Answering the essay question

Most essay questions can be answered by framing the specific response around several key words or ideas. Here are a few such key words or ideas:

M's: manpower, materials, methods, money, management
P's: purpose, program, policy, plan, procedure, practice, problems, pitfalls, personnel, public relations

- a. Six basic steps in handling problems:
    1. Preliminary plan and background development
    2. Collect information, data and facts
    3. Analyze and interpret information, data and facts
    4. Analyze and develop solutions as well as make recommendations
    5. Prepare report and sell recommendations
    6. Install recommendations and follow up effectiveness

- b. Pitfalls to avoid
    1. *Taking things for granted* – A statement of the situation does not necessarily imply that each of the elements is necessarily true; for example, a complaint may be invalid and biased so that all that can be taken for granted is that a complaint has been registered
    2. *Considering only one side of a situation* – Wherever possible, indicate several alternatives and then point out the reasons you selected the best one
    3. *Failing to indicate follow up* – Whenever your answer indicates action on your part, make certain that you will take proper follow-up action to see how successful your recommendations, procedures or actions turn out to be
    4. *Taking too long in answering any single question* – Remember to time your answers properly

IX. AFTER THE TEST

Scoring procedures differ in detail among civil service jurisdictions although the general principles are the same. Whether the papers are hand-scored or graded by machine we have described, they are nearly always graded by number. That is, the person who marks the paper knows only the number – never the name – of the applicant. Not until all the papers have been graded will they be matched with names. If other tests, such as training and experience or oral interview ratings have been given, scores will be combined. Different parts of the examination usually have different weights. For example, the written test might count 60 percent of the final grade, and a rating of training and experience 40 percent. In many jurisdictions, veterans will have a certain number of points added to their grades.

After the final grade has been determined, the names are placed in grade order and an eligible list is established. There are various methods for resolving ties between those who get the same final grade – probably the most common is to place first the name of the person whose application was received first. Job offers are made from the eligible list in the order the names appear on it. You will be notified of your grade and your rank as soon as all these computations have been made. This will be done as rapidly as possible.

People who are found to meet the requirements in the announcement are called "eligibles." Their names are put on a list of eligible candidates. An eligible's chances of getting a job depend on how high he stands on this list and how fast agencies are filling jobs from the list.

When a job is to be filled from a list of eligibles, the agency asks for the names of people on the list of eligibles for that job. When the civil service commission receives this request, it sends to the agency the names of the three people highest on this list. Or, if the job to be filled has specialized requirements, the office sends the agency the names of the top three persons who meet these requirements from the general list.

The appointing officer makes a choice from among the three people whose names were sent to him. If the selected person accepts the appointment, the names of the others are put back on the list to be considered for future openings.

That is the rule in hiring from all kinds of eligible lists, whether they are for typist, carpenter, chemist, or something else. For every vacancy, the appointing officer has his choice of any one of the top three eligibles on the list. This explains why the person whose name is on top of the list sometimes does not get an appointment when some of the persons lower on the list do. If the appointing officer chooses the second or third eligible, the No. 1 eligible does not get a job at once, but stays on the list until he is appointed or the list is terminated.

X. HOW TO PASS THE INTERVIEW TEST

The examination for which you applied requires an oral interview test. You have already taken the written test and you are now being called for the interview test – the final part of the formal examination.

You may think that it is not possible to prepare for an interview test and that there are no procedures to follow during an interview. Our purpose is to point out some things you can do in advance that will help you and some good rules to follow and pitfalls to avoid while you are being interviewed.

What is an interview supposed to test?

The written examination is designed to test the technical knowledge and competence of the candidate; the oral is designed to evaluate intangible qualities, not readily measured otherwise, and to establish a list showing the relative fitness of each candidate – as measured against his competitors – for the position sought. Scoring is not on the basis of "right" and "wrong," but on a sliding scale of values ranging from "not passable" to "outstanding." As a matter of fact, it is possible to achieve a relatively low score without a single "incorrect" answer because of evident weakness in the qualities being measured.

Occasionally, an examination may consist entirely of an oral test – either an individual or a group oral. In such cases, information is sought concerning the technical knowledges and abilities of the candidate, since there has been no written examination for this purpose. More commonly, however, an oral test is used to supplement a written examination.

Who conducts interviews?

The composition of oral boards varies among different jurisdictions. In nearly all, a representative of the personnel department serves as chairman. One of the members of the board may be a representative of the department in which the candidate would work. In some cases, "outside experts" are used, and, frequently, a businessman or some other representative of the general public is asked to serve. Labor and management or other special groups may be represented. The aim is to secure the services of experts in the appropriate field.

However the board is composed, it is a good idea (and not at all improper or unethical) to ascertain in advance of the interview who the members are and what groups they represent. When you are introduced to them, you will have some idea of their backgrounds and interests, and at least you will not stutter and stammer over their names.

What should be done before the interview?

While knowledge about the board members is useful and takes some of the surprise element out of the interview, there is other preparation which is more substantive. It *is* possible to prepare for an oral interview – in several ways:

1) Keep a copy of your application and review it carefully before the interview

This may be the only document before the oral board, and the starting point of the interview. Know what education and experience you have listed there, and the sequence and dates of all of it. Sometimes the board will ask you to review the highlights of your experience for them; you should not have to hem and haw doing it.

2) Study the class specification and the examination announcement

Usually, the oral board has one or both of these to guide them. The qualities, characteristics or knowledges required by the position sought are stated in these documents. They offer valuable clues as to the nature of the oral interview. For example, if the job involves supervisory responsibilities, the announcement will usually indicate that knowledge of modern supervisory methods and the qualifications of the candidate as a supervisor will be tested. If so, you can expect such questions, frequently in the form of a hypothetical situation which you are expected to solve. NEVER go into an oral without knowledge of the duties and responsibilities of the job you seek.

3) Think through each qualification required

Try to visualize the kind of questions you would ask if you were a board member. How well could you answer them? Try especially to appraise your own knowledge and background in each area, *measured against the job sought*, and identify any areas in which you are weak. Be critical and realistic – do not flatter yourself.

4) Do some general reading in areas in which you feel you may be weak

For example, if the job involves supervision and your past experience has NOT, some general reading in supervisory methods and practices, particularly in the field of human relations, might be useful. Do NOT study agency procedures or detailed manuals. The oral board will be testing your understanding and capacity, not your memory.

5) Get a good night's sleep and watch your general health and mental attitude

You will want a clear head at the interview. Take care of a cold or any other minor ailment, and of course, no hangovers.

What should be done on the day of the interview?

Now comes the day of the interview itself. Give yourself plenty of time to get there. Plan to arrive somewhat ahead of the scheduled time, particularly if your appointment is in the fore part of the day. If a previous candidate fails to appear, the board might be ready for you a bit early. By early afternoon an oral board is almost invariably behind schedule if there are many candidates, and you may have to wait.

Take along a book or magazine to read, or your application to review, but leave any extraneous material in the waiting room when you go in for your interview. In any event, relax and compose yourself.

The matter of dress is important. The board is forming impressions about you – from your experience, your manners, your attitude, and your appearance. Give your personal appearance careful attention. Dress your best, but not your flashiest. Choose conservative, appropriate clothing, and be sure it is immaculate. This is a business interview, and your appearance should indicate that you regard it as such. Besides, being well groomed and properly dressed will help boost your confidence.

Sooner or later, someone will call your name and escort you into the interview room. *This is it.* From here on you are on your own. It is too late for any more preparation. But remember, you asked for this opportunity to prove your fitness, and you are here because your request was granted.

What happens when you go in?

The usual sequence of events will be as follows: The clerk (who is often the board stenographer) will introduce you to the chairman of the oral board, who will introduce you to the other members of the board. Acknowledge the introductions before you sit down. Do not be surprised if you find a microphone facing you or a stenotypist sitting by. Oral interviews are usually recorded in the event of an appeal or other review.

Usually the chairman of the board will open the interview by reviewing the highlights of your education and work experience from your application – primarily for the benefit of the other members of the board, as well as to get the material into the record. Do not interrupt or comment unless there is an error or significant misinterpretation; if that is the case, do not hesitate. But do not quibble about insignificant matters. Also, he will usually ask you some question about your education, experience or your present job – partly to get you to start talking and to establish the interviewing "rapport." He may start the actual questioning, or turn it over to one of the other members. Frequently, each member undertakes the questioning on a particular area, one in which he is perhaps most competent, so you can expect each member to participate in the examination. Because time is limited, you may also expect some rather abrupt switches in the direction the questioning takes, so do not be upset by it. Normally, a board member will not pursue a single line of questioning unless he discovers a particular strength or weakness.

After each member has participated, the chairman will usually ask whether any member has any further questions, then will ask you if you have anything you wish to add. Unless you are expecting this question, it may floor you. Worse, it may start you off on an extended, extemporaneous speech. The board is not usually seeking more information. The question is principally to offer you a last opportunity to present further qualifications or to indicate that you have nothing to add. So, if you feel that a significant qualification or characteristic has been overlooked, it is proper to point it out in a sentence or so. Do not compliment the board on the thoroughness of their examination – they have been sketchy, and you know it. If you wish, merely say, "No thank you, I have nothing further to add." This is a point where you can "talk yourself out" of a good impression or fail to present an important bit of information. Remember, *you close the interview yourself.*

The chairman will then say, "That is all, Mr. _____, thank you." Do not be startled; the interview is over, and quicker than you think. Thank him, gather your belongings and take your leave. Save your sigh of relief for the other side of the door.

How to put your best foot forward

Throughout this entire process, you may feel that the board individually and collectively is trying to pierce your defenses, seek out your hidden weaknesses and embarrass and confuse you. Actually, this is not true. They are obliged to make an appraisal of your qualifications for the job you are seeking, and they want to see you in your best light. Remember, they must interview all candidates and a non-cooperative candidate may become a failure in spite of their best efforts to bring out his qualifications. Here are 15 suggestions that will help you:

1) Be natural – Keep your attitude confident, not cocky

If you are not confident that you can do the job, do not expect the board to be. Do not apologize for your weaknesses, try to bring out your strong points. The board is interested in a positive, not negative, presentation. Cockiness will antagonize any board member and make him wonder if you are covering up a weakness by a false show of strength.

2) Get comfortable, but don't lounge or sprawl

Sit erectly but not stiffly. A careless posture may lead the board to conclude that you are careless in other things, or at least that you are not impressed by the importance of the occasion. Either conclusion is natural, even if incorrect. Do not fuss with your clothing, a pencil or an ashtray. Your hands may occasionally be useful to emphasize a point; do not let them become a point of distraction.

3) Do not wisecrack or make small talk

This is a serious situation, and your attitude should show that you consider it as such. Further, the time of the board is limited – they do not want to waste it, and neither should you.

4) Do not exaggerate your experience or abilities

In the first place, from information in the application or other interviews and sources, the board may know more about you than you think. Secondly, you probably will not get away with it. An experienced board is rather adept at spotting such a situation, so do not take the chance.

5) If you know a board member, do not make a point of it, yet do not hide it

Certainly you are not fooling him, and probably not the other members of the board. Do not try to take advantage of your acquaintanceship – it will probably do you little good.

6) Do not dominate the interview

Let the board do that. They will give you the clues – do not assume that you have to do all the talking. Realize that the board has a number of questions to ask you, and do not try to take up all the interview time by showing off your extensive knowledge of the answer to the first one.

7) Be attentive

You only have 20 minutes or so, and you should keep your attention at its sharpest throughout. When a member is addressing a problem or question to you, give him your undivided attention. Address your reply principally to him, but do not exclude the other board members.

8) Do not interrupt

A board member may be stating a problem for you to analyze. He will ask you a question when the time comes. Let him state the problem, and wait for the question.

9) Make sure you understand the question

Do not try to answer until you are sure what the question is. If it is not clear, restate it in your own words or ask the board member to clarify it for you. However, do not haggle about minor elements.

10) Reply promptly but not hastily

A common entry on oral board rating sheets is "candidate responded readily," or "candidate hesitated in replies." Respond as promptly and quickly as you can, but do not jump to a hasty, ill-considered answer.

11) Do not be peremptory in your answers

A brief answer is proper – but do not fire your answer back. That is a losing game from your point of view. The board member can probably ask questions much faster than you can answer them.

12) Do not try to create the answer you think the board member wants

He is interested in what kind of mind you have and how it works – not in playing games. Furthermore, he can usually spot this practice and will actually grade you down on it.

13) Do not switch sides in your reply merely to agree with a board member

Frequently, a member will take a contrary position merely to draw you out and to see if you are willing and able to defend your point of view. Do not start a debate, yet do not surrender a good position. If a position is worth taking, it is worth defending.

14) Do not be afraid to admit an error in judgment if you are shown to be wrong

The board knows that you are forced to reply without any opportunity for careful consideration. Your answer may be demonstrably wrong. If so, admit it and get on with the interview.

15) Do not dwell at length on your present job

The opening question may relate to your present assignment. Answer the question but do not go into an extended discussion. You are being examined for a *new* job, not your present one. As a matter of fact, try to phrase ALL your answers in terms of the job for which you are being examined.

Basis of Rating

Probably you will forget most of these "do's" and "don'ts" when you walk into the oral interview room. Even remembering them all will not ensure you a passing grade. Perhaps you did not have the qualifications in the first place. But remembering them will help you to put your best foot forward, without treading on the toes of the board members.

Rumor and popular opinion to the contrary notwithstanding, an oral board wants you to make the best appearance possible. They know you are under pressure – but they also want to see how you respond to it as a guide to what your reaction would be under the pressures of the job you seek. They will be influenced by the degree of poise you display, the personal traits you show and the manner in which you respond.

EXAMINATION SECTION

EXAMINATION SECTION
TEST 1

DIRECTIONS: Each question or incomplete statement is followed by several suggested answers or completions. Select the one that BEST answers the question or completes the statement. *PRINT THE LETTER OF THE CORRECT ANSWER IN THE SPACE AT THE RIGHT.*

1. A library is in the process of conducting an annual performance evaluation. Which of the following would be an output measure that might be used in this process?

    A. Staff expenditures
    B. User satisfaction survey results
    C. Ratio of computer workstations to daily average users
    D. Ratio of interlibrary loan lending to borrowing

    1.____

2. The _____ record is a separate record attached to the bibliographic record for a serial title in which the receipt of individual issues or parts is entered on an ongoing basis.

    A. holdings
    B. check-in
    C. item
    D. periodical

    2.____

3. Of the following, which research tool would be most appropriate for finding where an author uses specific words or phrases?

    A. Abstract
    B. Gazetteer
    C. Dictionary
    D. Concordance

    3.____

4. In library cataloging, a separately published part of a bibliographic resource, usually representing a subject category within the whole and indicated by a topical heading or an alphanumeric heading, is a(n)

    A. class
    B. scope
    C. notch
    D. section

    4.____

5. The main advantage to paying an electronic journal publisher on a per-article basis, rather than subscribing to a package or database, is that

    A. hardware, browser, and networking requirements are simpler
    B. the library pays only for what it uses
    C. costs are shifted entirely to the user
    D. costs are more predictable over time

    5.____

6. The Dublin Core Metadata Initiative, an international effort to develop standard mechanisms for searching online resources, has named 15 core metadata elements to be used to direct searches. Which of the following is NOT one of these?

    A. Editor   B. Rights   C. Date   D. Format

    6.____

7. "Converting" electronic records means that

   A. there is a change to the underlying bit stream, but there is no change in the representation or intellectual content of the records
   B. they are moved from a proprietary legacy system that lacks software functionality to an open system
   C. they have been transferred from old storage media to new storage media with the same format specifications and without any loss in structure, content, or context
   D. they have been exported or imported from one software environment to another without the loss of structure, content, or context even though the underlying bit stream has likely been altered

8. The 3XX fields in the MARC system contain

   A. physical descriptions
   B. main entries
   C. subject added entries
   D. titles, editions, and imprints

9. In Internet user, instead of being taken to a desired Web page, instead is taken to a page that says *Error Message 404*. What has happened?

   A. Either the server is busy, or the site has moved.
   B. Special permission is needed to access the site.
   C. The file has been moved or deleted, or the URL in incorrect.
   D. The syntax used in the URL is incorrect.

10. An anthology is compiled by 6 authors. According to the MLA format, how many of the author's names should be included in a citation?

    A. 0
    B. 1
    C. 2
    D. 6

11. Which of the following is NOT an advantage of using HTML as a format for file preservation?

    A. Extensive authoring tools
    B. Improving tools for conversion-to-HTML
    C. Good standard for delivering simple text
    D. Can be viewed in any browser

12. In the MARC record, the same digits are assigned across fields in the second and third character positions of the tag to indicate data of the same type. For example, tags reading "X10" contain information about

    A. topical terms
    B. bibliographic titles
    C. uniform titles
    D. corporate names

13. A librarian wants to subscribe to an e-mail newsletter that contains annotations of information technology articles and other items written by a team of librarians and library staff. She is wary, however, of having her inbox clogged with unread material that arrives too frequently for her to read it all, and would prefer to have the newsletter arrive monthly. The librarian should subscribe to

    A. *Free Pint*
    B. *Edupage*
    C. *Current Cites*
    D. *NewsScan*

14. A journal's "impact factor," a measure of its relative importance, is most often defined as the _____ in a given year.

    A. number of electronic queries coming from a library database
    B. frequency of citations to its articles
    C. number of top-rated professionals or scholars who publish in it
    D. times the full-text is displayed on a library terminal

15. _____ is the online database designed and maintained since 1995 by the Library of Congress to make legislative information accessible to the public

    A. CQ
    B. NARA
    C. THOMAS
    D. FindLaw

16. The main software protocol that manages data on the Internet is

    A. TCP/IP
    B. HTTP
    C. HTML
    D. FTP

17. Which of the following is a repeatable MARC field?

    A. 100
    B. 246
    C. 250
    D. 260

18. A user seeking articles about transportation should be directed to Wilson's _____ Index.

    A. Social Sciences
    B. Business Periodicals
    C. Applied Science and Technology
    D. General Science

19. In the library literature, materials designated with the collecting level "4" in relation to a given subject are considered

    A. "out of scope"
    B. sources of basic information
    C. comprehensive and authoritative
    D. useful for the support of research in the given subject

20. In Web addresses, the hashmark is used to

    A. create a link to another location in the same document
    B. identify a port
    C. create a link to another Web page
    D. differentiate numerical characters

21. The content of a Web site is difficult to navigate, and users tend to get confused when trying to find information. The resource assessment guideline that needs to be addressed is

    A. Documentation and Credibility
    B. Ease of Use, Navigation, and Accessibility
    C. User Interface and Design
    D. Content

22. To extend the accessibility of any material that can be displayed at a library workstation to those with extremely poor vision, _____ can be used.

    A. screen reading software
    B. screen magnifying software
    C. TTY
    D. an on-screen keyboard

23. The software application needed to read files in Portable Document Format (PDF) is known as

    A. Acrobat Reader
    B. Real Page
    C. Pagemaker
    D. techexplorer Hypermedia Browser

24. In data that is prepared in the cataloging-in-publication (CIP) format and distributed in MARC format prior to a work's publication, the element that typically appears after the notes about bibliographical references or previous editions is the

    A. Library of Congress classification number
    B. statement of responsibility
    C. ISBN
    D. Dewey Decimal classification number

25. The reason for the slow pace of initial acceptance of WORM (write once, read many) technology in library archiving is that 25.____
    A. the amount of storage available on the disks is too variable to offer predictable capacity
    B. disks are not standardized and can be read only on the type of drive used to write them
    C. the data cannot be altered once it is stored
    D. the longevity of the disk media is still unknown

KEY (CORRECT ANSWERS)

1. D	6. A	11. A	16. A	21. B
2. B	7. D	12. D	17. B	22. A
3. D	8. A	13. C	18. C	23. A
4. D	9. C	14. B	19. D	24. C
5. B	10. B	15. C	20. A	25. B

TEST 2

DIRECTIONS: Each question or incomplete statement is followed by several suggested answers or completions. Select the one that BEST answers the question or completes the statement. *PRINT THE LETTER OF THE CORRECT ANSWER IN THE SPACE AT THE RIGHT.*

1. Which of the following is NOT an aggregator service?   1.___

   A. ScienceDirect
   B. JSTOR
   C. Britannica
   D. Blackwell's Electronic Journal Navigator

2. Technical service librarians are usually concerned with any of the following, EXCEPT   2.___

   A. repairing damaged materials
   B. checking in journals
   C. cataloging books
   D. checking books out

3. Materials that are published electronically are identified by their   3.___

   A. EAD
   B. DOI
   C. XLS
   D. ISBN

4. Which of the following is an example of "mobile code" that allows a Web designer to incorporate computer programs, such as Flash pages, into Web page content?   4.___

   A. Packet
   B. Worm
   C. Warez
   D. Applet

5. The abbreviation "NOP" on a publisher's invoice usually means the requested item   5.___

   A. is on back order
   B. is not in print
   C. the requested item is not published by the vendor
   D. has not yet been published, but will be in the future

6. A well-designed online catalog or bibliographic database allows the user to employ limiting parameters to restrict the retrieval or entries including the terms included in the search statement. Which of the following is NOT a common example of these "limiters?"   6.___

   A. Spelling
   B. Publication date
   C. Full-text
   D. Locally held

7. Which of the following is LEAST likely to be a guideline followed in setting up an electronic reserves (ER) system in an academic library?

    A. Restrict access to authorized users off-site, but maintain open access on-site.
    B. Limit offsite access by course and/or instructor name.
    C. Remove or suppress access at the end of every session.
    D. Post copyright warning notices.

8. Subsystems of the Internet include
    I. the World Wide Web
    II. Newsgroups
    III. Telnet
    IV. e-mail

    A. I only
    B. I, II and III
    C. II and III
    D. I, II, III and IV

9. Binary scanning at 300 dots per inch (dpi) is usually considered adequate for

    A. halftones
    B. illustrated text
    C. typed or laser-printed archival documents
    D. published text/line art

10. The systems librarian's responsibilities typically include each of the following, EXCEPT

    A. development and maintenance of hardware and software
    B. Webmaster
    C. training staff in the use of library systems
    D. interlibrary loan processing

11. A records survey is LEAST likely to be used for the purpose of determining the _____ of archival records.

    A. quality
    B. content
    C. physical quantities
    D. provenance

12. In the searching of an electronic database, which of the following might cause a "false drop?"

    A. The omission of older information
    B. Too-frequent updating of the database
    C. A word with more than one meaning
    D. Restrictions on database use

13. A group of librarians is meeting to determine the selection of electronic journals for a library's collection. One of the MOST likely disadvantages of including the reference librarian in this group is that he may not

   A. have close contact with users
   B. be accustomed to the collaborative approach
   C. be able to relinquish his primary responsibilities for long enough periods of time
   D. have experience selecting and supporting electronic resources

14. Most Internet service providers (ISPs) are built on _____ lines.

   A. 56 Kbps
   B. ISDN
   C. T-1
   D. T-3

15. Which of the following is a term used to denote a hard copy enlargement of an image on microform?

   A. Blowback
   B. Macroform
   C. Aperture card
   D. Blowup

16. On the Web or in an online bibliography, well-designed search software is capable of
   I. searching more than one database simultaneously
   II. removing duplicate record s from results when searching multiple databases
   III. viewing search terms highlighted in results
   IV. printing, e-mailing, and downloading results in various formats

   A. I only
   B. I and III
   C. III only
   D. I, II, III and IV

17. Subject heading systems do NOT

   A. assist searchers in understanding how a specific subject fits into a larger structure of knowledge
   B. divide knowledge over 30 broad categories
   C. describe what a book or article is about
   D. allow people to search by subject area

18. In order to ensure the integrity of digital archive, the origin and chain of custody of a particular file or record most be preserved. This feature of information integrity is known as

   A. content
   B. provenance
   C. content
   D. fixity

19. The creation of a Web page could involve
    I. using a dedicated Web authoring software program
    II. converting a word-processed document to HTML
    III. converting a magazine article, with images, to PDF
    IV. use the Web authoring capability of a portal

    A. I and II
    B. I, II and IV
    C. II and III
    D. II, III and IV

20. What is the general term for an indexable concept that is assigned to add depth to subject indexing, and that is not listed in the thesaurus of indexing terms because it either represents a proper name or a concept that is not yet authorized for inclusion in the bibliographic database?

    A. assigner
    B. identifier
    C. descriptor
    D. ideogram

21. The *World of Learning* is an example of a(n)

    A. concordance
    B. encyclopedia
    C. abstract
    D. directory

22. In the United States, the professional association for academic libraries and librarians is the

    A. Association of College and Research Libraries (ACRL)
    B. Association of Specialized and Cooperative Library Agencies (ASCLA)
    C. American Library Association (ALA)
    D. National Commission on Libraries and Information Science (NCLIS)

23. The module of the library automation system that is used by the public for interacting with the system is the

    A. circulation module
    B. serials module
    C. OPAC
    D. cataloging module

24. Which of the following is a synthetic classification system?

    A. Dewey Decimal
    B. Colon classification
    C. Library of Congress classification
    D. Sears List

25. Library issues concerning the USA Patriot Act include
    I. civil liberties related to privacy and confidentiality
    II. denial of access to information
    III. fair use
    IV. copyright law

    A. I and II
    B. II only
    C. II, III and IV
    D. I, II, III and IV

KEY (CORRECT ANSWERS)

1. C	6. A	11. A	16. D	21. D
2. D	7. A	12. C	17. B	22. A
3. B	8. D	13. C	18. B	23. C
4. D	9. C	14. C	19. B	24. B
5. C	10. D	15. A	20. B	25. A

EXAMINATION SECTION
TEST 1

DIRECTIONS: Each question or incomplete statement is followed by several suggested answers or completions. Select the one that BEST answers the question or completes the statement. *PRINT THE LETTER OF THE CORRECT ANSWER IN THE SPACE AT THE RIGHT.*

1. The heart of a MARC record for a separately-cataloged electronic journal is contained in the _____ fields

    A. 0XX
    B. 3XX
    C. 5XX
    D. 7XX

    1._____

2. Which of the following is NOT an online acquisitions tool?

    A. *JSTOR*
    B. *Blackwell's Collection Manager*
    C. *Books in Print*
    D. *GOBI*

    2._____

3. The in-house approach to digital imaging and preservation typically offers each of the following advantages, EXCEPT

    A. heightened security
    B. learning by doing
    C. quality assurance
    D. predictable per-image costs

    3._____

4. The publication date of a reference book is usually found on the

    A. back cover
    B. title page
    C. page immediately before the title page
    D. page immediately following the title page

    4._____

5. In the Dublin Core Metadata Initiative, an international effort to develop standard mechanisms for searching online resources, the "type" element provides information about the

    A. topic of the content of the resource, typically expressed as keywords or classification codes
    B. rights held in and over the resource
    C. nature or genre of the content of the resource
    D. extent or scope of the resource's content

    5._____

6. _____ indexing is a method in which the subject headings or descriptors assigned to documents represent simple concepts that the user must combine at the time of searching to retrieve information on a complex subject.

    A. String
    B. Assignment
    C. Pre-coordinate
    D. Post-coordinate

    6._____

7. A library server would most likely NOT be used as

   A. a terminal for searching online resources such as periodical databases
   B. a file server hosting work processing and other office software, along with staff documents and other files
   C. the host computer for the library's automation system
   D. a connection point between the library and the Internet

8. Under copyright law, any rights that eventually revert to the copyright holder when the time period or purpose stated in the contract has elapsed or been discharged are known as _____ rights.

   A. volume
   B. serial
   C. residual
   D. subsidiary

9. Research indicates that to most library professionals, _____ is the most frequently applied criterion for evaluating the appropriateness of bibliographic references.

   A. quality
   B. topicality
   C. novelty
   D. availability

10. The best way to minimize the substrate deformation and mistracking of magnetic media is to

    A. use acetate, rather than polyester
    B. limit playback as much as possible
    C. store the media in constant temperature and humidity
    D. store the media in a room that is warmer and more humid than the rest of the library

11. Which of the following is NOT an advantage associated with purchasing an electronic journal collection in the form of a commercially packaged product?

    A. Good way to track usage
    B. Searchability of articles from other publishers
    C. Lower price per title
    D. Single search interface

12. In the Dewey Decimal Classification System, works in Natural Sciences and Mathematics are classified in the number category

    A. 000
    B. 300
    C. 500
    D. 700

13. A library's OPAC allows users to turn off images in Web pages and see only the text during searches. This is an example of interface management called

    A. ghosting
    B. graceful degradation
    C. funneling
    D. cache emptying

14. Which of the following events in library automation occurred FIRST?

    A. The growing importance of "add-ons" related to the delivery of digital content
    B. Integration into the Web environment
    C. The development of the machine-readable catalog record (MARC)
    D. Integration of library systems with learning management systems

15. One of the main advantages associated with searching for information using print indexes is that they

    A. provide cross-references to other topics
    B. are usually faster than online searches
    C. tend to yield information that is more accurate
    D. are usually more current

16. Which of the following statements about online link resolvers is FALSE?

    A. They are applications designed to match source citations with target resources.
    B. Most do not store data, but merely establish links.
    C. Most accept citation information in the form of an OpenURL.
    D. They are designed to take into account which materials a user is authorized by subscription or licensing agreement to access.

17. The intended purpose of copyright law is NOT to

    A. deter others from plagiarizing a work
    B. ensure a fair return on an author's or publisher's investment of time and money into the creation of a work
    C. provide an author or publisher with the incentive to produce a work by granting a limited monopoly
    D. reward innovators at the expense of consumers

18. When using a library's OPAC, a patron moves the mouse to pass a cursor over an image in the Web page and holds the cursor over the image for several seconds. A text message pops up, replacing the information content of the image. This feature, designed for visually impaired users, is enabled by the use of _____ in coding the page.

    A. applets
    B. alt tags
    C. plug-ins
    D. SGML

19. A search of a database containing 100 records relevant to a topic retrieves 50 records, 25 of which are relevant to the topic. The search is said to have a _____ percent recall.

    A. 10
    B. 25
    C. 50
    D. 75

20. In a bibliography compiled in the MLA format, the authorship of a book by Tom and Bridget Jones would be indicated

    A. Jones, Tom and Bridget Jones
    B. Jones, Tom and Bridget
    C. Jones, Tom and Jones, Bridget
    D. Tom Jones and Bridget Jones

21. In most large libraries, the _____ record is attached to the bibliographic record for a serial title or multivolume item to track issues, parts, or volumes as they are acquired by the library.

    A. item
    B. check-in
    C. order
    D. holdings

22. Which of the following is an online bibliographic database vendor that charges on a per-search basis?

    A. EBSCO
    B. FirstSearch
    C. ProQuest
    D. Gale Group

23. What is the term for the blending of current and emerging technologies into a single multi-use device?

    A. Virtual reality
    B. Convergence
    C. Processing
    D. Artificial intelligence

24. Which of the following is an approach to interoperability that uses proxies as interfaces between existing systems?

    A. HotJava
    B. TeX
    C. InfoBus
    D. STARTS

25. The Metadata Object Description Schema, or MODS,
    I. is an XML schema
    II. was created by the Library of Congress for representing MARC-like semantics
    III. can be used to carry selected data from MARC21 records
    IV. cannot be used for the conversion of MARC to XML without loss of data

   A. I and II
   B. I, II and IV
   C. II and III
   D. I, II, III and IV

25.____

KEY (CORRECT ANSWERS)

1. C
2. A
3. D
4. D
5. C

6. D
7. A
8. C
9. B
10. C

11. B
12. C
13. B
14. C
15. A

16. B
17. D
18. B
19. B
20. A

21. D
22. B
23. B
24. C
25. D

TEST 2

DIRECTIONS: Each question or incomplete statement is followed by several suggested answers or completions. Select the one that BEST answers the question or completes the statement. *PRINT THE LETTER OF THE CORRECT ANSWER IN THE SPACE AT THE RIGHT.*

1. The main advantage to using an intermediary service for access to electronic journals is that

   A. one search engine will search the contents of journals from several publishers and/or disciplines
   B. the one-time start-up cost is predictable
   C. the databases will have citations and abstracts only for articles that are available in full-text
   D. the depth of backfiles is predictable

1.__

2. A library automation system needs to be able to search compatible resources from a single interface, and to search text files based on keywords.
The standard query language that is used for this is

   A. WAIS
   B. Gopher
   C. ODBC
   D. Z39.50

2.__

3. Under copyright law, the rights to publish a work in a form other than the original publication–for example, in installments in a periodical–are known as _____ rights.

   A. residual
   B. subsidiary
   C. site-specific
   D. residual

3.__

4. _____ indexing is a method in which multiple concepts are combined by the indexer to form subject headings or descriptors assigned to documents dealing with complex subjects.

   A. Derivative
   B. Pre-coordinate
   C. String
   D. Post-coordinate

4.__

5. Which of the following terms is associated with efforts to bridge the digital divide?

   A. E-rate
   B. Intellectual property
   C. Artificial intelligence
   D. Convergence

5.__

2 (#2)

6. After deciding to offer users online access to an electronic journals collection through the library's online catalog, a library must decide whether to use the "single-record" or "separate-record" approach to offering access to print and electronic versions. Advantages of the separate-record approach include the fact that it is
   I. better suited to handle linking relationships between formats
   II. it is prescribed by AACR2 (Anglo-American Cataloging Rules)
   III. used by the Government Printing Office (GPO)
   IV. preferred by the Cooperative Online Serials Program (CONSER)

   A. I only
   B. II and III
   C. I, II and IV
   D. I, II, III and IV

   6._____

7. One of the key issues in remote access to library automated systems today is

   A. authentication
   B. free speech
   C. cost
   D. training

   7._____

8. Which of the following is NOT a multiple-access database?

   A. A printed dictionary arranged alphabetically by headword
   B. A library catalog searchable by author, title, subject, and keywords
   C. A bibliographic database searchable by author, title, subject, or date
   D. A printed encyclopedia in alphabetical sections, with a subject or keyword index to the entire work at the end of the last volume.

   8._____

9. Which of the following services is LEAST likely to be offered by a jobber?

   A. Approval plans
   B. Continuation orders
   C. Technical processing
   D. Online searchable bibliographies

   9._____

10. Modern (5th generation) computers are most specifically characterized by the feature of

    A. transistors
    B. integrated chips
    C. multiprocessing
    D. data communications

    10._____

11. In library acquisitions, a purchase order becomes a contract when

    A. the seller receives the invoice
    B. it is accepted by the purchaser
    C. the purchaser signs the invoice
    D. it is accepted by the seller

    11._____

12. The primary metadata that describes a social science data set is a

    A. codebook   B. unicode
    C. chapbook   D. METS

    12._____

13. The contents of a single CD-ROM are roughly equivalent to the contents of about _____ books.

   A. 15
   B. 120
   C. 300
   D. 250

14. Which of the following is NOT a link resolver?

   A. ICate
   B. PURL
   C. SFX
   D. Linkfinder Plus

15. Historical works are classified in the Library of Congress Classification System under the broad category designated

   A. L
   B. H
   C. D
   D. S

16. The most widely used medium for offline data storage is

   A. CD-ROM
   B. RAID
   C. DVD-ROM
   D. magnetic tape

17. In archives, the legal term for a record or document that is no longer in the possession of its original creator or legitimate custodian is

   A. dangler
   B. estray
   C. abductee
   D. orphan

18. The largest unit in a database is a

   A. file
   B. record
   C. subfield
   D. field

19. Which of the following is NOT typically part of an item record?

   A. Price
   B. Volume number
   C. Vendor
   D. Barcode

20. Which of the following is an advantage associated with the "scan-first" approach to preservation-in which microfilm records are produced from digitized scans of original documents?   20.____

    A. Wide range of equipment and service vendors
    B. Unsettled standards for preservation
    C. Adjustments can be made prior to conversion
    D. Higher image resolution than analog photography

21. Communications from an author to the editor of a journal typically do NOT include   21.____

    A. proof of permission
    B. referee comments
    C. article appropriate query
    D. copyright assignment

22. Which of the following is NOT a primary source?   22.____

    A. Memoir/autobiography
    B. Encyclopedia
    C. Minutes from an organization or agency
    D. Speech

23. A user initiates an online search by typing "author = Shakespeare." This is an example of a _____ search.   23.____

    A. fielded
    B. Boolean
    C. full-text
    D. stop-list

24. Asyndetic references or bibliographies   24.____

    A. lack descriptors
    B. include embedded hypertext
    C. focus on semantic relationships between topics
    D. lack cross-references

25. The most universally accepted criteria for weeding library items are based on   25.____

    A. subject area
    B. date of publication
    C. the condition or physical description of the item
    D. content

KEY (CORRECT ANSWERS)

1.	A		11.	D
2.	D		12.	A
3.	B		13.	C
4.	B		14.	B
5.	A		15.	C
6.	C		16.	D
7.	A		17.	B
8.	A		18.	A
9.	D		19.	C
10.	C		20.	C

21. B
22. B
23. A
24. D
25. C

———

EXAMINATION SECTION
TEST 1

DIRECTIONS: Each question or incomplete statement is followed by several suggested answers or completions. Select the one that BEST answers the question or completes the statement. *PRINT THE LETTER OF THE CORRECT ANSWER IN THE SPACE AT THE RIGHT.*

1. A book about the life of another person is called a(n)

    A. monograph
    B. fiction
    C. biography
    D. autobiography
    E. reference

    1.____

2. A book about real experiences is usually referred to as a(n)

    A. reference
    B. monograph
    C. fiction
    D. non-fiction
    E. autobiography

    2.____

3. The Dewey Decimal system is a

    A. list of books, magazines, and non-print materials
    B. system for checking out books
    C. method for organizing materials on the same subject matter together
    D. system for filing cards
    E. system for networking

    3.____

4. A catalog card reading MOVIE see MOTION PICTURE means:

    A. All books on movies will be found under the subject heading MOTION PICTURE
    B. Additional books on movies will be found under the subject heading MOTION PICTURE
    C. Another library has the motion picture holdings
    D. Materials are expected on motion pictures
    E. All materials on movies are circulating

    4.____

5. A bibliography is a(n)

    A. encyclopedia
    B. networking
    C. means of circulating materials
    D. list of materials
    E. reference tool

    5.____

6. An annotation is a(n)

    A. review
    B. explanatory note
    C. precis
    D. format
    E. critique

    6.____

7. AMERICAN REFERENCE BOOKS ANNUAL provides a

    A. comprehensive reviewing service of reference books published in the United States
    B. monthly periodical furnishing reviews of popular reference tools
    C. publisher's guide to monthly reviewing sources
    D. professional journal published by the American Library Association
    E. bibliography of bibliographies

    7.____

8. An index is a(n)

    A. table of contents
    B. encyclopedia
    C. series of footnotes
    D. bibliography
    E. guide to locate material

9. The library catalog is a(n)

    A. shelf list
    B. index to the materials collection
    C. bibliography
    D. system for reserves
    E. collection of book orders

10. A shelf list is a

    A. record of materials in a library
    B. reserve list
    C. weeding list
    D. list of reference materials
    E. bibliography of reference sources

11. Technical services include

    A. acquisitions, cataloging, and materials preparation
    B. reference work and user services
    C. reader's advisory services
    D. circulation and reference services
    E. networking

12. A collection of materials such as pamphlets, clippings, or illustrations kept in special containers is referred to as a

    A. card catalog   B. card file   C. vertical file
    D. container collection   E. clipping file

13. An electromagnetic recording made for playback on a television set is referred to as a(n)

    A. audio tape   B. cassette   C. video-recording
    D. superdisk   E. fiche

14. A word, name, object, group of words, or acronym describing a subject is usually referred to as a

    A. cross reference   B. subject heading
    C. nom de plume   D. serial
    E. catalog card

15. A collection of materials with restricted circulation usually found in college and university libraries is called a(n) _____ collection.

    A. reserved materials   B. patron   C. student
    D. open stack   E. rotating reserve

16. An independent publication of forty-nine pages or less, bound in paper covers, is called a

    A. serial   B. monograph   C. microcard
    D. pamphlet   E. fiche

3 (#1)

17. Library work directly concerned with assistance to readers in securing information and in using library resources is termed   17.____

    A. circulation services B. technical services
    C. reader's advisory services D. user services
    E. networking

18. A three-dimensional representation of a real object reproduced in the original size or to scale is called a(n)   18.____

    A. model B. film C. microform
    D. ultrafiche E. videotape

19. The act of filling out required forms to become an eligible library borrower is called   19.____

    A. serialization B. direction C. registration
    D. reference work E. signing

20. A direction in a catalog that guides the user to related names or subjects is termed a _____ reference.   20.____

    A. shelf B. see-also C. title
    D. see E. subject

21. A record of a work in the catalog under the title is called a   21.____

    A. subject card B. number entry C. author card
    D. subject entry E. title entry

22. The printed scheme of a classification system is referred to as a   22.____

    A. classification schedule B. numbering schedule
    C. lettering schedule D. cutter number
    E. copyright

23. The entry of a work in the catalog under the subject heading is called a   23.____

    A. subject card B. subject heading C. subject entry
    D. reference entry E. subject guide

24. The department in a library responsible for officially listing prospective borrowers is the _____ department.   24.____

    A. reference B. registration C. welcoming
    D. circulation E. technical

25. Library work that deals with patrons and the use of the library collection is called _____ services.   25.____

    A. technical B. reader C. circulation
    D. reference E. public

KEY (CORRECT ANSWERS)

1.	C	11.	A
2.	D	12.	C
3.	C	13.	C
4.	A	14.	B
5.	D	15.	A
6.	B	16.	D
7.	A	17.	D
8.	E	18.	A
9.	B	19.	C
10.	A	20.	B

21. E
22. A
23. C
24. B
25. D

TEST 2

DIRECTIONS: Each question or incomplete statement is followed by several suggested answers or completions. Select the one that BEST answers the question or completes the statement. *PRINT THE LETTER OF THE CORRECT ANSWER IN THE SPACE AT THE RIGHT.*

1. Material held for a borrower for a limited time is termed _____ material.   1._____
   - A. reference
   - B. reserved
   - C. circulation
   - D. special
   - E. held

2. A notice sent to a borrower to remind him to return heldover due material is a(n)   2._____
   - A. warning
   - B. notice
   - C. overdue notice
   - D. warning notice
   - E. call slip

3. Material returned to the library before the date due is   3._____
   - A. Penalized
   - B. returned
   - C. accepted
   - D. unneeded
   - E. subject to examination

4. Real objects, specimens, or artifacts are called   4._____
   - A. toys
   - B. realia
   - C. games
   - D. opaque material
   - E. models

5. A film with a series of pictures in sequence which creates the illusion of motion when projected is classified as a   5._____
   - A. photogram
   - B. motion picture
   - C. videotape
   - D. cassette
   - E. slide

6. Laying books on the shelves in proper order is called   6._____
   - A. placing   B. weeding   C. reading   D. shifting   E. shelving

7. A publication issued in successive parts usually to be continued indefinitely is referred to as a   7._____
   - A. paper   B. monograph   C. serial   D. pamphlet   E. edition

8. A record of the loan of material is called a   8._____
   - A. call slip   B. reserve   C. contract   D. copy   E. charge

9. Information arranged in tabular, outline, or graphic form on a sheet of paper is called a   9._____
   - A. classification
   - B. charge
   - C. chart
   - D. catalog
   - E. cartoon

10. The method used to lend materials to borrowers and maintain the necessary records is the _____ system.   10._____
    - A. classification
    - B. circulation control
    - C. reference
    - D. borrowing
    - E. returnable

11. Any entry, other than a subject entry, that is made in a catalog in addition to the main entry is called a(n)

    A. added entry B. call number C. central reference
    D. reference entry E. explanatory entry

12. The record of the number of items charged out of a library is termed

    A. record statistics B. circulation statistics
    C. circulation control D. record control
    E. itemizing

13. A number assigned to each book or item as it is received by the library is referred to as a(n) _____ number.

    A. call B. accession C. entry
    D. acquisition E. ordering

14. A master file of all registered borrowers in a library system is called the _____ file.

    A. personnel B. charging C. classification
    D. central registration E. circulation control

15. A person who charges out materials from a library is called the

    A. lender B. technician C. professional librarian
    D. clerk E. borrower

16. A catalog in which all entries are filed in alphabetical order is called a(n) _____ catalog.

    A. card B. Library of Congress C. alphabetical
    D. dictionary E. subject

17. The day material is to be returned to a library is usually referred to as the _____ day.

    A. library B. date-due C. return
    D. book E. library-due

18. The act of annulling the library's record of a loan is called

    A. discharging B. cancelling C. stamping
    D. recording E. unloaning

19. The penalty charge for material returned after the date due is called a(n)

    A. charge B. fine C. tax D. levy E. arrangement

20. A set of materials containing rules designed to be played in a competitive situation is called a

    A. rolodome B. game C. sketch D. linedex E. materialsset

21. A catalog in more than one part is termed a _____ catalog.

    A. divided B. split C. Library of Congress
    D. Dewey E. Sears

22. A metal file containing a number of flat metal leaves that hold single cardboard strips listing titles and holdings is called a   22.____

    A. linedesk   B. linetop   C. rolotop
    D. rotofile   E. linedex

23. A metal file containing a number of shallow drawers in which serial check-in cards are kept is usually referred to as a   23.____

    A. linedesk   B. rotofile   C. box   D. kardex   E. linetop

24. The strip of paper pasted in the book or on the book packet, on which the date due is stamped, is called the   24.____

    A. date slip   B. date card   C. date strip
    D. call slip   E. card strip

25. Film on which materials have been photographed in greatly reduced size is called   25.____

    A. minifilm   B. microfilm   C. photogram
    D. miniaturization   E. photoreduction

KEY (CORRECT ANSWERS)

1.	B	11.	A
2.	C	12.	B
3.	C	13.	B
4.	B	14.	D
5.	B	15.	E
6.	E	16.	D
7.	C	17.	B
8.	E	18.	A
9.	C	19.	B
10.	B	20.	B

21. A
22. E
23. D
24. A
25. B

EXAMINATION SECTION
TEST 1

DIRECTIONS: Each question or incomplete statement is followed by several suggested answers or completions. Select the one that BEST answers the question or completes the statement. *PRINT THE LETTER OF THE CORRECT ANSWER IN THE SPACE AT THE RIGHT.*

1. The BEST known encyclopedia in the Western world, first published in the 18th century, is   1.____

    A. WORLD BOOK ENCYCLOPEDIA
    B. COMPTON'S PICTURED ENCYCLOPEDIA
    C. ENCYCLOPEDIA BRITANNICA
    D. ENCYCLOPEDIA AMERICANA

2. Authority-control records are important in an online catalog environment because they   2.____

    A. help prevent *blind* cross-references
    B. expand the capacity of the database
    C. keep the system from overloading
    D. provide access to fugitive materials

3. The NEW ENCYCLOPEDIA BRITANNICA does NOT include the   3.____

    A. Micropaedia   B. Monopaedia
    C. Macropaedia   D. Propaedia

4. Which of the following is NOT the name of an online catalog?   4.____

    A. Geobase   B. Dynix   C. Geac   D. OCLC

5. Nom de plume is synonymous with   5.____

    A. pseudonym   B. nickname
    C. given name   D. telonism

6. Component-word searching is another way of saying _____ searching.   6.____

    A. key-word   B. permuterm
    C. subject   D. author/title

7. The ENCYCLOPEDIA AMERICANA is ESPECIALLY useful for   7.____

    A. finding information about movie stars
    B. finding little-known material about the United States
    C. finding tide charts
    D. doing comprehensive world research

8. The citation indexes (SCIENCE CITATION INDEX, etc.) are unique in that they   8.____

    A. allow searching by the name of an institution
    B. provide access to foreign language journals
    C. allow searching of an author's references
    D. contain millions of unique records

9. The following are all children's and young adults' encyclopedias EXCEPT

   A. MERIT STUDENTS ENCYCLOPEDIA
   B. WORLD BOOK ENCYCLOPEDIA
   C. COMPTON'S ENCYCLOPEDIA AND FACT BOOK
   D. COLLIER'S ENCYCLOPEDIA

10. A good online public access catalog (OPAC) can be expected to provide all of the following EXCEPT

    A. author and title access to books and audio-visual materials
    B. the loan status of materials that circulate
    C. information regarding who a book has been loaned to
    D. the place and publisher of each book in the catalog

11. Of the points to consider in a systematic evaluation of an encyclopedia, the LEAST important one is

    A. cost
    B. viewpoint and objectivity
    C. subject coverage
    D. number of pages

12. Widespread searching of bibliographic databases dates back to

    A. the 1950's
    B. 1960
    C. the mid-1980's
    D. the early 1970's

13. The format of a reference set means the

    A. writing style
    B. binding and size
    C. authority of contributors
    D. viewpoint and objectivity

14. The FIRST bibliographic databases were by-products of

    A. progress in NASA technology
    B. online card catalogs such as OCLC
    C. information dissemination centers
    D. the computerized typesetting operation

15. A patron asks your advice as a librarian on a set of encyclopedias he is considering for his family.
    The MOST helpful response for you is to

    A. give limited advice and provide the patron with professional reviews of the set under question
    B. give no advice for fear of repercussions from sales-persons and publishers
    C. endorse or condemn the set whole-heartedly, depending on your own opinion
    D. refer the patron to the director of the library

16. The four basic components of the online industry include all of the following EXCEPT

    A. libraries and information centers
    B. library school administrators
    C. end-users who request information
    D. database producers

17. McGraw-Hill's ENCYCLOPEDIA OF WORLD ART is an example of a _____ encyclope-   17._____
    dia.

    A. children's   B. subject
    C. supermarket   D. foreign

18. Which of the following bibliographic databases is NOT produced by a federal government   18._____
    agency or federally-supported institution?

    A. ERIC   B. COMPENDEX   C. AGRICOLA   D. MEDLINE

19. A ready-reference work is one which   19._____

    A. is allowed to circulate outside of the library
    B. is especially difficult to use
    C. arrives on a monthly basis
    D. is useful for *quick* questions of a factual nature

20. All of the following are examples of source documents EXCEPT   20._____

    A. patents   B. conference papers
    C. indexes   D. newspapers

21. The STATISTICAL ABSTRACT OF THE UNITED STATES is a compendium in the sense   21._____
    that it

    A. contains statistics on a wide range of subjects
    B. is published on an annual basis
    C. is a summary of U.S. Census data
    D. can be used for research in education

22. The number EJ121478, as part of an ERIC record, would indicate that the material refer-   22._____
    enced

    A. is a journal article
    B. is a book
    C. is an ERIC document on microfiche
    D. was entered in the database in 1978

23. Which of the following almanacs is published in London, England?   23._____

    A. WHITAKER'S ALMANAC
    B. INFORMATION PLEASE ALMANAC
    C. WORLD ALMANAC AND BOOK OF FACTS
    D. THE PEOPLE'S ALMANAC

24. A thesaurus which accompanies an index such as ERIC is a list of   24._____

    A. corporate authors   B. journals indexed
    C. stop words   D. assigned descriptors

25. Ready-reference materials include all of the following EXCEPT   25._____

    A. STATISTICAL ABSTRACT OF THE UNITED STATES
    B. INFORMATION PLEASE ALMANAC
    C. BIOLOGICAL ABSTRACTS
    D. THE NEW YORK RED BOOK

KEY (CORRECT ANSWERS)

1. C
2. A
3. B
4. A
5. A

6. A
7. B
8. C
9. D
10. C

11. D
12. D
13. B
14. D
15. A

16. B
17. B
18. B
19. D
20. C

21. C
22. A
23. A
24. D
25. C

TEST 2

DIRECTIONS: Each question or incomplete statement is followed by several suggested answers or completions. Select the one that BEST answers the question or completes the statement. *PRINT THE LETTER OF THE CORRECT ANSWER IN THE SPACE AT THE RIGHT.*

1. The U.S. National Library of Medicine produces all of the following databases EXCEPT 1._____

    A. EMBASE   B. AIDSLINE   C. CANCERLIT   D. MEDLINE

2. H.W. Wilson's CURRENT BIOGRAPHY provides 2._____

    A. essay-length biographical information
    B. reference to information in BIOGRAPHY INDEX
    C. no more information on an individual than is provided by WHO'S WHO
    D. reviews of best-selling biographies

3. The database which provides access to fugitive materials in education is 3._____

    A. Academic Index
    B. Education Index
    C. ERIC
    D. Mental Measurements Yearbook

4. All of the following are covered in CONTEMPORARY AUTHORS EXCEPT 4._____

    A. screenwriters   B. poets
    C. dramatists   D. technical writers

5. Boolean logic utilizes all of the following logical operators EXCEPT 5._____

    A. if   B. or   C. not   D. and

6. A prescriptive dictionary is one which 6._____

    A. discusses in great detail the origin of a word
    B. adheres to tradition and historical authority for word definitions and approved usage
    C. attempts to relate every possible definition and usage of a word
    D. is published only in the United States

7. Free-text searching in a bibliographic database means 7._____

    A. searching several descriptors at one time
    B. using Boolean logic in your search
    C. searching without the use of controlled vocabulary
    D. searching only titles and abstracts

8. ABRIDGED INDEX MEDICUS differs from INDEX MEDICUS in that it 8._____

    A. contains citations to English-language journals only
    B. contains only information from the last twelve months
    C. contains citations to foreign-language journals only
    D. is not published by the National Library of Medicine

9. The two PRINCIPAL operations of public services are

   A. circulation and reference
   B. reference and serials management
   C. circulation and collection development
   D. reference and classification

10. Of the following reasons for an academic library to acquire the DICTIONARY OF AMERICAN SLANG, which is the LEAST valid?

    A. Most regular dictionaries do not indicate the variations of meaning of given slang terms or words.
    B. Students often come across expressions which are not defined well in ordinary dictionaries.
    C. It is a good source to check on the language used by an author to convey a character's background or social class.
    D. Students and librarians alike enjoy reading through it during their leisure time.

11. Collection maintenance includes all of the following EXCEPT

    A. taking inventory   B. reshelving books
    C. identifying overdues   D. shelf-reading

12. A gazetteer is a

    A. biographical dictionary
    B. good source for looking up phases of the moon
    C. geographical dictionary
    D. guide to motels throughout the United States

13. A Dewey Decimal Classification number never has MORE than how many digits to the LEFT of the decimal?

    A. Four   B. Five   C. Three   D. Two

14. In MOST government depository libraries, the government documents are arranged on the shelves

    A. by Superintendent of Documents numbers
    B. by Library of Congress call numbers
    C. by Dewey Decimal numbers
    D. alphabetically by title

15. The Library of Congress Classification System is different from the Dewey Decimal Classification System in that it

    A. arranges books on the shelf by subject
    B. does not include author numbers
    C. is not frequently used by libraries in the United States
    D. was developed to meet the needs of a specific library's collection

16. The BEST reference source for finding, in detail, the organization and activities of all U.S. government agencies is

    A. POLITICS IN AMERICA
    B. THE STATESMAN'S YEARBOOK
    C. UNITED STATES GOVERNMENT MANUAL
    D. MOODY'S MUNICIPAL AND GOVERNMENT MANUAL

17. The added entries in a catalog record could be for

    A. joint authors, titles, or series
    B. joint authors, series, or subjects
    C. joint authors, titles, or subjects
    D. titles, publishers, or series

18. Which of the following illustrates a directional question?

    A. How far is Syracuse from Lake Ontario?
    B. Where is the public telephone?
    C. Where can I find a biographical dictionary of presidents?
    D. Is Italy to the east of Spain?

19. You are performing an online bibliographic search for a patron and have brought up a set consisting of 300 records.
    Of the following, which is the LEAST valid way of limiting the search in order to avoid printing such a large set?

    A. Limit the search to a certain range of years
    B. Redefine the search using more specific descriptors
    C. Print only the first 40 records of the set
    D. Cut out references to articles in languages the patron cannot read

20. All of the following are examples of primary sources EXCEPT

    A. diaries   B. biographies
    C. letters   D. memoirs

21. *What is the population of Mexico City?* would MOST likely be classified as what type of reference question?

    A. Ready reference   B. Directional
    C. Research on a topic D. Instructional

22. Something you would NOT expect to find in a vertical file is

    A. a monograph   B. a pamphlet
    C. a folded map   D. newspaper clippings

23. Logical product, logical sum, and logical difference are all part of what type of searching?

    A. Permuterm logic   B. Keyword-in-context (KWIC)
    C. Statistical logic D. Boolean logic

24. Keyword-in-context (KWIC) indexing is also called _____ indexing.

    A. title   B. comprehensive
    C. subject   D. permutation

25. The MARC format was developed at the

　　A. National Library of Medicine
　　B. British Library
　　C. Library of Congress
　　D. Smithsonian Institute

26. Patrons of a general library are usually MOST aware of which of the following library activities?

　　A. Circulation　　　　B. Accession
　　C. Cataloging　　　　D. Reference

27. Three of the following four are consequences of the copy-righting of books by the U.S. government.
Which is NOT such a consequence?

　　A. Protecting author's rights
　　B. Encouraging writing
　　C. Securing deposit material for the government
　　D. Government endorsement of the copyrighted texts

28. The term *cataloging in publication* refers to a cataloging program under which cataloging information

　　A. appears in the PUBLISHERS' WEEKLY
　　B. appears in the National Union Catalog
　　C. appears in the publication itself
　　D. is prepared by the publisher

29. The MAJOR use of a formal statement of a library's objective is

　　A. serving as a guideline for program development and services
　　B. justifying library staffing to the board and public
　　C. convincing the governing body of the need for financial support
　　D. training library staff in improved methods and practices

30. Circulation statistics should be gathered PRIMARILY for the purpose of

　　A. justifying the library budget
　　B. improving library service
　　C. cutting library costs
　　D. analyzing personnel performance

KEY (CORRECT ANSWERS)

1.	A	16.	C
2.	A	17.	A
3.	C	18.	B
4.	D	19.	C
5.	A	20.	B
6.	B	21.	A
7.	C	22.	A
8.	A	23.	D
9.	A	24.	D
10.	D	25.	C
11.	C	26.	A
12.	C	27.	D
13.	C	28.	C
14.	A	29.	A
15.	D	30.	B

TEST 3

DIRECTIONS: Each question or incomplete statement is followed by several suggested answers or completions. Select the one that BEST answers the question or completes the statement. *PRINT THE LETTER OF THE CORRECT ANSWER IN THE SPACE AT THE RIGHT.*

1. A typical reference in the READER'S GUIDE TO PERIODICAL LITERATURE would include all of the following EXCEPT

    A. author
    B. title of the article
    C. journal name
    D. journal abstract

2. An example of a subject authority list used in cataloging is the

    A. THESAURUS OF ERIC DESCRIPTORS
    B. LIBRARY OF CONGRESS SUBJECT HEADINGS
    C. NEW YORK TIMES INDEX
    D. CINAHL SUBJECT HEADING LIST

3. An example of a nonperiodical serial is

    A. EUROPA YEARBOOK
    B. AQUACULTURE MAGAZINE
    C. THE WASHINGTON POST
    D. JOURNAL OF THE AMERICAN MEDICAL ASSOCIATION

4. The Superintendent of Documents classification system arranges government documents on the shelves

    A. alphabetically by title
    B. by government agency
    C. alphabetically by author
    D. according to date of printing

5. Which of the following is an example of an open-ended question?

    A. Would you like books or magazine articles?
    B. You say you need to know the elevation of Denver?
    C. What kind of information about sharks are you looking for?
    D. Have you ever used our online catalog?

6. Scientific Information's weekly CURRENT CONTENTS consists of

    A. reproductions of journal contents pages
    B. a subject index for scientific journals
    C. author and title indexes for current periodicals
    D. scientific journal abstracts

7. All of the following are bibliographic utilities involved in resource sharing EXCEPT

    A. OCLC   B. RLIN   C. DYNIX   D. UTLAS

8. The MAIN objective of reference negotiation is to

   A. save the librarian's time
   B. steer patrons away from heavily used sources
   C. find out what the patron specifically needs
   D. instruct patrons in the proper use of reference materials

9. Which of the following PROPERLY demonstrates a logical product and logical difference search statement?

   A. Dogs and cats, not birds
   B. (Dogs or cats) and not birds
   C. Dogs and not birds or cats
   D. Dogs and (cats or birds)

10. The generally accepted definition of a serial includes all of the following EXCEPT

    A. yearbooks
    B. newspapers
    C. theses
    D. journals

11. ESSAY AND GENERAL LITERATURE INDEX is MOST useful for locating

    A. a specific chapter of a book
    B. magazine and journal articles
    C. biographical essays
    D. a pamphlet or newsletter

12. What do LIBRARY JOURNAL, SHEEHY'S GUIDE TO REFERENCE BOOKS, and ARBA have in common?
    They

    A. are all periodicals
    B. discuss management of online catalogs
    C. provide critical evaluation of reference materials
    D. discuss only highly recommended reference sources

13. SHORT STORY INDEX covers stories published

    A. on all subjects except science fiction
    B. in collections and the NEW YORK TIMES
    C. in collections and periodicals
    D. by American authors only

14. One way in which nonperiodical serials (such as yearbooks) are different from periodical serials (such as journals) is that nonperiodicals are

    A. published several times a year
    B. usually a collection of articles
    C. usually ordered by subscription
    D. usually acquired through a standing order

15. Of the general serial sources listed below, which is the only one that includes newspapers?

    A. STANDARD PERIODICAL DIRECTORY
    B. GALE DIRECTORY OF PUBLICATIONS
    C. ULRICH'S INTERNATIONAL PERIODICALS DIRECTORY
    D. IRREGULAR SERIALS AND ANNUALS

16. The READER'S GUIDE TO PERIODICAL LITERATURE indexes

    A. magazines and newspapers
    B. popular magazines
    C. scholarly journals
    D. short story anthologies

17. Ethnic numbers are added to classification symbols so as to arrange books by

    A. subject   B. place of printing
    C. author   D. language

18. End-matter items could include all of the following EXCEPT

    A. appendices   B. bibliographies
    C. tables of contents D. indexes

19. Which of the following BEST describes a jobber?
    A

    A. company which produces databases
    B. corporate body responsible for placing a book on the market
    C. wholesale bookseller who stocks books and supplies them to libraries
    D. person skilled in writing computer programs

20. The word *an* is a stopword on the Medline database.
    This means that

    A. it cannot be used as a search term in the database
    B. Medline includes articles such as *an* and *the* when alphabetizing by title
    C. if you type in that word, you will exit the database
    D. you cannot use Medline when searching for a title that begins with *an*

21. Of the following queries, which could NOT be answered by consulting a regular dictionary?

    A. What is the Golden Rule?
    B. How deep is a fathom?
    C. Does "humble" come from the same root as "human"?
    D. What are the rules for writing a sonnet?

22. An accurate definition of annals would be a(n)

    A. serial publication issued once a year
    B. anonymous publication
    C. record of events arranged in chronological order
    D. bibliography of an author's writings arranged by date of publication

23. West's FEDERAL PRACTICE DIGEST is an index to 23._____
   A. United States Supreme Court cases
   B. United States statutes
   C. New York State statutes
   D. The Code of Federal Regulations

24. MOST federal government documents are printed by 24._____
   A. the Government Printing Office
   B. the Library of Congress
   C. the United States Printing Office
   D. Congress

25. Setting aside a separate section for oversized books is an example of 25._____
   A. subject cataloging
   B. parallel arrangement
   C. a special materials collection
   D. Dewey Decimal Classification

KEY (CORRECT ANSWERS)

1.	D	11.	A
2.	B	12.	C
3.	A	13.	C
4.	B	14.	D
5.	C	15.	B
6.	A	16.	B
7.	C	17.	D
8.	C	18.	C
9.	A	19.	C
10.	C	20.	A

21. D
22. C
23. A
24. A
25. B

EXAMINATION SECTION
TEST 1

DIRECTIONS: Each question or incomplete statement is followed by several suggested answers or completions. Select the one that BEST answers the question or completes the statement. *PRINT THE LETTER OF THE CORRECT ANSWER IN THE SPACE AT THE RIGHT.*

1. An employee requests a book which is not in the department library.
   Of the following, the MOST advisable course of action for you to take is to

   A. attempt to get the book for him by means of the department's affiliation with the public library
   B. explain that the book is not available from the department's library
   C. suggest that he try his local public library and give him a list of local libraries
   D. tell him where he may purchase the book and offer to make the purchase for him

   1.____

2. The catalog for the use of department employees has just been thoroughly checked and revised by a professional librarian. After trying to find the name of a book in the catalog, an employee tells you that he cannot find it.
   Of the following, the MOST advisable action for you to take FIRST is to

   A. call the public library for the exact title
   B. look it up in the catalog yourself
   C. look through the stacks for the book
   D. tell him you are sorry but the book is not in the department library

   2.____

3. You find that three pages are missing from one of the copies of a very popular book in the department library.
   Of the following, the MOST advisable action for you to take is to

   A. discard the book since its usefulness is now sharply curtailed
   B. order another copy of the book but keep the old copy until the new one is received
   C. report the fact to the head of the department and request further instructions
   D. type copies of the pages from another volume of the book and tape them in the appropriate place

   3.____

4. The department library is scheduled to close at 5 P.M. It is now 4:55, and an employee reading a book shows no signs of leaving.
   Of the following, the MOST advisable action for you to take is to

   A. tell him it is time to leave
   B. tell him the time and ask him if he wishes to borrow the book
   C. turn the lights off and on, indirectly suggesting that he leave
   D. wait until he decides to leave

   4.____

5. The dealer from whom you have been buying books for the department library has informed you that henceforth he can give you only a fifteen percent instead of a twenty percent discount.
   Of the following, the MOST advisable course of action for you to take FIRST is to

   5.____

A. accept the fifteen percent discount
B. inform the head of your department
C. investigate the discount given by other book dealers
D. order directly from the publishers

6. Your supervisor is a professional librarian and is responsible for the selection of material to be added to the department library in which you are an employee. Shortly after you start on the job, an employee of the department brings you a written request to have several books of his choice added to the library.
Of the following, the MOST advisable course of action for you to take is to

   A. order the books immediately
   B. pass the suggestion along to your supervisor
   C. refuse to accept his suggestion
   D. tell him that he will have to buy the books

7. You object to your supervisor's plan to change the system in the department library from closed to open stacks.
Of the following, the MOST advisable course of action for you to take is to

   A. ask other members of the staff to support your objections
   B. await further instructions and then do as you are told
   C. discuss your objections with your supervisor
   D. send a brief report of your objections to the department head

8. Two weeks after you begin working in the department library, you learn that books in library bindings last twice as long as those with the publishers' bindings.
Of the following, the MOST advisable course of action for you to follow is to

   A. buy only paperbound books
   B. have all new books put in library bindings
   C. put in library bindings only rare editions
   D. put in library bindings only those books likely to get hard use

9. Your superior is away on an official trip. You have been asked to type and e-mail several hundred letters before he returns. Just as you begin the job, the computer breaks down.
Of the following, the MOST advisable course of action for you to take is to

   A. arrange to have the computer serviced as soon as possible
   B. write the letters by hand
   C. postpone the job until after your supervisor returns
   D. write to your supervisor for advice

10. Your supervisor in the department library is out for the day. You receive a telephone call from another city department asking if they may borrow one of the books in your library.
Of the following, the MOST advisable action for you to take FIRST is to tell the department

    A. that books are not permitted out of the department
    B. that you will check and call back the next day
    C. to send a representative to inquire the next day
    D. to write a letter to the department head

11. Two months have passed since the head of the department has borrowed one of the books in the department library. Of the following, the MOST advisable action for you to take is to

    A. ask the department head if he wishes to keep the book out longer
    B. leave a note for the department head telling him that the book should be returned immediately
    C. wait another month and then write the book off as lost
    D. wait until you receive another request for the book

12. Your supervisor tells you that he would like to have all old book cards replaced, all torn pages mended, and the books put in good condition in all other respects by the following day. You know that this is an impossible task.
    Of the following, the MOST advisable course of action for you to take is to

    A. attempt to finish as much of the job as possible
    B. explain the difficulties involved to the supervisor and await further instruction
    C. ignore the request since it is completely unreasonable
    D. make a complaint to the head of the department

13. The library in which you work has received about fifty new books. These books must be cataloged, but you have had no experience in this type of work. However, you have been told that a professional librarian will join the staff in about six weeks.
    Of the following, the MOST advisable course of action for you to take in the meantime is to

    A. close the library for a week and try to do the cataloging yourself
    B. lend the books only to those who can get special permission
    C. let the users take the books even though they are not cataloged
    D. put all the books in storage until they can be cataloged

14. The hospital library in which you work has a large back-log of books that need to be mended. You are unable to do more than a small part of the job by yourself. One of the patients in the hospital has done book binding and mending. He offers to help you because he sees the need for doing the job and because he wants something to do with his hands.
    Of the following, the MOST advisable course of action for you to take is to

    A. accept his offer on condition that the doctor approves
    B. ask him to push the book cart around the wards so you will be free to do the mending
    C. refuse his offer
    D. write a letter to his former employer to find out whether he is a good bookbinder

15. You accidentally spill a glass of water over an open book.
    Of the following, the MOST advisable action for you to take FIRST in most cases is to

    A. discard the book to prevent the water from spoiling other material
    B. hang the book up by its binding
    C. press the covers together to squeeze out the water
    D. separate the wet pages with blotters

16. In mending a book, you overturn a jar of glue on a new book.
    Of the following, the MOST advisable action for you to take FIRST is to

    A. allow the glue to harden so that it may be peeled off
    B. attempt to wipe off the glue with any clean scrap paper
    C. discard the book to prevent other materials from being spoiled
    D. report the incident immediately to your supervisor

17. Of the following, the situation LEAST likely to result in injury to books is one in which

    A. all books support each other standing upright
    B. short books are placed between tall ones
    C. the books are as close together as possible
    D. the books lean against the sides of the shelves

18. Of the following, a damp cloth may BEST be used to clean a cloth book cover that has been coated with

    A. benzene   B. gold leaf
    C. turpentine   D. varnish

19. Decay of leather bindings may be MOST effectively delayed by

    A. a short tanning period
    B. air conditioning
    C. rubbing periodically with a damp cloth
    D. treatment with heat

20. When paste is used to mend a page, it is MOST desirable that the page should then be

    A. aired   B. heated   C. pressed   D. sprayed

21. A book that is perfectly clean but has been used by someone with chicken pox can probably BEST be handled by

    A. burning, followed by proper disposal of the ashes
    B. forty-eight hour exposure to ultraviolet light
    C. keeping it out of circulation for six months
    D. treating it the same as any other book

22. The BEST combination of temperature and humidity for books is temperature _____ degrees, humidity _____.

    A. 50-60; 20-30%   B. 60-70; 10-20%
    C. 60-70; 50-60%   D. 70-80; 70-80%

23. When a new book is received, it is LEAST important to keep a record of the

    A. author's name
    B. cost of the book
    C. number of pages
    D. source from which it was obtained

24. You have just received from the publisher a new book for the department library, but you find that the binding is torn.
Of the following, the MOST advisable action for you to take is to

    A. mend the binding and take no further action
    B. mend the binding but claim a price discount
    C. report the damage to the department head
    D. send the book back to the publisher

24.____

25. Of the following, a characteristic of MOST photographic charging systems is that

    A. book cards are not used
    B. charging is done by one person
    C. date due is stamped on borrower's card
    D. transaction cards are not used

25.____

KEY (CORRECT ANSWERS)

1. A
2. B
3. D
4. B
5. C

6. B
7. C
8. D
9. A
10. B

11. A
12. B
13. C
14. A
15. D

16. B
17. A
18. D
19. B
20. C

21. D
22. C
23. C
24. D
25. B

TEST 2

DIRECTIONS: Each question or incomplete statement is followed by several suggested answers or completions. Select the one that BEST answers the question or completes the statement. *PRINT THE LETTER OF THE CORRECT ANSWER IN THE SPACE AT THE RIGHT.*

1. In a card catalog, a reference from one subject heading to another is MOST commonly called a(n) _____ reference.

    A. cross   B. direct   C. primary   D. indirect

2. A book which is shortened by omission of detail but which retains the general sense of the original is called a(n)

    A. compendium   B. manuscript
    C. miniature   D. abridgment

3. An anonymous book is a

    A. book published before 1500
    B. book whose author is unknown
    C. copy which is defective
    D. work that is out of print

4. All the letters, figures, and symbols assigned to a book to indicate its location on library shelves comprise the _____ number.

    A. call   B. Cutter   C. index   D. inventory

5. The term *format* does NOT refer to a book's

    A. binding   B. size
    C. theme   D. typography

6. The term *card catalog* USUALLY refers to a

    A. catalog consisting of loose-leaf pages upon which the cards are pasted
    B. catalog in which entries are on separate cards arranged in a definite order
    C. catalog of the cards available from the Library of Congress
    D. record on cards of the works which have been weeded out of the library collection

7. The term *circulation record* USUALLY refers to a record of

    A. daily attendance
    B. the books borrowed
    C. the most popular books
    D. the books out on interlibrary loan

8. Reading shelves USUALLY involves checking the shelves to see that all the books

    A. are in the correct order
    B. are suitable for the library's patrons
    C. are there
    D. have been cataloged correctly

9. In an alphabetical catalog of book titles and authors' names, the name *de Santis* would be filed

   A. after *DeWitt*
   B. after *Sanders*
   C. before AND THEN THERE WERE NONE
   D. before *Deutsch*

10. In typing, the Shift key on the computer keyboard is used to

    A. change the font size
    B. indent a line of text
    C. type numbers
    D. type capitals

11. The abbreviation e.g. means *most nearly*

    A. as follows
    B. for example
    C. refer to
    D. that is

12. The abbreviation ff. means *most nearly*

    A. and following pages
    B. formerly
    C. frontispiece
    D. the end

13. The abbreviation ibid, means *most nearly*

    A. consult the index
    B. in the same place
    C. see below
    D. turn the page

14. *Ex libris* is a Latin phrase meaning

    A. former librarian
    B. from the books
    C. without charge
    D. without liberty

15. An expurgated edition of a book is one which

    A. contains many printing errors
    B. includes undesirable passages
    C. is not permitted in public libraries
    D. omits objectionable material

16. The re-charging of a book to a borrower is USUALLY called

    A. fining
    B. processing
    C. reissue
    D. renewal

17. A sheet of paper that is pierced with holes is

    A. borated
    B. collated
    C. perforated
    D. serrated

18. *Glossary* means *most nearly* a(n)

    A. dictionary of selected terms in a particular book or field
    B. list of chapter headings in the order in which they appear in a book
    C. section of the repairing division which coats books with a protective lacquer
    D. alphabetical table of the contents of a book

19. *Accessioning* means *most nearly*

    A. acquiring books
    B. arranging books for easy access
    C. donating books as gifts
    D. listing books in the order of purchase

20. *Bookplate* means *most nearly*

    A. a label in a book showing who owns it
    B. a metal device for holding books upright
    C. a rounded zinc surface upon which a page is printed
    D. the flat part of the binding of a book

21. *Thesaurus* means *most nearly* a book which

    A. contains instructions on how to prepare a thesis
    B. contains words grouped according to similarity of meaning
    C. describes the techniques of dramatic acting
    D. gives quotations from well-known works of literature

22. *Salacious* means *most nearly*

    A. careful   B. delicious   C. lewd   D. salty

23. *Pseudonym* means *most nearly*

    A. false report   B. fictitious name
    C. libelous statement   D. psychic phenomenon

24. *Gamut* means *most nearly* a(n)

    A. bookworm   B. simpleton
    C. vagrant   D. entire range

25. *Monograph* means *most nearly* a

    A. machine for duplicating typewritten material by means of a stencil
    B. picture reproduced on an entire page of a manuscript
    C. single chart used to represent statistical data
    D. systematic treatise on a particular subject

KEY (CORRECT ANSWERS)

1.	A		11.	B
2.	D		12.	A
3.	B		13.	B
4.	A		14.	B
5.	C		15.	D
6.	B		16.	D
7.	B		17.	C
8.	A		18.	A
9.	D		19.	D
10.	D		20.	A

21. B
22. C
23. B
24. D
25. D

TEST 3

DIRECTIONS: Each question or incomplete statement is followed by several suggested answers or completions. Select the one that BEST answers the question or completes the statement. *PRINT THE LETTER OF THE CORRECT ANSWER IN THE SPACE AT THE RIGHT.*

Questions 1-15.

DIRECTIONS: Questions 1 through 15 are to be answered SOLELY on the basis of the information contained in the following passage.

Machines may be useful for bibliographic purposes, but they will be useful only if we study the bibliographic requirements to be met and the machines available, in terms of each job which needs to be done. Many standard tools now available are more efficient than high-speed machines if the machines are used as gadgets rather than as the mechanical elements of well-considered systems.

It does not appear impossible for us to learn to think in terms of scientific management to such an extent that we may eventually be able to do much of the routine part of bibliographic work mechanically with greater efficiency, both in terms of cost per unit of service and in terms of management of the intellectual content of literature. There are many bibliographic tasks which will probably not be done mechanically in the near future because the present tools appear to present great advantages over any machine in sight; for example, author bibliography done on the electronic machines would appear to require almost as much work in instructing the machine as is required to look in an author catalog. The major field of usefulness of the machines would appear to be that of subject bibliography, and particularly in research rather than quick reference jobs.

Machines now available or in sight cannot answer a quick reference question either as fast or as economically as will consultation of standard reference works such as dictionaries, encyclopedias, or almanacs, nor would it appear worthwhile to instruct a machine and run the machine to pick out one recent book or "any recent book" in a broad subject field. It would appear, therefore, that high-speed electronic or electrical machinery may be used for bibliographic purposes only in research institutions, at least for the next five or ten years, and their use will probably be limited to research problems in those institutions. It seems quite probable that during the next decade electronic machines, including the Rapid Selector, which was designed with bibliographic purposes in mind, will find application in administrative, office, and business uses to a much greater extent than they will in bibliographic operations.

The shortcomings of machines used as gadgets have been stressed in this paper. Nevertheless, the use of machines for bibliographic purposes is developing, and it is developing rapidly. It appears quite certain that several of the machines and mechanical devices can now perform certain of the routine operations involved in bibliographic work more accurately and more efficiently than these operations can be performed without them.

At least one machine, the Rapid Selector, appears potentially capable of performing higher orders of bibliographic work than we have been able to perform in the past, if and when we learn: (a) what is really needed for the advancement of learning in the way of bibliographic services; and (b) how to utilize the machine efficiently.

2 (#3)

There is no magic in machines as such. There will be time-lag in their application, just as there was with the typewriter. The speed and efficiency in handling the mechanical part of bibliographic work, which will determine the point of diminishing returns, depend in large measure on how long it will be before we approach these problems from the point of view of scientific management.

This report cannot solve the problem of bibliographic organization. Machines alone cannot solve the problem. We need to develop systems of handling the mass of bibliographic material, but such systems cannot be developed until we discover and establish our objectives, our plans, our standards, our methods and controls, within the framework of each situation. This may take twenty years or it may take one hundred, but it will come. The termination of how long the time-lag will be rests upon our time-lag in gathering objective information upon which scientific management of literature can be based.

1. On the basis of the above passage, machines will *probably* be MOST useful in

    A. determining the cost per unit of service
    B. quick reference jobs
    C. subject bibliography
    D. title cataloging

2. On the basis of the above passage, the Rapid Selector will *probably* be LEAST used during the next ten years in

    A. administration   B. bibliographic work
    C. business   D. office work

3. It may be inferred from the above passage that is is NOT practical to use machines to do author bibliography because

    A. experienced machine operators are not available
    B. more than one machine is needed for such a task
    C. the results obtained from a machine are unreliable
    D. too much work is involved in instructing the machine

4. On the basis of the above passage, one of the criteria of efficiency is the

    A. amount of work required   B. cost per unit of service
    C. net cost of service   D. number of machines available

5. On the basis of the above passage, the LEAST efficient of the following for quick reference jobs are

    A. bibliographies   B. dictionaries
    C. encyclopedias   D. machines

6. On the basis of the above passage, in the next few years, high-speed electronic machinery will probably be used for bibliographic purposes only by

    A. civil engineers
    B. institutions of higher education
    C. publishers
    D. research institutions

7. On the basis of the above passage, the Rapid Selector was designed for use in handling

   A. bibliographic operations
   B. computing problems
   C. photographic reproduction
   D. standard reference works

8. On the basis of the above passage, progress on the development of machines to do bibliographic tasks has reached the point at which

   A. all present tools have become obsolete
   B. certain jobs are better performed with machines than without them
   C. machines are as efficient in doing quick reference jobs as in doing special research jobs
   D. machines are no longer regarded as being too expensive

9. The one of the following which is NOT stated by the above passage to be essential in developing ways of handling bibliographic material is

   A. discovering methods and controls
   B. establishing objectives
   C. establishing standards
   D. obtaining historical data

10. The above passage indicates that machines alone will NOT be able to solve the problem of

    A. bibliographic organization
    B. reference work
    C. scientific management
    D. system analysis

11. On the basis of the above passage, the viewpoint of scientific management is essential in

    A. developing the mechanical handling of bibliographic work
    B. operating the Rapid Selector
    C. repairing electronic machines
    D. showing that people are always superior to machines in bibliographic work

12. On the basis of the above passage, there are machines in existence which

    A. are particularly useful for statistical analysis in library work
    B. are the result of scientific management of bibliographic work
    C. have not been efficiently utilized for bibliographic work
    D. may be installed in a medium-sized library

13. On the basis of the above passage, the scientific management of literature awaits the

    A. assembling of objective information
    B. compilation of new reference books
    C. development of more complex machines
    D. development of simplified machinery

14. Based on the above passage, it may be INFERRED that the author's attitude toward the   14._____
use of machines in bibliographic work is that they

    A. have limited usefulness at the present time
    B. will become useful only if scientific management is applied
    C. will probably always be restricted to routine operations
    D. will probably never be useful

15. The author of the above passage believes that high-speed machines are BEST adapted   15._____
to bibliographic work when they are used

    A. as gadgets
    B. in place of standard reference works
    C. to perform complex operations
    D. to perform routine operations

Questions 16-25.

DIRECTIONS: Questions 16 through 25 deal with the classification of non-fiction books according to the Dewey Classification as outlined below. For each book listed, print in the space on the right the letter in front of the class to which it belongs.

Classification

16.	Ernst. WORDS: ENGLISH ROOTS AND HOW THEY GROW	A.	000 General Works	16._____
17.	Faulkner. FROM VERSAILLES TO THE NEW DEAL	B.	100 Philosophy	17._____
18.	Fry. CHINESE ART	C.	200 Religion	18._____
19.	Kant. CRITIQUE OF PURE REASON	D.	300 Social Science	19._____
20.	Millikan. THE ELECTRON	E.	400 Philology	20._____
21.	Morgan. THEORY OF THE GENE	F.	500 Pure Science	21._____
22.	Raine. THE YEAR ONE; POEMS	G.	600 Applied Science, Useful Arts	22._____
23.	Richards. PRINCIPLES OF LITERARY CRITICISM	H.	700 Fine Arts	23._____
24.	Steinberg. BASIC JUDAISM	I.	800 Literature, Belleslettres	24._____
25.	Strachey. QUEEN VICTORIA	J.	900 History, Biography	25._____

KEY (CORRECT ANSWERS)

1. C
2. B
3. D
4. B
5. D

6. D
7. A
8. B
9. D
10. A

11. A
12. C
13. A
14. A
15. D

16. E
17. J
18. H
19. B
20. F

21. F
22. I
23. I
24. C
25. J

EXAMINATION SECTION
TEST 1

DIRECTIONS: Each question or incomplete statement is followed by several suggested answers or completions. Select the one that BEST answers the question or completes the statement. *PRINT THE LETTER OF THE CORRECT ANSWER IN THE SPACE AT THE RIGHT.*

1. When conducting a needs assessment for the purpose of education planning, an agency's FIRST step is to identify or provide

    A. a profile of population characteristics
    B. barriers to participation
    C. existing resources
    D. profiles of competing resources

    1.____

2. Research has demonstrated that of the following, the most effective medium for communicating with external publics is/are

    A. video news releases
    B. television
    C. radio
    D. newspapers

    2.____

3. Basic ideas behind the effort to influence the attitudes and behaviors of a constituency include each of the following, EXCEPT the idea that

    A. words, rather than actions or events, are most likely to motivate
    B. demands for action are a usual response
    C. self-interest usually figures heavily into public involvement
    D. the reliability of change programs is difficult to assess

    3.____

4. An agency representative is trying to craft a pithy message to constituents in order to encourage the use agency program resources. Choosing an audience for such messages is easiest when the message

    A. is project- or behavior-based
    B. is combined with other messages
    C. is abstract
    D. has a broad appeal

    4.____

5. Of the following factors, the most important to the success of an agency's external education or communication programs is the

    A. amount of resources used to implement them
    B. public's prior experiences with the agency
    C. real value of the program to the public
    D. commitment of the internal audience

    5.____

6. A representative for a state agency is being interviewed by a reporter from a local news network. The representative is being asked to defend a program that is extremely unpopular in certain parts of the municipality. When a constituency is known to be opposed to a position, the most useful communication strategy is to present

    6.____

A. only the arguments that are consistent with constituents' views
B. only the agency's side of the issue
C. both sides of the argument as clearly as possible
D. both sides of the argument, omitting key information about the opposing position

7. The most significant barriers to effective agency community relations include
    I. widespread distrust of communication strategies
    II. the media's "watchdog" stance
    III. public apathy
    IV. statutory opposition

    A. I only
    B. I and II
    C. II and III
    D. III and IV

8. In conducting an education program, many agencies use workshops and seminars in a classroom setting. Advantages of classroom-style teaching over other means of educating the public include each of the following, EXCEPT:

    A. enabling an instructor to verify learning through testing and interaction with the target audience
    B. enabling hands-on practice and other participatory learning techniques
    C. ability to reach an unlimited number of participants in a given length of time
    D. ability to convey the latest, most up-to-date information

9. The _____ model of community relations is characterized by an attempt to persuade the public to adopt the agency's point of view.

    A. two-way symmetric
    B. two-way asymmetric
    C. public information
    D. press agency/publicity

10. Important elements of an internal situation analysis include the
    I. list of agency opponents
    II. communication audit
    III. updated organizational almanac
    IV. stakeholder analysis

    A. I and II
    B. I, II and III
    C. II and III
    D. I, II, III and IV

11. Government agency information efforts typically involve each of the following objectives, EXCEPT to

    A. implement changes in the policies of government agencies to align with public opinion
    B. communicate the work of agencies
    C. explain agency techniques in a way that invites input from citizens
    D. provide citizen feedback to government administrators

12. Factors that are likely to influence the effectiveness of an educational campaign include the
    I. level of homogeneity among intended participants
    II. number and types of media used
    III. receptivity of the intended participants
    IV. level of specificity in the message or behavior to be taught

    A. I and II
    B. I, II and III
    C. II and III
    D. I, II, III and IV

13. An agency representative is writing instructional objectives that will later help to measure the effectiveness of an educational program. Which of the following verbs, included in an objective, would be MOST helpful for the purpose of measuring effectiveness?

    A. Know
    B. Identify
    C. Learn
    D. Comprehend

14. A state education agency wants to encourage participation in a program that has just received a boost through new federal legislation. The program is intended to include participants from a wide variety of socioeconomic and other demographic characteristics. The agency wants to launch a broad-based program that will inform virtually every interested party in the state about the program's new circumstances. In attempting to deliver this message to such a wide-ranging constituency, the agency's best practice would be to

    A. broadcast the same message through as many different media channels as possible
    B. focus on one discrete segment of the public at a time
    C. craft a message whose appeal is as broad as the public itself
    D. let the program's achievements speak for themselves and rely on word-of-mouth

15. Advantages associated with using the World Wide Web as an educational tool include
    I. an appeal to younger generations of the public
    II. visually-oriented, interactive learning
    III. learning that is not confined by space, time, or institutional association
    IV. a variety of methods for verifying use and learning

    A. I only
    B. I and II
    C. I, II and III
    D. I, II, III and IV

16. In agencies involved in health care, community relations is a critical function because it

    A. serves as an intermediary between the agency and consumers
    B. generates a clear mission statement for agency goals and priorities
    C. ensures patient privacy while satisfying the media's right to information
    D. helps marketing professionals determine the wants and needs of agency constituents

17. After an extensive campaign to promote its newest program to constituents, an agency learns that most of the audience did not understand the intended message. Most likely, the agency has

   A. chosen words that were intended to inform, rather than persuade
   B. not accurately interpreted what the audience really needed to know
   C. overestimated the ability of the audience to receive and process the message
   D. compensated for noise that may have interrupted the message

18. The necessary elements that lead to conviction and motivation in the minds of participants in an educational or information program include each of the following, EXCEPT the _____ of the message.

   A. acceptability
   B. intensity
   C. single-channel appeal
   D. pervasiveness

19. Printed materials are often at the core of educational programs provided by public agencies. The primary disadvantage associated with print is that it

   A. does not enable comprehensive treatment of a topic
   B. is generally unreliable in term of assessing results
   C. is often the most expensive medium available
   D. is constrained by time

20. Traditional thinking on public opinion holds that there is about _____ percent of the public who are pivotal to shifting the balance and momentum of opinion they are concerned about an issue, but not fanatical, and interested enough to pay attention to a reasoned discussion.

   A. 2
   B. 10
   C. 33
   D. 51

21. One of the most useful guidelines for influencing attitude change among people is to

   A. inviting the target audience to come to you, rather than approaching them
   B. use moral appeals as the primary approach
   C. use concrete images to enable people to see the results of behaviors or indifference
   D. offer tangible rewards to people for changes in behaviors

22. An agency is attempting to evaluate the effectiveness of its educational program. For this purpose, it wants to observe several focus groups discussing the same program. Which of the following would NOT be a guideline for the use of focus groups?

   A. Focus groups should only include those who have participated in the program.
   B. Be sure to accurately record the discussion.
   C. The same questions should be asked at each focus group meeting.
   D. It is often helpful to have a neutral, non-agency employee facilitate discussions.

23. Research consistently shows that _____ is the determinant most likely to make a newspaper editor run a news release.

    A. novelty
    B. prominence
    C. proximity
    D. conflict

    23.____

24. Which of the following is NOT one of the major variables to take into account when considering a population needs assessment?

    A. State of program development
    B. Resources available
    C. Demographics
    D. Community attitudes

    24.____

25. The first step in any communications audit is to

    A. develop a research instrument
    B. determine how the organization currently communicates
    C. hire a contractor
    D. determine which audience to assess

    25.____

KEY (CORRECT ANSWERS)

1. A
2. D
3. A
4. A
5. D

6. C
7. D
8. C
9. B
10. C

11. A
12. D
13. B
14. B
15. C

16. A
17. B
18. C
19. B
20. B

21. C
22. A
23. C
24. C
25. D

TEST 2

DIRECTIONS: Each question or incomplete statement is followed by several suggested answers or completions. Select the one that BEST answers the question or completes the statement. *PRINT THE LETTER OF THE CORRECT ANSWER IN THE SPACE AT THE RIGHT.*

1. A public relations practitioner at an agency has just composed a press release highlighting a program's recent accomplishments and success stories. In pitching such releases to print outlets, the practitioner should
    I. e-mail, mail, or send them by messenger
    II. address them to "editor" or "news director"
    III. have an assistant call all media contacts by telephone
    IV. ask reporters or editors how they prefer to receive them

    A. I and II   B. I and IV   C. II, III and IV   D. III only

    1.___

2. The "output goals" of an educational program are MOST likely to include

    A. specified ratings of services by participants on a standardized scale
    B. observable effects on a given community or clientele
    C. the number of instructional hours provided
    D. the number of participants served

    2.___

3. An agency wants to evaluate satisfaction levels among program participants, and mails out questionnaires to everyone who has been enrolled in the last year. The primary problem associated with this method of evaluative research is that it

    A. poses a significant inconvenience for respondents
    B. is inordinately expensive
    C. does not allow for follow-up or clarification questions
    D. usually involves a low response rate

    3.___

4. A communications audit is an important tool for measuring

    A. the depth of penetration of a particular message or program
    B. the cost of the organization's information campaigns
    C. how key audiences perceive an organization
    D. the commitment of internal stakeholders

    4.___

5. The "ABC's" of written learning objectives include each of the following, EXCEPT

    A. Audience   B. Behavior   C. Conditions   D. Delineation

    5.___

6. When attempting to change the behaviors of constituents, it is important to keep in mind that
    I. most people are skeptical of communications that try to get them to change their behaviors
    II. in most cases, a person selects the media to which he exposes himself
    III. people tend to react defensively to messages or programs that rely on fear as a motivating factor
    IV. programs should aim for the broadest appeal possible in order to include as many participants as possible

    A. I and II   B. I, II and III   C. II and III   D. I, II, III and IV

    6.___

7. The "laws" of public opinion include the idea that it is

   A. useful for anticipating emergencies
   B. not sensitive to important events
   C. basically determined by self-interest
   D. sustainable through persistent appeals

8. Which of the following types of evaluations is used to measure public attitudes before and after an information/educational program?

   A. retrieval study
   B. copy test
   C. quota sampling
   D. benchmark study

9. The primary source for internal communications is/are usually

   A. flow charts
   B. meetings
   C. voice mail
   D. printed publications

10. An agency representative is putting together informational materials brochures and a newsletteroutlining changes in one of the state's biggest benefits programs. In assembling print materials as a medium for delivering information to the public, the representative should keep in mind each of the following trends:
    I. For various reasons, the reading capabilities of the public are in general decline
    II. Without tables and graphs to help illustrate the changes, it is unlikely that the message will be delivered effectively
    III. Professionals and career-oriented people are highly receptive to information written in the form of a journal article or empirical study
    IV. People tend to be put off by print materials that use itemized and bulleted (•) lists.

    A. I and II   B. I, II and III   C. II and III   D. I, II, III and IV

11. Which of the following steps in a problem-oriented information campaign would typically be implemented FIRST?

    A. Deciding on tactics
    B. Determining a communications strategy
    C. Evaluating the problem's impact
    D. Developing an organizational strategy

12. A common pitfall in conducting an educational program is to

    A. aim it at the wrong target audience
    B. overfund it
    C. leave it in the hands of people who are in the business of education, rather than those with expertise in the business of the organization
    D. ignore the possibility that some other organization is meeting the same educational need for the target audience

13. The key factors that affect the credibility of an agency's educational program include

    A. organization
    B. scope
    C. sophistication
    D. penetration

14. Research on public opinion consistently demonstrates that it is

    A. easy to move people toward a strong opinion on anything, as long as they are approached directly through their emotions
    B. easier to move people away from an opinion they currently hold than to have them form an opinion about something they have not previously cared about
    C. easy to move people toward a strong opinion on anything, as long as the message appeals to their reason and intellect
    D. difficult to move people toward a strong opinion on anything, no matter what the approach

15. In conducting an education program, many agencies use meetings and conferences to educate an audience about the organization and its programs. Advantages associated with this approach include
    I. a captive audience that is known to be interested in the topic
    II. ample opportunities for verifying learning
    III. cost-efficient meeting space
    IV. the ability to provide information on a wider variety of subjects

    A. I and II
    B. I, III and IV
    C. II and III
    D. I, II, III and IV

16. An agency is attempting to evaluate the effectiveness of its educational programs. For this purpose, it wants to observe several focus groups discussing particular programs. For this purpose, a focus group should never number more than _____ participants.

    A. 5   B. 10   C. 15   D. 20

17. A _____ speech is written so that several agency members can deliver it to different audiences with only minor variations.

    A. basic   B. printed   C. quota   D. pattern

18. Which of the following statements about public opinion is generally considered to be FALSE?

    A. Opinion is primarily reactive rather than proactive.
    B. People have more opinions about goals than about the means by which to achieve them.
    C. Facts tend to shift opinion in the accepted direction when opinion is not solidly structured.
    D. Public opinion is based more on information than desire.

19. An agency is trying to promote its educational program. As a general rule, the agency should NOT assume that

    A. people will only participate if they perceive an individual benefit
    B. promotions need to be aimed at small, discrete groups
    C. if the program is good, the audience will find out about it
    D. a variety of methods, including advertising, special events, and direct mail, should be considered

20. In planning a successful educational program, probably the first and most important question for an agency to ask is:

    A. What will be the content of the program?
    B. Who will be served by the program?
    C. When is the best time to schedule the program?
    D. Why is the program necessary?

21. Media kits are LEAST likely to contain

    A. fact sheets
    B. memoranda
    C. photographs with captions
    D. news releases

22. The use of pamphlets and booklets as media for communication with the public often involves the disadvantage that

    A. the messages contained within them are frequently nonspecific
    B. it is difficult to measure their effectiveness in delivering the message
    C. there are few opportunities for people to refer to them
    D. color reproduction is poor

23. The most important prerequisite of a good educational program is an

    A. abundance of resources to implement it
    B. individual staff unit formed for the purpose of program delivery
    C. accurate needs assessment
    D. uneducated constituency

24. After an education program has been delivered, an agency conducts a program evaluation to determine whether its objectives have been met. General rules about how to conduct such an education program evaluation include each of the following, EXCEPT that it

   A. must be done immediately after the program has been implemented
   B. should be simple and easy to use
   C. should be designed so that tabulation of responses can take place quickly and inexpensively
   D. should solicit mostly subjective, open-ended responses if the audience was large

25. Using electronic media such as television as means of educating the public is typically recommended ONLY for agencies that
   I. have a fairly simple message to begin with
   II. want to reach the masses, rather than a targeted audience
   III. have substantial financial resources
   IV. accept that they will not be able to measure the results of the campaign with much precision

   A. I and II
   B. I, II and III
   C. II and IV
   D. I, II, III and IV

KEY (CORRECT ANSWERS)

1.	B	11.	C
2.	C	12.	D
3.	D	13.	A
4.	C	14.	D
5.	D	15.	B
6.	B	16.	B
7.	C	17.	D
8.	D	18.	D
9.	D	19.	C
10.	A	20.	D

21. B
22. B
23. C
24. D
25. D

EXAMINATION SECTION
TEST 1

DIRECTIONS: Each question or incomplete statement is followed by several suggested answers or completions. Select the one that BEST answers the question or completes the statement. *PRINT THE LETTER OF THE CORRECT ANSWER IN THE SPACE AT THE RIGHT.*

1. A supervisor may be required to help train a newly appointed clerk. Which of the following is LEAST important for a newly appointed clerk to know in order to perform his work efficiently?

    A. Acceptable ways of answering and recording telephone calls
    B. The number of files in the storage files unit
    C. The filing methods used by his unit
    D. Proper techniques for handling visitors

    1.____

2. In your agency you have the responsibility of processing clients who have appointments with agency representatives. On a particularly busy day, a client comes to your desk and insists that she must see the person handling her case although she has no appointment.
   Under the circumstances, your FIRST action should be to

    A. show her the full appointment schedule
    B. give her an appointment for another day
    C. ask her to explain the urgency
    D. tell her to return later in the day

    2.____

3. Which of the following practices is BEST for a supervisor to use when assigning work to his staff?

    A. Give workers with seniority the most difficult jobs
    B. Assign all unimportant work to the slower workers
    C. Permit each employee to pick the job he prefers
    D. Make assignments based on the workers' abilities

    3.____

4. In which of the following instances is a supervisor MOST justified in giving commands to people under his supervision? When

    A. they delay in following instructions which have been given to them clearly
    B. they become relaxed and slow about work, and he wants to speed up their production
    C. he must direct them in an emergency situation
    D. he is instructing them on jobs that are unfamiliar to them

    4.____

5. Which of the following supervisory actions or attitudes is MOST likely to result in getting subordinates to try to do as much work as possible for a supervisor?
   He

    A. shows that his most important interest is in schedules and production goals
    B. consistently pressures his staff to get the work out
    C. never fails to let them know he is in charge
    D. considers their abilities and needs while requiring that production goals be met

    5.____

6. Assume that a supervisor has been explaining certain regulations to a new clerk under his supervision.
The MOST efficient way for the supervisor to make sure that the clerk has understood the explanation is to

   A. give him written materials on the regulations
   B. ask him if he has any further questions about the regulations
   C. ask him specific questions based on what has just been explained to him
   D. watch the way he handles a situation involving these regulations

7. One of your unit clerks has been assigned to work for a Mr. Jones in another office for several days. At the end of the first day, Mr. Jones, saying the clerk was not satisfactory, asks that she not be assigned to him again. This clerk is one of your most dependable workers, and no previous complaints about her work have come to you from any other outside assignments.
To get to the root of this situation, your FIRST action should be to

   A. ask Mr. Jones to explain in what way her work was unsatisfactory
   B. ask the clerk what she did that Mr. Jones considered unsatisfactory
   C. check with supervisors for whom she previously worked to see if your own rating of her is in error
   D. tell Mr. Jones to pick the clerk he would prefer to have work for him the next time

8. A senior typist, still on probation, is instructed to type, as quickly as possible, one section of a draft of a long, complex report. Her part must be typed and readable before another part of the report can be written. Asked when she can have the report ready, she gives her supervisor an estimate of a day longer than she knows it will actually take. She then finishes the job a day sooner than the date given her supervisor.
The judgment shown by the senior typist in giving an overestimate of time in a situation like this is, in general,

   A. *good* because it prevents the supervisor from thinking she works slowly
   B. *good* because it keeps unrealistic supervisors from expecting too much
   C. *bad* because she should have used the time left to further check and proofread her work
   D. *bad* because schedules and plans for other parts of the project may have been based on her false estimate

9. Suppose a new clerk, still on probation, is placed under your supervision and refuses to do a job you ask him to do. What is the FIRST thing you should do?

   A. Explain that you are the supervisor and he must follow your instructions.
   B. Tell him he may be suspended if he refuses.
   C. Ask someone else to do the job and rate him accordingly.
   D. Ask for his reason for objecting to the request.

10. As a supervisor of a small group of people, you have blamed worker A for something that you later find out was really done by worker B.
The BEST thing for you to do now would be to

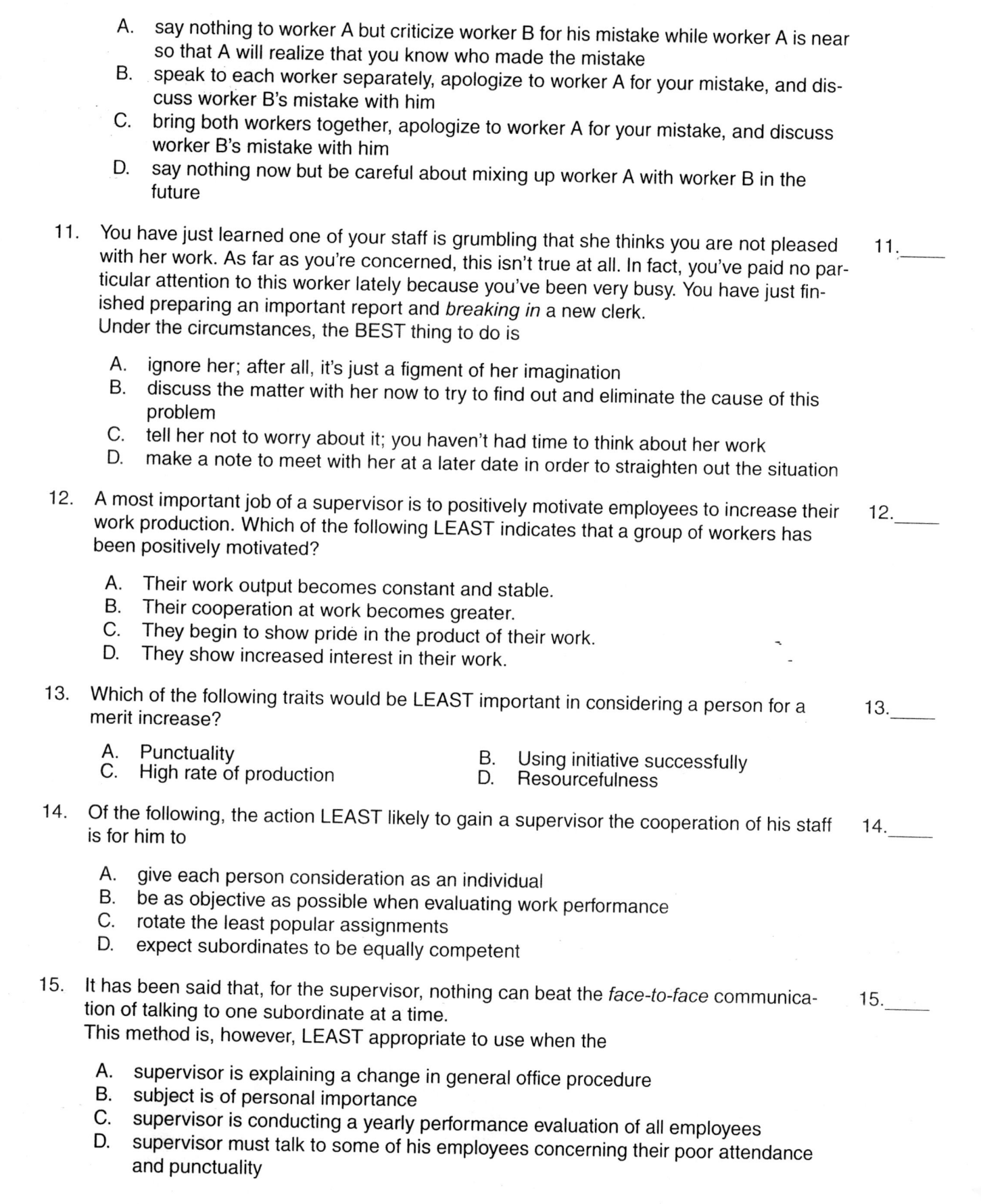

A. say nothing to worker A but criticize worker B for his mistake while worker A is near so that A will realize that you know who made the mistake
B. speak to each worker separately, apologize to worker A for your mistake, and discuss worker B's mistake with him
C. bring both workers together, apologize to worker A for your mistake, and discuss worker B's mistake with him
D. say nothing now but be careful about mixing up worker A with worker B in the future

11. You have just learned one of your staff is grumbling that she thinks you are not pleased with her work. As far as you're concerned, this isn't true at all. In fact, you've paid no particular attention to this worker lately because you've been very busy. You have just finished preparing an important report and *breaking in* a new clerk.
Under the circumstances, the BEST thing to do is

A. ignore her; after all, it's just a figment of her imagination
B. discuss the matter with her now to try to find out and eliminate the cause of this problem
C. tell her not to worry about it; you haven't had time to think about her work
D. make a note to meet with her at a later date in order to straighten out the situation

11.____

12. A most important job of a supervisor is to positively motivate employees to increase their work production. Which of the following LEAST indicates that a group of workers has been positively motivated?

A. Their work output becomes constant and stable.
B. Their cooperation at work becomes greater.
C. They begin to show pride in the product of their work.
D. They show increased interest in their work.

12.____

13. Which of the following traits would be LEAST important in considering a person for a merit increase?

A. Punctuality
C. High rate of production
B. Using initiative successfully
D. Resourcefulness

13.____

14. Of the following, the action LEAST likely to gain a supervisor the cooperation of his staff is for him to

A. give each person consideration as an individual
B. be as objective as possible when evaluating work performance
C. rotate the least popular assignments
D. expect subordinates to be equally competent

14.____

15. It has been said that, for the supervisor, nothing can beat the *face-to-face* communication of talking to one subordinate at a time.
This method is, however, LEAST appropriate to use when the

A. supervisor is explaining a change in general office procedure
B. subject is of personal importance
C. supervisor is conducting a yearly performance evaluation of all employees
D. supervisor must talk to some of his employees concerning their poor attendance and punctuality

15.____

16. While you are on the telephone answering a question about your agency, a visitor comes to your desk and starts to ask you a question. There is no emergency or urgency in either situation, that of the phone call or that of answering the visitor's question.
In this case, you should

    A. continue to answer the person on the telephone until you are finished and then tell the visitor you are sorry to have kept him waiting
    B. excuse yourself to the person on the telephone and tell the visitor that you will be with him as soon as you have finished on the phone
    C. explain to the person on the telephone that you have a visitor and must shorten the conversation
    D. continue to answer the person on the phone while looking up occasionally at the visitor to let him know that you know he is waiting

17. While speaking on the telephone to someone who called, you are disconnected.
The FIRST thing you should do is

    A. hang up but try to keep your line free to receive the call back
    B. immediately get the dialtone and continually dial the person who called you until you reach him
    C. signal the switchboard operator and ask her to re-establish the connection
    D. dial 0 for Operator and explain that you were disconnected

18. The type of speech used by an office worker in telephone conversations greatly affects the communicator.
Of the following, the BEST way to express your ideas when telephoning is with a vocabulary that consists mainly of _____ words.

    A. formal, intellectual sounding
    B. often used colloquial
    C. technical, emphatic
    D. simple, descriptive

19. Suppose a clerk under your supervision has taken a personal phone call and is at the same time needed to answer a question regarding an assignment being handled by another member of your office. He appears confused as to what he should do. How should you instruct him later as to how to handle a similar situation?
You should tell him to

    A. tell the caller to hold on while he answers the question
    B. tell the caller to call back a little later
    C. return the call during an assigned break
    D. finish the conversation quickly and answer the question

20. You are asked to place a telephone call by your supervisor. When you place the call, you receive what appears to be a wrong number.
Of the following, you should FIRST

    A. check the number with your supervisor to see if the number he gave you is correct
    B. ask the person on the other end what his number is and who he is
    C. check with the person on the other end to see if the number you dialed is the number you received
    D. apologize to the person on the other end for disturbing him and hang up

Questions 21-30.

WORD MEANING

DIRECTIONS: Each Question 21 through 30 contains a word in capitals followed by four suggested meanings of the word. For each question, choose the BEST meaning and write the letter of the best meaning in the space at the right.

21. ACCURATE
    A. correct   B. useful   C. afraid   D. careless   21.____

22. ALTER
    A. copy   B. change   C. repeat   D. agree   22.____

23. DOCUMENT
    A. outline   B. agreement   C. blueprint   D. record   23.____

24. INDICATE
    A. listen   B. show   C. guess   D. try   24.____

25. INVENTORY
    A. custom   B. discovery   C. warning   D. list   25.____

26. ISSUE
    A. annoy   B. use up   C. give out   D. gain   26.____

27. NOTIFY
    A. inform   B. promise   C. approve   D. strengthen   27.____

28. ROUTINE
    A. path   B. mistake   C. habit   D. journey   28.____

29. TERMINATE
    A. rest   B. start   C. deny   D. end   29.____

30. TRANSMIT
    A. put in   B. send   C. stop   D. go across   30.____

Questions 31-35.

READING COMPREHENSION

DIRECTIONS: Questions 31 through 35 test how well you understand what you read. It will be necessary for you to read carefully because your answers to these questions should be based SOLELY on the information given in the following paragraphs.

The recipient gains an impression of a typewritten letter before he begins to read the message. Factors which provide for a good first impression include margins and spacing that are visually pleasing, formal parts of the letter which are correctly placed according to the style of the letter, copy which is free of obvious erasures and over-strikes, and transcript that is even and clear. The problem for the typist is that of how to produce that first, positive impression of her work.

There are several general rules which a typist can follow when she wishes to prepare a properly spaced letter on a sheet of letterhead. Ordinarily, the width of a letter should not be less the four inches nor more than six inches. The side margins should also have a desirable relation to the bottom margin and the space between the letterhead and the body of the letter. Usually the most appealing arrangement is when the side margins are even and the bottom margin is slightly wider than the side margins. In some offices, however, standard line length is used for all business letters, and the secretary then varies the spacing between the date line and the inside address according to the length of the letter.

31. The BEST title for the above paragraphs would be:

    A. Writing Office Letters
    B. Making Good First Impressions
    C. Judging Well-Typed Letters
    D. Good Placing and Spacing for Office Letters

32. According to the above paragraphs, which of the following might be considered the way in which people very quickly judge the quality of work which has been typed?
    By

    A. measuring the margins to see if they are correct
    B. looking at the spacing and cleanliness of the typescript
    C. scanning the body of the letter for meaning
    D. reading the date line and address for errors

33. What, according to the above paragraphs, would be definitely UNDESIRABLE as the average line length of a typed letter?

    A. 4" B. 5" C. 6" D. 7"

34. According to the above paragraphs, when the line length is kept standard, the secretary

    A. does not have to vary the spacing at all since this also is standard
    B. adjusts the spacing between the date line and inside address for different lengths of letters
    C. uses the longest line as a guideline for spacing between the date line and inside address
    D. varies the number of spaces between the lines

35. According to the above paragraphs, side margins are MOST pleasing when they

    A. are even and somewhat smaller than the bottom margin
    B. are slightly wider than the bottom margin
    C. vary with the length of the letter
    D. are figured independently from the letterhead and the body of the letter

7 (#1)

Questions 36-40.

CODING

DIRECTIONS: Name of Applicant   H A N G S B R U K E
Test Code   c o m p l e x i t y
File Number   0 1 2 3 4 5 6 7 8 9

Assume that each of the above capital letters is the first letter of the name of an applicant, that the small letter directly beneath each capital letter is the test code for the applicant, and that the number directly beneath each code letter is the file number for the applicant.

In each of the following Questions 36 through 40, the test code letters and the file numbers in Columns 2 and 3 should correspond to the capital letters in Column 1. For each question, look at each Column carefully and mark your answer as follows:

If there is an error only in Column 2, mark your answer A.
If there is an error only in Column 3, mark your answer B.
If there is an error in both Columns 2 and 3, mark your answer C.
If both Columns 2 and 3 are correct, mark your answer D.

The following sample question is given to help you understand the procedure.

SAMPLE QUESTION

Column 1	Column 2	Column 3
AKEHN	otyci	18902

In Column 2, the final test code letter *i* should be *m*. Column 3 is correctly coded to Column 1. Since there is an error only in Column 2, the answer is A.

	Column 1	Column 2	Column 3	
36.	NEKKU	mytti	29987	36._____
37.	KRAEB	txlye	86095	37._____
38.	ENAUK	ymoit	92178	38._____
39.	REANA	xeomo	69121	39._____
40.	EKHSE	ytcxy	97049	40._____

Questions 41-50.

ARITHMETICAL REASONING

DIRECTIONS: Solve the following problems.

41. If a secretary answered 28 phone calls and typed the addresses for 112 credit statements in one morning, what is the RATIO of phone calls answered to credit statements typed for that period of time?   41._____

   A. 1:4   B. 1:7   C. 2:3   D. 3:5

42. According to a suggested filing system, no more than 10 folders should be filed behind any one file guide, and from 15 to 25 file guides should be used in each file drawer for easy finding and filing.
The MAXIMUM number of folders that a five-drawer file cabinet can hold to allow easy finding and filing is

   A. 550   B. 750   C. 1,100   D. 1,250

43. An employee had a starting salary of $32,902. He received a salary increase at the end of each year, and at the end of the seventh year, his salary was $36,738. What was his AVERAGE annual increase in salary over these seven years?

   A. $510   B. $538   C. $548   D. $572

44. The 55 typists and 28 senior clerks in a certain agency were paid a total of $1,943,200 in salaries for the year. If the average annual salary of a typist was $22,400, the AVERAGE annual salary of a senior clerk was

   A. $25,400   B. $26,600   C. $26,800   D. $27,000

45. A typist has been given a three-page report to type. She has finished typing the first two pages. The first page has 283 words, and the second page has 366 words.
If the total report consists of 954 words, how many words will she have to type on the third page of the report?

   A. 202   B. 287   C. 305   D. 313

46. In one day, Clerk A processed 30% more forms than Clerk B, and Clerk C processed 1 1/4 as many forms as Clerk A.
If Clerk B processed 40 forms, how many MORE forms were processed by Clerk C than Clerk B?

   A. 12   B. 13   C. 21   D. 25

47. A clerk who earns a gross salary of $452 every week has the following deductions taken from her paycheck: 17 1/2% for City, State, Federal taxes, and for Social Security, $1.20 for health insurance, and $6.10 for union dues. The amount of her take-home pay is

   A. $286.40   B. $312.40   C. $331.60   D. $365.60

48. In 2006 an agency spent $200 to buy pencils at a cost of $1 a dozen.
If the agency used 3/4 of these pencils in 2006 and used the same number of pencils in 2007, how many MORE pencils did it have to buy to have enough pencils for all of 2007?

   A. 1,200   B. 2,400   C. 3,600   D. 4,800

49. A clerk who worked in Agency X earned the following salaries: $30,070 the first year, $30,500 the second year, and $30,960 the third year. Another clerk who worked in Agency Y for three years earned $30,550 a year for two years and $30,724 the third year. The DIFFERENCE between the average salaries received by both clerks over a three-year period is

   A. $98   B. $102   C. $174   D. $282

50. An employee who works over 40 hours in any week receives overtime payment for the extra hours at time and one-half (1 1/2 times) his hourly rate of pay. An employee who earns $7.80 an hour works a total of 45 hours during a certain week.
His TOTAL pay for that week would be

    A. $312.00   B. $351.00   C. $370.50   D. $412.00

50. _____

KEY (CORRECT ANSWERS)

1. B	11. B	21. A	31. D	41. A
2. C	12. A	22. B	32. B	42. D
3. D	13. A	23. D	33. D	43. C
4. C	14. D	24. B	34. B	44. A
5. D	15. A	25. D	35. A	45. C
6. C	16. B	26. C	36. B	46. D
7. A	17. A	27. A	37. C	47. D
8. D	18. D	28. C	38. D	48. B
9. D	19. C	29. D	39. A	49. A
10. B	20. C	30. B	40. C	50. C

TEST 2

DIRECTIONS: Each question or incomplete statement is followed by several suggested answers or completions. Select the one that BEST answers the question or completes the statement. *PRINT THE LETTER OF THE CORRECT ANSWER IN THE SPACE AT THE RIGHT.*

1. To tell a newly employed clerk to fill a top drawer of a four-drawer cabinet with heavy folders which will be often used and to keep lower drawers only partly filled is

    A. *good* because a tall person would have to bend unnecessarily if he had to use a lower drawer
    B. *bad* because the file cabinet may tip over when the top drawer is opened
    C. *good* because it is the most easily reachable drawer for the average person
    D. *bad* because a person bending down at another drawer may accidentally bang his head on the bottom of the drawer when he straightens up

2. If you have requisitioned a *ream* of paper in order to duplicate a single page office announcement, how many announcements can be printed from the one package of paper?

    A. 200   B. 500   C. 700   D. 1,000

3. In the operations of a government agency, a voucher is ORDINARILY used to

    A. refer someone to the agency for a position or assignment
    B. certify that an agency's records of financial transactions are accurate
    C. order payment from agency funds of a stated amount to an individual
    D. enter a statement of official opinion in the records of the agency

4. Of the following types of cards used in filing systems, the one which is generally MOST helpful in locating records which might be filed under more than one subject is the _____ card.

    A. cut   B. tickler
    C. cross-reference   D. visible index

5. The type of filing system in which one does NOT need to refer to a card index in order to find the folder is called

    A. alphabetic   B. geographic   C. subject   D. locational

6. Of the following, records management is LEAST concerned with

    A. the development of the best method for retrieving important information
    B. deciding what records should be kept
    C. deciding the number of appointments a client will need
    D. determining the types of folders to be used

7. If records are continually removed from a set of files without *charging* them to the borrower, the filing system will soon become ineffective.
   Of the following terms, the one which is NOT applied to a form used in a charge-out system is a

    A. requisition card   B. out-folder
    C. record retrieval form D. substitution card

8. A new clerk has been told to put 500 cards in alphabetical order. Another clerk suggests that she divide the cards into four groups such as A to F, G to L, M to R, and S to Z, and then alphabetize these four smaller groups.
The suggested method is

    A. *poor* because the clerk will have to handle the sheets more than once and will waste time
    B. *good* because it saves time, is more accurate, and is less tiring
    C. *good* because she will not have to concentrate on it so much when it is in smaller groups
    D. *poor* because this method is much more tiring than straight alphabetizing

9. The term that describes the equipment attached to an office computer is

    A. interface   B. network   C. hardware   D. software

10. Suppose a clerk has been given pads of pre-printed forms to use when taking phone messages for others in her office. The clerk is then observed using scraps of paper and not the forms for writing her messages.
It should be explained that the BEST reason for using the forms is that

    A. they act as a checklist to make sure that the important information is taken
    B. she is expected to do her work in the same way as others in the office
    C. they make sure that unassigned paper is not wasted on phone messages
    D. learning to use these forms will help train her to use more difficult forms

11. Of the following, the one which is spelled incorrectly is

    A. alphabetization   B. reccommendation
    C. redaction   D. synergy

12. Of the following, the MAIN reason a stock clerk keeps a perpetual inventory of supplies in the storeroom is that such an inventory will

    A. eliminate the need for a physical inventory
    B. provide a continuous record of supplies on hand
    C. indicate whether a shipment of supplies is satisfactory
    D. dictate the terms of the purchase order

13. As a supervisor, you may be required to handle different types of correspondence. Of the following types of letters, it would be MOST important to promptly seal which kind of letters?

    A. One marked *confidential*
    B. Those containing enclosures
    C. Any letter to be sent airmail
    D. Those in which carbons will be sent along with the original

14. While opening incoming mail, you notice that one letter indicates that an enclosure was to be included but, even after careful inspection, you are not able to find the information to which this refers.
Of the following, the thing that you should do FIRST is

A. replace the letter in its envelope and return it to the sender
B. file the letter until the sender's office mails the missing information
C. type out a letter to the sender informing them of their error
D. make a notation in the margin of the letter that the enclosure was omitted

15. You have been given a checklist and assigned the responsibility of inspecting certain equipment in the various offices of your agency.
Which of the following is the GREATEST advantage of the checklist?

A. It indicates which equipment is in greatest demand.
B. Each piece of equipment on the checklist will be checked only once.
C. It helps to insure that the equipment listed will not be overlooked.
D. The equipment listed suggests other equipment you should look for.

16. Your supervisor has asked you to locate a telephone number for an attorney named Jones, whose office is located at 311 Broadway and whose name is not already listed in your files.
The BEST method for finding the number would be for you to

A. call the information operator and have her get it for you
B. look in the alphabetical directory (white pages) under the name Jones at 311 Broadway
C. refer to the heading Attorney in the yellow pages for the name Jones at 311 Broadway
D. ask your supervisor who referred her to Mr. Jones, then call that person for the number

17. An example of material that should NOT be sent by first class mail is a

A. carbon copy of a letter
B. postcard
C. business reply card
D. large catalogue

18. Which of the following BEST describes *office work simplification?*

A. An attempt to increase the rate of production by speeding up the movements of employees
B. Eliminating wasteful steps in order to increase efficiency
C. Making jobs as easy as possible for employees so they will not be overworked
D. Eliminating all difficult tasks from an office and leaving only simple ones

19. The duties of a supervisor who is assigned the job of timekeeper may include all of the following EXCEPT

A. computing and recording regular hours worked each day in accordance with the normal work schedule
B. approving requests for vacation leave, sick leave, and annual leave
C. computing and recording overtime hours worked beyond the normal schedule
D. determining the total regular hours and total extra hours worked during the week

20. Suppose a clerk under your supervision accidentally opens a personal letter while handling office mail.
Under such circumstances, you should tell the clerk to put the letter back into the envelope and

A. take the letter to the person to whom it belongs and make sure he understands that the clerk did not read it
B. try to seal the envelope so it won't appear to have been opened
C. write on the envelope *Sorry - opened by mistake,* and put his initials on it
D. write on the envelope *Sorry - opened by mistake,* but not put his initials on it

Questions 21-25.

SPELLING

DIRECTIONS: Each Question 21 through 25 consists of three words. In each question, one of the words may be spelled incorrectly or all three may be spelled correctly. For each question, if one of the words is spelled incorrectly, write the letter of the incorrect word in the space at the right. If all three words are spelled correctly, write the letter D in the space at the right.

SAMPLE I: (A) guide   (B) departmint   (C) stranger

SAMPLE II: (A) comply   (B) valuable   (C) window

In the Sample Question I, *departmint* is incorrect.
It should be spelled *department*. Therefore, B is the answer to Sample Question I.
In the Sample Question II, all three words are spelled correctly. Therefore, D is the answer to Sample Question II.

21. A. argument   B. reciept   C. complain   21.____
22. A. sufficient   B. postpone   C. visible   22.____
23. A. expirience   B. dissatisfy   C. alternate   23.____
24. A. occurred   B. noticable   C. appendix   24.____
25. A. anxious   B. guarantee   C. calender   25.____

Questions 26-30.

ENGLISH USAGE

DIRECTIONS: Each Question 26 through 30 contains a sentence. Read each sentence carefully to decide whether it is correct. Then, in the space at the right, mark your answer:
(A) if the sentence is incorrect because of bad grammar or sentence structure
(B) if the sentence is incorrect because of bad punctuation
(C) if the sentence is incorrect because of bad capitalization
(D) if the sentence is correct

Each incorrect sentence has only one type of error. Consider a sentence correct if it has no errors, although there may be other correct ways of saying the same thing.

SAMPLE QUESTION I: One of our clerks were promoted yesterday.

The subject of this sentence is *one,* so the verb should be *was promoted* instead of *were promoted*. Since the sentence is incorrect because of bad grammar, the answer to Sample Question I is A.

SAMPLE QUESTION II: Between you and me, I would prefer not going there.

Since this sentence is correct, the answer to Sample Question II is D.

26. The National alliance of Businessmen is trying to persuade private businesses to hire youth in the summertime. 26.___

27. The supervisor who is on vacation, is in charge of processing vouchers. 27.___

28. The activity of the committee at its conferences is always stimulating. 28.___

29. After checking the addresses again, the letters went to the mailroom. 29.___

30. The director, as well as the employees, are interested in sharing the dividends. 30.___

Questions 31-40.

FILING

DIRECTIONS: Each Question 31 through 40 contains four names. For each question, choose the name that should be FIRST if the four names are to be arranged in alphabetical order in accordance with the Rules for Alphabetical Filing given below. Read these rules carefully. Then, for each question, indicate in the correspondingly numbered space at the right the letter before the name that should be FIRST in alphabetical order.

RULES FOR ALPHABETICAL FILING

Names of People

(1) The names of people are filed in strict alphabetical order, first according to the last name, then according to first name or initial, and finally according to middle name or initial. For example: George Allen comes before Edward Bell, and Leonard P. Reston comes before Lucille B. Reston.

(2) When last names are the same, for example A. Green and Agnes Green, the one with the initial comes before the one with the name written out when the first initials are identical.

(3) When first and last names are alike and the middle name is given, for example John David Doe and John Devoe Doe, the names should be filed in the alphabetical order of the middle names.

(4) When first and last names are the same, a name without a middle initial comes before one with a middle name or initial. For example: John Doe comes before both John A. Doe and John Alan Doe.

(5) When first and last names are the same, a name with a middle initial comes before one with a middle name beginning with the same initial. For example: Jack R. Hertz comes before Jack Richard Hertz.

(6) Prefixes such as De, O', Mac, Mc, and Van are filed as written and are treated as part of the names to which they are connected. For example: Robert O'Dea is filed before David Olsen.

(7) Abbreviated names are treated as if they were spelled out. For example: Chas. is filed as Charles and Thos. is filed as Thomas.

(8) Titles and designations such as Dr., Mr., and Prof, are disregarded in filing.

<u>Names of Organizations</u>

(1) The names of business organizations are filed according to the order in which each word in the name appears. When an organization name bears the name of a person, it is filed according to the rules for filing names of people as given above. For example: William Smith Service Co. comes before Television Distributors, Inc.

(2) Where bureau, board, office or department appears as the first part of the title of a governmental agency, that agency should be filed under the word in the title expressing the chief function of the agency. For example: Bureau of the Budget would be filed as if written Budget, (Bureau of the). The Department of Personnel would be filed as if written Personnel, (Department of).

(3) When the following words are part of an organization, they are disregarded: the, of, and.

(4) When there are numbers in a name, they are treated as if they were spelled out. For example: 10th Street Bootery is filed as Tenth Street Bootery.

```
SAMPLE QUESTION:  (A) Jane Earl        (2)
                  (B) James A. Earle   (4)
                  (C) James Earl       (1)
                  (D) J. Earle         (3)
```

The numbers in parentheses show the proper alphabetical order in which these names should be filed. Since the name that should be filed FIRST is James Earl, the answer to the sample question is C.

31. A. Majorca Leather Goods
     B. Robert Maiorca and Sons
     C. Maintenance Management Corp.
     D. Majestic Carpet Mills

31._____

32. A. Municipal Telephone Service
    B. Municipal Reference Library
    C. Municipal Credit Union
    D. Municipal Broadcasting System

33. A. Robert B. Pierce   B. R. Bruce Pierce
    C. Ronald Pierce   D. Robert Bruce Pierce

34. A. Four Seasons Sports Club
    B. 14 Street Shopping Center
    C. Forty Thieves Restaurant
    D. 42nd St. Theaters

35. A. Franco Franceschini   B. Amos Franchini
    C. Sandra Franceschia   D. Lilie Franchinesca

36. A. Chas. A. Levine   B. Kurt Levene
    C. Charles Levine   D. Kurt E. Levene

37. A. Prof. Geo. Kinkaid   B. Mr. Alan Kinkaid
    C. Dr. Albert A. Kinkade   D. Kincade Liquors Inc.

38. A. Department of Public Events
    B. Office of the Public Administrator
    C. Queensborough Public Library
    D. Department of Public Health

39. A. Martin Luther King, Jr. Towers
    B. Metro North Plaza
    C. Manhattanville Houses
    D. Marble Hill Houses

40. A. Dr. Arthur Davids
    B. The David Check Cashing Service
    C. A.C. Davidsen
    D. Milton Davidoff

Questions 41-45.

READING COMPREHENSION

DIRECTIONS: Questions 41 through 45 test how well you understand what you read. It will be necessary for you to read carefully because your answers to these questions should be based SOLELY on the information given in the following paragraph.

Work standards presuppose an ability to measure work. Measurement in office management is needed for several reasons. First, it is necessary to evaluate the overall efficiency of the office itself. It is then essential to measure the efficiency of each particular section or unit and that of the individual worker. To plan and control the work of sections and units, one must have measurement. A program of measurement goes hand in hand with a program of standards. One can have measurement without standards, but one cannot have work standards without measurement. Providing data on amount of work done and time expended, measure-

ment does not deal with the amount of energy expended by an individual although in many cases such energy may be in direct proportion to work output. Usually from two-thirds to three-fourths of all work can be measured. However, less than two-thirds of all work is actually measured because measurement difficulties are encountered when office work is non-repetitive and irregular, or when it is primarily mental rather than manual. These obstacles are often used as excuses for non-measurement far more frequently than is justified.

41. According to the paragraph, an office manager cannot set work standards unless he can

    A. plan the amount of work to be done
    B. control the amount of work that is done
    C. estimate accurately the quantity of work done
    D. delegate the amount of work to be done to efficient workers

42. According to the paragraph, the type of office work that would be MOST difficult to measure would be

    A. checking warrants for accuracy of information
    B. recording payroll changes
    C. processing applications
    D. making up a new system of giving out supplies

43. According to the paragraph, the actual amount of work that is measured is _____ of all work.

    A. less than two-thirds
    B. two-thirds to three-fourths
    C. less than three-sixths
    D. more than three-fourths

44. Which of the following would be MOST difficult to determine by using measurement techniques?

    A. The amount of work that is accomplished during a certain period of time
    B. The amount of work that should be planned for a period of time
    C. How much time is needed to do a certain task
    D. The amount of incentive a person must have to do his job

45. The one of the following which is the MOST suitable title for the paragraph is:

    A. How Measurement of Office Efficiency Depends on Work Standards
    B. Using Measurement for Office Management and Efficiency
    C. Work Standards and the Efficiency of the Office Worker
    D. Managing the Office Using Measured Work Standards

Questions 46-50.

INTERPRETING STATISTICAL DATA

DIRECTIONS: Answer Questions 46 through 50 using the information given in the table below.

AGE COMPOSITION IN THE LABOR FORCE IN CITY A
(1990-2000)

	Age Group	1990	1995	2000
Men	14 - 24	8,430	10,900	14,340
	25 - 44	22,200	22,350	26,065
	45+	17,550	19,800	21,970
Women	14 - 24	4,450	6,915	7,680
	25 - 44	9,080	10,010	11,550
	45+	7,325	9,470	13,180

46. The GREATEST increase in the number of people in the labor force between 1990 and 1995 occurred among

    A. men between the ages of 14 and 24
    B. men age 45 and over
    C. women between the ages of 14 and 24
    D. women age 45 and over

47. If the total number of women of all ages in the labor force increases from 2000 to 2005 by the same number as it did from 1995 to 2000, the TOTAL number of women of all ages in the labor force in 2005 will be

    A. 27,425   B. 29,675   C. 37,525   D. 38,425

48. The total increase in numbers of women in the labor force from 1990 to 1995 differs from the total increase of men in the same years by being _____ than that of men.

    A. 770 less   B. 670 more   C. 770 more   D. 1,670 more

49. In the year 1990, the proportion of married women in each group was as follows: 1/5 of the women in the 14-24 age group, 1/4 of those in the 25-44 age group, and 2/5 of those 45 and over.
How many married women were in the labor force in 1990?

    A. 4,625   B. 5,990   C. 6,090   D. 7,910

50. The 14-24 age group of men in the labor force from 1990 to 2000 increased by APPROXIMATELY

    A. 40%   B. 65%   C. 70%   D. 75%

KEY (CORRECT ANSWERS)

1.	B	11.	B	21.	B	31.	C	41.	C
2.	B	12.	B	22.	D	32.	D	42.	D
3.	C	13.	A	23.	A	33.	B	43.	A
4.	C	14.	D	24.	B	34.	D	44.	D
5.	A	15.	C	25.	C	35.	C	45.	B
6.	C	16.	C	26.	C	36.	B	46.	A
7.	C	17.	D	27.	B	37.	D	47.	D
8.	B	18.	B	28.	D	38.	B	48.	B
9.	C	19.	B	29.	A	39.	A	49.	C
10.	A	20.	C	30.	A	40.	B	50.	C

EXAMINATION SECTION
TEST 1

DIRECTIONS: Each question or incomplete statement is followed by several suggested answers or completions. Select the one that BEST answers the question or completes the statement. *PRINT THE LETTER OF THE CORRECT ANSWER IN THE SPACE AT THE RIGHT.*

1. As head of the filing unit in your department, you have been receiving complaints that material which should be in the files cannot be located. On investigating this matter, you find that one of your new clerks has been careless in placing material in the files.
   The BEST of the following actions which you might take FIRST is to

   A. admonish this clerk and tell him that he will be given a below-average service rating if his carelessness continues
   B. remind this clerk that he is a probationary employee and that his services may be terminated at the end of his probationary period if his carelessness continues
   C. call the attention of this clerk to the effects of filing and impress upon him the necessity for accuracy in filing
   D. give this clerk another assignment in the unit where accuracy is less essential

2. The GREATEST amount of improvement in the efficiency and morale of a unit will be brought about by the supervisor who

   A. reminds his employees constantly that they must follow departmental regulations
   B. frequently praises an employee in the presence of the other employees in the unit
   C. invariably gives mild reproof and constructive criticism to subordinates when he discovers that they have made a mistake
   D. assigns duties to employees in conformance with their abilities and interests as far as practicable

3. Assume that you are the supervisor of a unit which performs routine clerical work. For you to encourage your subordinates to make suggestions for increasing the efficiency of the unit is

   A. *undesirable;* employees who perform routine work may resent having additional duties and responsibilities assigned to them
   B. *desirable;* by presenting criticism of each other's work, the employees may develop a competitive spirit and in this way increase their efficiency
   C. *undesirable;* the employees may conclude that the supervisor is not capable of efficiently supervising the work of the unit
   D. *desirable;* increased interest in their assignment may be acquired by the employees, and the work of the unit may be performed more efficiently

4. The MOST accurate of the following statements regarding the chief purpose for maintaining a perpetual inventory of office supplies is that it

   A. eliminates the necessity for making a physical inventory of office supplies
   B. makes available at all times a record of the balance of office supplies on hand
   C. reduces the amount of clerical work required in distributing supplies
   D. reduces the amount of paper work involved in requisitioning supplies

5. Of the following, a centralized filing system is LEAST suitable for filing

   A. material which is confidential in nature
   B. routine correspondence
   C. periodic reports of the divisions of the department
   D. material used by several divisions of the department

6. Form letters should be used mainly when

   A. an office has to reply to a great many similar inquiries
   B. the type of correspondence varies widely
   C. it is necessary to have letters which are well-phrased and grammatically correct
   D. letters of inquiry have to be answered as soon as possible after they are received

7. Assume that you have recommended that one of your subordinates be given a below-average service rating. The subordinate disagreed with your recommendation and requests that you discuss the service rating report with him.
   In taking up this matter with the employee, the BEST of the following procedures for you to follow is to

   A. discuss the general standards of evaluation you have used, rather than his specific deficiencies
   B. tell him that it would be too time-consuming to discuss his report with him, but inform him that objective standards were used in evaluating all employees and that the reports will be reviewed by an impartial board which will make any changes it deems necessary
   C. explain the standards of evaluation you have used and discuss this subordinate's work with him in relation to these standards
   D. point out to your subordinate that you are in a better position than he to compare his work with that of the other employees in your unit

8. Suppose that you are assigned to prepare a form from which certain information will be posted in a ledger. It would be MOST helpful to the person posting the information in the ledger if, in designing the form, you were to

   A. use the same color paper for both the form and the ledger
   B. make the form the same size as the pages of the ledger
   C. have the information on the form in the same order as that used in the ledger
   D. include in the form a box which is to be initialed when the data on the form have been posted in the ledger

9. A misplaced record is a lost record.
   Of the following, the MOST valid implication of this statement in regard to office work is that

   A. all records in an office should be filed in strict alphabetical order
   B. accuracy in filing is essential
   C. only one method of filing should be used throughout the office
   D. files should be locked when not in use

10. John Smith is applying for a provisional appointment as a clerk in your department. He presents a letter of recommendation from a former employer stating: *John Smith was rarely late or absents he has a very pleasing manner, and never got into an argument with his fellow employees.*
The above information concerning this applicant

   A. proves clearly that he produces more work than the average employee
   B. indicates that he was probably attempting to conceal his inefficiency from his former employer
   C. presents no conclusive evidence of his ability to do clerical work
   D. indicates clearly that with additional training he will make a good supervisor

11. It is not possible to draw a hard and fast line between training courses for greater efficiency on the present job.
This statement means MOST NEARLY that

   A. to be worthwhile, a training course should prepare the employee for promotion as well as for greater efficiency on the present job
   B. training courses should be designed only to increase employee efficiency on the present job
   C. training courses should be given only to employees who are competing for promotion
   D. by attending a training course for promotion, employees may become more efficient in their present work

12. Approximate figures serve as well as exact figures to indicate trends and make comparisons.
Of the following, the MOST accurate statement on the basis of this statement is that

   A. it takes less time to obtain approximate figures than exact figures
   B. exact figures are rarely used as they require too much computation
   C. for certain purposes, approximate figures are as revealing as exact figures
   D. approximate figures can usually be used in place of exact figures

13. Suppose that you are placed in charge of a unit in your department. You find that many of the employees have been disregarding the staff regulation requiring employees to be at their desks at 9:05 A.M.
Of the following, the LEAST desirable course of action for you to take would be to

   A. call a meeting of the staff and explain why it is essential that all employees be at their desks at 9:05 A.M.
   B. post conspicuously on the bulletin board a notice calling the employees' attention to the frequent violation of this regulation and requesting them to observe this regulation
   C. recommend an above-average service rating for all employees who consistently comply with this regulation, provided their work is satisfactory
   D. summon the offenders and explain to them how their violation of this regulation results in decreasing the efficiency of the unit

14. Suppose that certain office responsibilities require you to be frequently absent from the unit you supervise. You have, therefore, decided to designate one of your staff members to act as unit head in your absence.
Of the following factors, the one which is MOST important in selecting the employee best fitted for this assignment is his

   A. manner and personal appearance
   B. estimated ability to perform work of a supervisory nature
   C. ability to perform his present duties
   D. relative seniority in the service

15. One of the assignments in the unit you supervise is the checking of a list of 500 unalphabetized names against an alphabetical 5x8 card index containing several thousand names. The clerk performing this task is to make sure that there is a card in the file for each name on the list.
The one of the following which you should suggest as the BEST procedure for the clerk to follow is for him to

   A. rewrite the names on the list in alphabetical order, look for the corresponding card in the file, and place a check mark next to each name on the list for which he finds a card
   B. take each name on the list in turn, look for the corresponding card in the file, and place a check mark in the corner of each card he finds
   C. go through all the cards in the file in consecutive order and place a check mark next to each name on the list for which he finds a card
   D. take each name on the list in turn, look for the corresponding card in the file, and place a check mark next to each name on the list for which he finds a card

16. Suppose that you are in charge of a unit which maintains a rather intricate filing system. A new file clerk has been added to your staff.
Of the following assignments that may be given to this clerk, the one which requires the LEAST amount of knowledge of the filing system is

   A. placing material in the files
   B. removing papers from the files
   C. classifying and coding material for filing
   D. keeping a record of material taken from, and returned to, the files

17. In undertaking to improve the method of performing a certain job or operation, the new office manager should first ascertain the

   A. present method of performing the job
   B. purpose of the job
   C. number and titles of employees assigned to the job
   D. methods used by other agencies to perform the same kind of job

18. The proofreading of a large number of papers has been assigned to two clerks. These clerks have been instructed to indicate all necessary corrections on a slip of paper, attach this correction slip to the papers, and send them to the typist for correction.
Of the following additional steps that might be taken before sending the papers to the xerox operator, the BEST one is that the

A. clerks should proofread each paper in its entirety after the corrections have been made on it
B. typist should make the necessary corrections and return the correction slip and the corrected papers to the clerks; the clerks should then examine the papers to see that all the requested corrections have been made properly
C. typist should make the necessary corrections, placing a check mark opposite each correction noted on the correction slip; she should then review the correction slip to make sure that no correction has been omitted
D. typist should make the necessary corrections, place a check mark opposite each correction noted on the correction slip, and return the papers and the correction slip to the clerks; the clerks should then review the correction slip to make sure that a check mark has been placed opposite each item on the correction slip

19. Suppose you are the supervisor of a unit in a department. You notice that a clerk with long service in the department is arguing with a recently appointed clerk regarding the procedure to be followed in performing a certain task. Each is convinced he is right. The argument is disturbing the other employees.
Of the following, the BEST action for you to take in dealing with this problem is to

   A. call the clerks to your desk, discuss the matter with them, and then state which procedure is the correct one
   B. support the employee with the longer service, for to do otherwise will impair the morale of the office
   C. call the clerks to your desk and tell them to settle their differences without disturbing the others
   D. order the clerks to discontinue their argument immediately and to bring the matter up at the next staff conference, where the staff will determine which procedure is the correct one

20. Assume that you devised a new procedure which you expected would result in a substantial reduction in the amount of paper used in performing the work of the unit you supervise. After trying out this new procedure in your unit for several weeks, you find that the quantity of paper saved is considerably less than you anticipated.
Of the following, the BEST action for you to take first is to

   A. inform your staff that they are probably using paper unnecessarily, and that in view of the current paper shortage, you expect them to conserve paper as much as possible
   B. suspend the use of this new procedure until you can discover why it has not worked out as you anticipated
   C. invite your subordinates to submit suggestions as to how the procedure may be improved
   D. analyze the various processes involved in the new procedure to determine whether there are any factors which you may have overlooked

21. Assume that you are the head of the bureau of information in a department. You are faced with the problem of replacing the clerk assigned to the information desk.
Of the following available employees, the one who should be given the assignment is

A. John Jones, a new clerk who specialized in English at college and recently received a Master of Arts degree; at present, he has no permanent assignment
B. Mary Smith, an excellent stenographer who has had much experience as secretary to one of the bureau heads; she is intelligent, pleasant in manner, and learns quickly
C. Richard Roe, a clerk who has been rated as *tactful, dependable,* and *resourceful* by the various bureau heads who have prepared his service rating reports during the four years that he has been in the department
D. Jane Doe, who is a diligent typist when she works alone but who disturbs the other typists by her constant stream of chatter when she works near them

22. The one of the following which is the MOST accurate statement regarding routine operations in an office is that

A. routine assignments should not last more than two or three days each week
B. methods for performing routine work should be standardized as much as is practicable
C. routine work performed by one employee should be checked by another employee
D. changes in the procedures of a unit should not affect the existing routine operations of the unit

23. Modern management realizes the importance of sound personnel practices in business administration. It has found that production is largely dependent upon the effective utilization of an employee's interests, capabilities, and skills.
Of the following, the MOST logical implication of the above statement is that

A. there should be one bureau in each business organization to take charge of both production and personnel administration
B. production cannot be increased without the utilization of a sound personnel policy
C. production will increase if the number of persons assigned to work in a business organization is increased
D. maximum efficiency in an organization cannot be achieved without proper placement of employees

24. One of the stenographers under your supervision has completed all of her assignments, and there is no additional typing to be done.
It would be LEAST desirable for you to suggest that she

A. straighten up the supply cabinet to improve its appearance
B. check the files for material that is surplus or outdated
C. read the daily newspaper to keep up with current events
D. practice shorthand or typing to improve her speed

25. Of the following, the BEST way for a supervisor to determine when further on-the-job training in a particular work area is needed is by

A. evaluating the employees' work performance
B. asking the employees
C. determining the ratio of idle time to total work time
D. classifying the jobs in the work area

Questions 26-30.

DIRECTIONS: Each of Questions 26 through 30 consists of a statement containing five words in capital letters. One of these words in capital letters is not in keeping with the meaning which the statement is evidently intended to carry. The five words in capital letters in each statement are reprinted after the statement. In the space at the right, write the letter preceding the one of the five words which does most to spoil the true meaning of the statement.

26. Within each major DIVISION in a properly set-up public or private organization, provision is made so that each NECESSARY activity is CARED for and lines of AUTHORITY and responsibility are clear-cut and INFINITE.

    A. division   B. necessary   C. cared
    D. authority   E. infinite

27. In public service, the scale of salaries paid must be INCIDENTAL to the services rendered, with due CONSIDERATION for the attraction of the desired MANPOWER and for the MAINTENANCE of a standard of living COMMENSURATE with the work to be performed.

    A. incidental   B. consideration   C. manpower
    D. maintenance   E. commensurate

28. An understanding of the AIMS of an organization by the staff will AID greatly in increasing the DEMAND of the correspondence work of the office, and will to a large extent DETERMINE the NATURE of the correspondence.

    A. aims   B. aid   C. demand
    D. determine   E. nature

29. BECAUSE the Civil Service Commission strongly feels that the MERIT system is a key factor in the MAINTENANCE of democratic government, it has adopted as one of its major DEFENSES the progressive democratization of its own PROCEDURES in dealing with candidates for positions in the public service.

    A. Because   B. merit   C. maintenance
    D. defenses   E. procedures

30. Retirement and pensions systems are ESSENTIAL not only to provide employees with a means of support in the future, but also to prevent longevity and CHARITABLE considerations from UPSETTING the PROMOTIONAL opportunities for RETIRED members of the career service.

    A. essential   B. charitable   C. upsetting
    D. promotional   E. retired

31. Suppose that the amount of money spent for supplies in 2005 for a division of a department was $15,650. This represented an increase of 12% over the amount spent for supplies for this division in 2004. The amount of money spent for supplies for this division in 2004 was MOST NEARLY

    A. $13,973   B. $13,772   C. $14,346   D. $13,872

32. Suppose that a group of five clerks have been assigned to insert 24,000 letters into envelopes. The clerks perform this work at the following rates of speed: Clerk A, 1100 letters an hour; Clerk B, 1450 letters an hour; Clerk C, 1200 letters an hour; Clerk D, 1300 letters an hour; Clerk E, 1250 letters an hour. At the end of two hours of work, Clerks C and D are assigned to another task. Fron the time that Clerks C and D were taken off the assignment, the number of hours required for the remaining clerks to complete this assignment is

   A. less than 3 hours
   B. 3 hours
   C. more than 3 hours, but less than 4 hours
   D. more than 4 hours

33. The employees were SKEPTICAL about the usefulness of the new procedure. The word *skeptical,* as used in this sentence, means MOST NEARLY

   A. enthusiastic   B. indifferent
   C. doubtful   D. misinformed

34. He presented ABSTRUSE reasons in defense of his proposal. The word *abstruse,* as used in this sentence, means MOST NEARLY

   A. unnecessary under the circumstances
   B. apparently without merit or value
   C. hard to be understood
   D. obviously sound

35. A program of AUSTERITY is in effect in many countries. The word *austerity,* as used in this sentence, means MOST NEARLY

   A. rigorous self-restraint   B. military censorship
   C. rugged individualism   D. self-indulgence

36. The terms of the contract were ABROGATED at the last meeting of the board. The word *abrogated,* as used in this sentence, means MOST NEARLY

   A. discussed   B. summarized
   C. agreed upon   D. annulled

37. The enforcement of STRINGENT regulations is a difficult task. The word *stringent,* as used in this sentence, means MOST NEARLY

   A. unreasonable   B. strict
   C. unpopular   D. obscure

38. You should not DISPARAGE the value of his suggestions. The word *disparage,* as used in this sentence, means MOST NEARLY

   A. ignore   B. exaggerate
   C. belittle   D. reveal

39. The employee's conduct was considered REPREHENSIBLE by his superior. The word *reprehensible,* as used in this sentence, means MOST NEARLY

A. worthy of reward or honor
B. in accordance with rules and regulations
C. detrimental to efficiency and morale
D. deserving of censure or rebuke

40. He said he would EMULATE the persistence of his co-workers. The word *emulate*, as used in this sentence, means MOST NEARLY

   A. strive to equal
   B. acknowledge
   C. encourage
   D. attach no significance to

41. The revised regulations on discipline contained several MITIGATING provisions. The word *mitigating*, as used in this sentence, means MOST NEARLY

   A. making more effective
   B. containing contradictions
   C. rendering less harsh
   D. producing much criticism

42. The arrival of the inspector at the office on that day was FORTUITOUS. The word *fortuitous*, as used in this sentence, means MOST NEARLY

   A. accidental
   B. unfortunate
   C. prearranged
   D. desirable

43. A clerk who comes across the abbreviation *et.al.* should know that it stands for

   A. for example
   B. and others
   C. disposition pending
   D. and every month thereafter

Questions 44-50.

DIRECTIONS: Questions 44 through 50 are to be answered SOLELY on the basis of the following information.

Assume that the following regulations were established in your department to compute vacation allowances for services rendered by its employees during the period from June 1, 2007 through May 31, 2008. You are to determine the answer to each of the questions on the basis of these regulations.

<u>VACATION REGULATIONS</u>
(For the Period June 1, 2007 - May 31, 2008)

The vacation allowance for this period is to be taken after May 31, 2008.

Standard Vacation Allowance
   Permanent per annum employees shall be granted 25 days vacation for a full year's service in such status. Employees who have served less than a full year in a permanent per annum status shall receive an allowance of 2 days for each month of such service.
   Per diem employees shall be granted 1 1/2 days vacation for each month of service in such status.
   Temporary employees shall be granted one day of vacation for each month of service in such status.

10 (#1)

No vacation credit shall accrue to employees for the time they are on leave of absence.

Additional Allowance for Overtime

One day of vacation allowance shall be granted for each seven hours of accrued overtime. Where there is a balance of less than 7 hours of accrued overtime, one-half day of vacation shall be granted for each 3 1/2 hours of such overtime. In no case shall the additional vacation allowed for accrued overtime exceed 6 days.

Deductions for Excessive Sick Leave

Sick leave allowance for all employees, regardless of length of service, shall be 12 days for the year. Sick leave taken in excess of 12 days shall be deducted from vacation allowance. Any unused sick leave balance will be canceled on May 31, 2008.

Deductions for Excessive Lateness

Deductions for excessive lateness shall be made from vacation allowance in accordance with the following schedule:

No. of Times Late	Deduction from Vacation Allowance
0-50	no deduction
51-60	1/2 day
61-70	1 day
71-80	1 1/2 days
81-90	2 days
91-100	2 1/2 days
101-120	4 days
121-140	6 days
141 or over	penalty to be determined by Secretary of Department

Unused Vacation

Unused vacation allowance earned during the previous year shall be added to the current vacation allowance, up to a maximum of twelve days.

Note that the vacation allowances are for services rendered during the year ending May 31, 2008, and that computations for all employees are to be made as of that date.

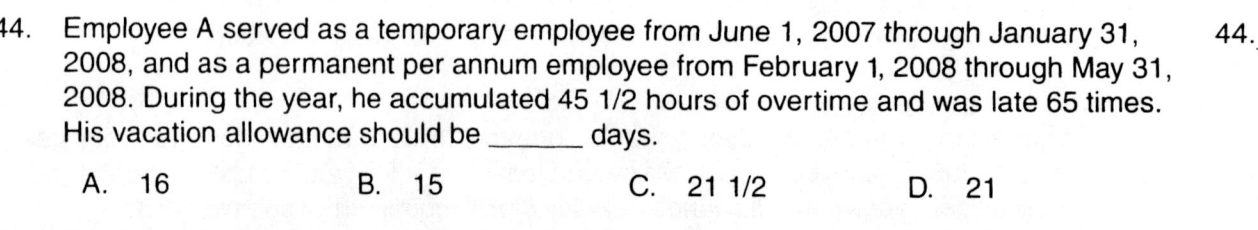

44. Employee A served as a temporary employee from June 1, 2007 through January 31, 2008, and as a permanent per annum employee from February 1, 2008 through May 31, 2008. During the year, he accumulated 45 1/2 hours of overtime and was late 65 times. His vacation allowance should be _____ days.   44.___

    A. 16   B. 15   C. 21 1/2   D. 21

45. Employee B was newly appointed to the department as a per diem employee on September 1, 2007. During the year, he took 15 days of sick leave and was late 48 times. His vacation allowance should be _____ days.   45.___

A.	less than 10	B.	10 1/2
C.	15	D.	12 1/2

46. Employee C has been a permanent per annum employee throughout the year. He had 15 days of vacation due him from the previous year. During the year, he was late 85 times, he took 10 days of sick leave, and he accumulated 38 1/2 hours of overtime.
His vacation allowance should be _____ days.

46._____

A.	38 1/2	B.	42 1/2
C.	40 1/2	D.	more than 43

47. Employee D was newly appointed to the department as a permanent per annum employee on July 1, 2007. He was on leave of absence from December 1, 2007 through February 28, 2008. During the year, he took 6 days of sick leave, he was late 70 times, and he accumulated 21 hours of overtime.
His vacation allowance should be _____ days.

47._____

A. 24 B. 18 C. 17 1/2 D. 19 1/2

48. Employee E served as a per diem employee from June 1, 2007 through July 31, 2007, and as a permanent per annum employee from August 1, 2007 to May 31, 2008. He had 6 days of vacation due him from the previous year. During the year, he took 13 days of sick leave, he accumulated 70 hours of overtime, and he was late 132 times.
His vacation allowance should be _____ days.

48._____

A.	less than 29	B.	29
C.	30	D.	more than 30

49. The maximum total vacation allowance which a permanent per annum employee can have due him by May 31, 2008 is _____ days.

49._____

A. 43 B. 25 C. 31 D. 37

50. An employee who has served as a temporary employee for 6 months and as a permanent per annum employee for 6 months will earn exactly

50._____

A. two-thirds as much vacation as an employee who has been on a permanent per annum basis for the whole year
B. as much vacation as an employee who has been on a per diem basis for the whole year
C. as much vacation as an employee who has been on a per diem basis for 4 months and on a permanent per annum basis for 8 months
D. as much vacation as an employee who has been on a per diem basis for 8 months and on a permanent per annum basis for 5 months

Questions 51-60.

DIRECTIONS: Each of Questions 51 through 60 may be classified under one of the following four categories:

A. faulty because of incorrect grammar or sentence structure
B. faulty because of incorrect punctuation
C. faulty because of incorrect spelling
D. correct

Examine each sentence carefully to determine under which of the above four options it is best classified. Then, in the space at the right, write the letter preceding the option which is the BEST of the four suggested above. Each incorrect sentence contains but one type of error. Consider a sentence to be correct if it contains none of the types of errors mentioned, even though there may be other correct ways of expressing the same thought.

51. Although the department's supply of scratch pads and stationery have diminished considerably, the allotment for our division has not been reduced. 51.___

52. You have not told us whom you wish to designate as your secretary. 52.___

53. Upon reading the minutes of the last meeting, the new proposal was taken up for consideration. 53.___

54. Before beginning the discussion, we locked the door as a precautionery measure. 54.___

55. The supervisor remarked, "Only those clerks, who perform routine work, are permitted to take a rest period." 55.___

56. Not only will this duplicating machine make accurate copies, but it will also produce a quantity of work equal to fifteen transcribing typists. 56.___

57. "Mr. Jones," said the supervisor, "we regret our inability to grant you an extention of your leave of absence." 57.___

58. Although the employees find the work monotonous and fatigueing, they rarely complain. 58.___

59. We completed the tabulation of the receipts on time despite the fact that Miss Smith our fastest operator was absent for over a week. 59.___

60. The reaction of the employees who attended the meeting, as well as the reaction of those who did not attend, indicates clearly that the schedule is satisfactory to everyone concerned. 60.___

KEY (CORRECT ANSWERS)

1.	C	16.	D	31.	A	46.	C
2.	D	17.	B	32.	B	47.	B
3.	D	18.	B	33.	C	48.	A
4.	B	19.	A	34.	C	49.	A
5.	A	20.	D	35.	A	50.	B
6.	A	21.	C	36.	D	51.	A
7.	C	22.	B	37.	B	52.	D
8.	C	23.	D	38.	C	53.	A
9.	B	24.	C	39.	D	54.	C
10.	C	25.	A	40.	A	55.	B
11.	D	26.	E	41.	C	56.	A
12.	C	27.	A	42.	A	57.	C
13.	C	28.	C	43.	B	58.	C
14.	B	29.	D	44.	D	59.	B
15.	D	30.	E	45.	B	60.	D

EXAMINATION SECTION
TEST 1

DIRECTIONS: Each question or incomplete statement is followed by several suggested answers or completions. Select the one that BEST answers the question or completes the statement. *PRINT THE LETTER OF THE CORRECT ANSWER IN THE SPACE AT THE RIGHT.*

1. Records of one type or another are kept in every office. The MOST important of the following reasons for the supervisor of a clerical or stenographic unit to keep statistical records of the work done in his unit is generally to

    A. supply basic information needed in planning the work of the unit
    B. obtain statistics for comparison with other units
    C. serve as the basis for unsatisfactory employee evaluation
    D. provide the basis for special research projects on program budgeting

    1.____

2. It is better for an employee to report and be responsible directly to several supervisors than to report and be responsible to only one supervisor.
   This statement directly CONTRADICTS the supervisory principle generally known as

    A. span of control   B. unity of command
    C. delegation of authority D. accountability

    2.____

3. The one of the following which would MOST likely lead to friction among clerks in a unit is for the unit supervisor to

    A. defend the actions of his clerks when discussing them with his own supervisor
    B. praise each of his clerks "in confidence" as the best clerk in the unit
    C. get his men to work together as a team in completing the work of the unit
    D. consider the point of view of the rank and file clerks when assigning unpleasant tasks

    3.____

4. You become aware that one of the employees you supervise has failed to follow correct procedure and has been permitting various reports to be prepared, typed, and transmitted improperly.
   The BEST action for you to take FIRST in this situation is to

    A. order the employee to review all departmental procedures and reprimand him for having violated them
    B. warn the employee that he must obey regulations because uniformity is essential for effective departmental operation
    C. confer with the employee both about his failure to follow regulations and his reasons for doing so
    D. watch the employee's work very closely in the future but say nothing about this violation

    4.____

5. The supervisory clerk who would be MOST likely to have poor control over his subordinates is the one who

    A. goes to unusually great lengths to try to win their approval
    B. pitches in with the work they are doing during periods of heavy workload when no extra help can be obtained

    5.____

C. encourages and helps his subordinates toward advancement
D. considers suggestions from his subordinates before establishing new work procedures involving them

6. Suppose that a clerk who has been transferred to your office from another division in your agency because of difficulties with his supervisor has been placed under your supervision.
The BEST course of action for you to take FIRST is to

   A. instruct the clerk in the duties he will be performing in your office and make him feel "wanted" in his new position
   B. analyze the clerk's past grievance to determine if the transfer was the best solution to the problem
   C. advise him of the difficulties that his former supervisor had with other employees and encourage him not to feel badly about the transfer
   D. warn him that you will not tolerate any nonsense and that he will be under continuous surveillance while assigned to you

7. A certain office supervisor takes the initiative to represent his employees' interests related to working conditions, opportunities for advancement, etc. to his own supervisor and the administrative levels of the agency. This supervisor's actions will MOST probably have the effect of

   A. preventing employees from developing individual initiative in their work goals
   B. encouraging employees to compete openly for the special attention of their supervisor
   C. depriving employees of the opportunity to be represented by persons and/or unions of their own choosing
   D. building employee confidence in their supervisor and a spirit of cooperation in their work

8. Suppose that you have been promoted, assigned as a supervisor of a certain unit and asked to reorganize its functions so that specific routine procedures can be established. Before deciding which routines to establish, the FIRST of the following steps you should take is to

   A. decide who will perform each task in the routine
   B. determine the purpose to be served by each routine procedure
   C. outline the sequence of steps in each routine to be established
   D. calculate if more staff will be needed to carry out the new procedures

9. When routine procedures covering the ordinary work of an office are established, the supervisor of the office tends to be relieved of the need to

   A. make repeated decisions on the handling of recurring similar situations
   B. check the accuracy of the work completed by his subordinates
   C. train his subordinates in new work procedures
   D. plan and schedule the work of his office

10. Of the following, the method which would be LEAST helpful to a supervisor in effectively applying the principles of on-the-job safety to the daily work of his unit is for him to

A. initiate corrections of unsafe layouts of equipment and unsafe work processes
B. take charge of operations that are not routine to make certain that safety precautions are established and observed
C. continue to "talk safety" and promote safety consciousness in his subordinates
D. figure the cost of all accidents which could possibly occur on the job

11. A clerk is assigned to serve as receptionist for a large and busy office. Although many members of the public visit this office, the clerk often experiences periods of time in which he has nothing to do.
In these circumstances, the MOST advisable of the following actions for the supervisor to take is to

   A. assign a number of relatively low priority clerical jobs to the receptionist to do in the slow periods
   B. regularly rotate this assignment so that all the clerks experience this lighter work load
   C. assign the receptionist job as part of the duties of a number of clerks whose desks are nearest the reception room
   D. overlook the situation, since most of the receptionist's time is spent in performing a necessary and meaningful function

12. For a supervisor to require all stenographers in a stenographic pool to produce the same amount of work on a particular day is

   A. *advisable;* since it will prove that the supervisor plays no favorites
   B. *fair;* since all the stenographers are receiving approximately the same salary, their output should be equivalent
   C. *not necessary;* since the fast workers will compensate for the slow workers
   D. *not realistic;* since individual differences in abilities and work assignment must be taken into consideration

13. The establishment of a centralized typing pool to service the various units in an organization is MOST likely to be worthwhile when there is

   A. wide fluctuation from time to time in the needs of the various units for typing service
   B. a large volume of typing work to be done in each of the units
   C. a need by each unit for different kinds of typing service
   D. a training program in operation to develop and maintain typing skills

14. A newly appointed supervisor should learn as much as possible about the backgrounds of his subordinates. This statement is generally CORRECT because

   A. knowing their backgrounds assures they will be treated objectively, equally, and without favor
   B. effective handling of subordinates is based upon knowledge of their individual differences
   C. subordinates perform more efficiently under one supervisor than under another
   D. subordinates have confidence in a supervisor who knows all about them

15. The use of electronic computers in modern businesses has produced many changes in office and information management. Of the following, it would NOT be correct to state that computer utilization

A. broadens the scope of managerial and supervisory authority
B. establishes uniformity in the processing and reporting of information
C. cuts costs by reducing the personnel needed for efficient office operation
D. supplies management rapidly with up-to-date data to facilitate decision-making

16. The CHIEF advantage of having a single, large open office instead of small partitioned ones for a clerical unit or stenographic pool is that the single, large open office

    A. affords privacy without isolation for all office workers not directly dealing with the public
    B. assures the smoother, more continuous inter-office flow of work that is essential for efficient work production
    C. facilitates the office supervisor's visual control over and communication with his subordinates
    D. permits a more decorative and functional arrangement of office furniture and machines

17. When a supervisor provides a new employee with the information necessary for a basic knowledge and a general understanding of practices and procedures of the agency, he is applying the type of training generally known as _____ training.

    A. pre-employment   B. induction
    C. on-the-job   D. supervisory

18. Many government agencies require the approval by a central forms control unit of the design and reproduction of new office forms.
    The one of the following results of this procedure that is a DISADVANTAGE is that requiring prior approval of a central forms control unit USUALLY

    A. limits the distribution of forms to those offices with justifiable reasons for receiving them
    B. permits checking whether existing forms or modifications of them are in line with current agency needs
    C. encourages reliance on only the central office to set up all additional forms when needed
    D. provides for someone with a specialized knowledge of forms design to review and criticize new and revised forms

19. Suppose that a large quantity of information is in the files which are located a good distance from your desk. Almost every worker in your office must use these files constantly. Your duties in particular require that you daily refer to about 25 of the same items. They are short, one-page items distributed throughout the files.
    In this situation, your BEST course would be to

    A. take the items that you use daily from the files and keep them on your desk, inserting "out cards" in their place
    B. go to the files each time you need the information so that the items will be there when other workers need them
    C. make xerox copies of the information you use most frequently and keep them in your desk for ready reference
    D. label the items you use most often with different colored tabs for immediate identification

20. Of the following, the MOST important advantage of preparing manuals of office procedures in loose-leaf form is that this form

   A. permits several employees to use different sections simultaneously
   B. facilitates the addition of new material and the removal of obsolete material
   C. is more readily arranged in alphabetical order
   D. reduces the need for cross-references to locate material carried under several headings

21. Suppose that you establish a new clerical procedure for the unit you supervise. Your keeping a close check on the time required by your staff to handle the new procedure is wise MAINLY because such a check will find out

   A. whether your subordinates know how to handle the new procedure
   B. whether a revision of the unit's work schedule will be necessary as a result of the new procedure
   C. what attitude your employees have toward the new procedure
   D. what alterations in job descriptions will be necessitated by the new procedure

22. From the viewpoint of an office supervisor, the BEST of the following reasons for distributing the incoming mail *before* the beginning of the regular work day is that

   A. distribution can be handled quickly and most efficiently at that time
   B. distribution later in the day may be distracting to or interfere with other employees
   C. the employees who distribute the mail can then perform other tasks during the rest of the day
   D. office activities for the day based on the mail may then be started promptly

23. Suppose you are the head of a unit with ten staff members who are located in several different rooms. If you want to inform your staff of a *minor* change in procedure, the BEST and LEAST expensive way of doing so would usually be to

   A. send a mimeographed copy to each staff member
   B. call a special staff meeting and announce the change
   C. circulate a memo, having each staff member initial it
   D. have a clerk tell each member of the staff about the change

24. The numbered statements below relate to the stenographic skill of taking dictation. According to authorities on secretarial practices, which of these are GENERALLY recommended guides to development of efficient stenographic skills?
   A stenographer should
   I. date her notebook daily to facilitate locating certain notes at a later time
   II. make corrections of grammatical mistakes while her boss is dictating to her
   III. draw a line through the dictated matter in her notebook after she has transcribed it
   IV. write in longhand unfamiliar names and addresses dictated to her
   The CORRECT answer is:

   A. I, II, III
   B. II, III, IV
   C. I, III, IV
   D. All of the above

25. A bureau of a city agency is about to move to a new location.
   Of the following, the FIRST step that should be taken in order to provide a good layout for the office at the new location is to

A. decide the exact amount of space to be assigned to each unit of the bureau
B. decide whether to lay out a single large open office or one consisting of small partitioned units
C. ask each unit chief in the bureau to examine the new location and submit a request for the amount of space he needs
D. prepare a detailed plan of the dimensions of the floor space to be occupied by the bureau at the new location

---

KEY (CORRECT ANSWERS)

1. A
2. B
3. B
4. C
5. A

6. A
7. D
8. B
9. A
10. D

11. A
12. D
13. A
14. B
15. A

16. C
17. B
18. C
19. C
20. B

21. B
22. D
23. C
24. C
25. D

TEST 2

DIRECTIONS: Each question or incomplete statement is followed by several suggested answers or completions. Select the one that BEST answers the question or completes the statement. *PRINT THE LETTER OF THE CORRECT ANSWER IN THE SPACE AT THE RIGHT.*

1. Suppose you are the supervisor of the mailroom of a large agency where the mail received daily is opened by machine, sorted by hand for delivery and time-stamped. Letters and any enclosures are removed from envelopes and stapled together before distribution. One of your newest clerks asks you what should be done when a letter makes reference to an enclosure, but no enclosure is in the envelope.
   You should tell him that in this situation the BEST procedure is to

   A. make an entry of the sender's name and address in the "missing enclosures" file and forward the letter to its proper destination
   B. return the letter to its sender, attaching a request for the missing enclosure
   C. put the letter aside until a proper investigation may be made concerning the missing enclosure
   D. route the letter to the person for whom it is intended, noting the absence of the enclosure on the letter margin

   1.____

2. The term "work flow," when used in connection with office management or the activities in an office, GENERALLY means the

   A. use of charts in the analysis of various office functions
   B. rate of speed at which work flows through a single section of an office
   C. step-by-step physical routing of work through its various procedures
   D. number of individual work units which can be produced by the average employee

   2.____

3. Physical conditions can have a definite effect on the efficiency and morale of an office. Which of the following statements about physical conditions in an office is CORRECT?

   A. Hard, non-porous surfaces reflect more noise than linoleum on the top of a desk.
   B. Painting in tints of bright yellow is more appropriate for sunny, well-lit offices than for dark, poorly-lit offices.
   C. Plate glass is better than linoleum for the top of a desk.
   D. The central typing room needs less light than a conference room does.

   3.____

4. In a certain filing system, documents are consecutively numbered as they are filed, a register is maintained of such consecutively numbered documents, and a record is kept of the number of each document removed from the files and its destination.
   This system will NOT help in

   A. finding the present whereabouts of a particular document
   B. proving the accuracy of the data recorded on a certain document
   C. indicating whether observed existing documents were ever filed
   D. locating a desired document without knowing what its contents are

   4.____

5. In deciding the kind and number of records an agency should keep, the administrative staff must recognize that records are of value in office management PRIMARILY as

   5.____

A. informational bases for agency activities
B. data for evaluating the effectiveness of the agency
C. raw material on which statistical analyses are to be based
D. evidence that the agency is carrying out its duties and responsibilities

6. Complaints are often made by the public about the city government's procedures. Although in most cases such procedures cannot be changed since various laws and regulations require them, it may still be possible to reduce the number of complaints. Which one of the following actions by personnel dealing with applicants for city services is LEAST likely to reduce complaints concerning city procedures?

    A. Treating all citizens alike and explaining to them that no exceptions to required procedures can be made
    B. Explaining briefly to the citizen why he should comply with regulations
    C. Being careful to avoid mistakes which may make additional interviews or correspondence necessary
    D. Keeping the citizen informed of the progress of his correspondence when immediate disposition cannot be made

7. In answering a complaint made by a member of the public that a certain essential procedure required by your agency is difficult to follow, it would be BEST for you to stress MOST

    A. that a change in the rules may be considered if enough complaints are received
    B. why the operation of a large agency sometimes proves a hardship in individual cases
    C. the necessity for the procedure
    D. the origin of the procedure

8. When talking to a citizen, it is BEST for an employee of government to

    A. use ordinary conversational phrases and a natural manner
    B. try to copy the pronunciation and level of education shown by the citizen
    C. try to speak in a very cultured manner and tone
    D. use technical terms to show his familiarity with his own work

9. Employees who service the public should maintain an attitude which is both sympathetic and objective.
   An UNSYMPATHETIC and SUBJECTIVE attitude would be shown by a public employee who

    A. says "no" with a smile when a citizen's request must be denied
    B. listens attentively to a long complaint from a citizen about the government's "red tape"
    C. responds with sarcasm when a citizen asks a question which has an obvious answer
    D. suggests a definite solution to a citizen's problems

10. You are a supervisor in a city agency and are holding your first interview with a new employee.
    In this interview, you should strive MAINLY to

A. show the new employee that you are an efficient and objective supervisor, with a completely impersonal attitude toward your subordinates
B. complete the entire orientation process including the giving of detailed job-duty instructions
C. make it clear to the employee that all your decisions are based on your many years of experience
D. lay the groundwork for a good employee-supervisor relationship by gaining the new employee's confidence

11. A senior clerk or senior typist may be required to help train a newly-appointed clerk. Which of the following is LEAST important for a newly-appointed clerk to know in order to perform his work efficiently?

    A. Acceptable ways of answering and recording telephone calls
    B. The number of files in the storage files unit
    C. The filing methods used by his unit
    D. Proper techniques for handling visitors

12. In your agency, you have the responsibility of processing clients who have appointments with agency representatives. On a particularly busy day, a client comes to your desk and insists that she must see the person handling her case although she has no appointment.
Under the circumstances, your FIRST action should be to

    A. show her the full appointment schedule
    B. give her an appointment for another day
    C. ask her to explain the urgency
    D. tell her to return later in the day

13. Which of the following practices is BEST for a supervisor to use when assigning work to his staff?

    A. Give workers with seniority the most difficult jobs
    B. Assign all unimportant work to the slower workers
    C. Permit each employee to pick the job he prefers
    D. Make assignments based on the workers' abilities

14. In which of the following instances is a supervisor MOST justified in giving commands to people under his supervision? When

    A. they delay in following instructions which have been given to them clearly
    B. they become relaxed and slow about work, and he wants to speed up their production
    C. he must direct them in an emergency situation
    D. he is instructing them on jobs that are unfamiliar to them

15. Which of the following supervisory actions or attitudes is MOST likely to result in getting subordinates to try to do as much work as possible for a supervisor? He

    A. shows that his most important interest is in schedules and production goals
    B. consistently pressures his staff to get the work out
    C. never fails to let them know he is in charge
    D. considers their abilities and needs while requiring that production goals be met

16. Assume that a senior clerk has been explaining certain regulations to a new clerk under his supervision.
The MOST efficient way for the senior clerk to make sure that the clerk has understood the explanation is to

    A. give him written materials on the regulations
    B. ask him if he has any further questions about the regulations
    C. ask him specific questions based on what has just been explained to him
    D. watch the way he handles a situation involving these regulations

17. One of your unit clerks has been assigned to work for a Mr. Jones in another office for several days. At the end of the first day, Mr. Jones, saying the clerk was not satisfactory, asks that she not be assigned to him again. This clerk is one of your most dependable workers, and no previous complaints about her work have come to you from any other outside assignments.
To get to the root of this situation, your FIRST action should be to

    A. ask Mr. Jones to explain in what way her work was unsatisfactory
    B. ask the clerk what she did that Mr. Jones considered unsatisfactory
    C. check with supervisors for whom she previously worked to see if your own rating of her is in error
    D. tell Mr. Jones to pick the clerk he would prefer to have work for him the next time

18. A senior typist, still on probation, is instructed to type, as quickly as possible, one section of a draft of a long, complex report. Her part must be typed and readable before another part of the report can be written. Asked when she can have the report ready, she gives her supervisor an estimate of a day longer than she knows it will actually take. She then finishes the job a day sooner than the date given her supervisor.
The judgment shown by a senior typist in giving an overestimate of time in a situation like this is, in general,

    A. *good,* because it prevents the supervisor from thinking she works slowly
    B. *good,* because it keeps unrealistic supervisors from expecting too much
    C. *bad,* because she should have used the time left to further check and proofread her work
    D. *bad,* because schedules and plans for other parts of the project may have been based on her false estimate

19. Suppose a new clerk, still on probation, is placed under your supervision and refuses to do a job you ask him to do.
What is the FIRST thing you should do?

    A. Explain that you are the supervisor, and he must follow your instructions.
    B. Tell him he may be suspended if he refuses.
    C. Ask someone else to do the job, and rate him accordingly.
    D. Ask for his reason for objecting to the request.

20. As a supervisor of a small group of people, you have blamed worker A for something that you later find out was really done by worker B.
The BEST thing for you to do now would be to

    A. say nothing to worker A, but criticize worker B for his mistake while worker A is near so that A will realize that you know who made the mistake
    B. speak to each worker separately, apologize to worker A for your mistake, and discuss worker B's mistake with him
    C. bring both workers together, apologize to worker A for your mistake, and discuss worker B's mistake with him
    D. say nothing new but be careful about mixing up worker A with worker B in the future

21. You have just learned one of your staff is grumbling that she thinks you are not pleased with her work. As far as you are concerned, this is not true at all. In fact, you have paid no particular attention to this worker lately because you have been very busy. You have just finished preparing an important report and "breaking in" a new clerk.
Under the circumstances, the BEST thing to do is

    A. ignore her; after all, it is just a figment of her imagination
    B. discuss the matter with her now to try to find out and eliminate the cause of this problem
    C. tell her not to worry about it; you have not had time to think about her work
    D. make a note to meet with her at a later date in order to straighten out the situation

22. A most important job of a supervisor is to positively motivate employees to increase their work production. Which of the following LEAST indicates that a group of workers has been positively motivated?

    A. Their work output becomes constant and stable.
    B. Their cooperation at work becomes greater.
    C. They begin to show pride in the product of their work.
    D. They show increased interest in their work.

23. Which of the following traits would be LEAST important in considering a person for a merit increase?

    A. Punctuality
    B. Using initiative successfully
    C. High rate of production
    D. Resourcefulness

24. Of the following, the action LEAST likely to gain a supervisor the cooperation of his staff is for him to

    A. give each person consideration as an individual
    B. be as objective as possible when evaluating work performance
    C. rotate the least popular assignments
    D. expect subordinates to be equally competent

25. It has been said that, for the supervisor, nothing can beat the "face-to-face" communication of talking to one subordinate at a time.
This method is, however, LEAST appropriate to use when the
   A. supervisor is explaining a change in general office procedure
   B. subject is of personal importance
   C. supervisor is conducting a yearly performance evaluation of all employees
   D. supervisor must talk to some of his employees concerning their poor attendance and punctuality

KEY (CORRECT ANSWERS)

1. D
2. C
3. A
4. B
5. A

6. A
7. C
8. A
9. C
10. D

11. B
12. C
13. D
14. C
15. D

16. C
17. A
18. D
19. D
20. B

21. B
22. A
23. A
24. D
25. A

TEST 3

DIRECTIONS: Each question or incomplete statement is followed by several suggested answers or completions. Select the one that BEST answers the question or completes the statement. *PRINT THE LETTER OF THE CORRECT ANSWER IN THE SPACE AT THE RIGHT.*

1. While you are on the telephone answering a question about your agency, a visitor comes to your desk and starts to ask you a question. There is no emergency or urgency in either situation, that of the phone call or that of answering the visitor's question.
   In this case, you should

   A. continue to answer the person on the telephone until you are finished and then tell the visitor you are sorry to have kept him waiting
   B. excuse yourself to the person on the telephone and tell the visitor that you will be with him as soon as you have finished on the phone
   C. explain to the person on the telephone that you have a visitor and must shorten the conversation
   D. continue to answer the person on the phone while looking up occasionally at the visitor to let him know that you know he is waiting

   1.____

2. While speaking on the telephone to someone who called, you are disconnected.
   The FIRST thing you should do is

   A. hang up, but try to keep your line free to receive the call back
   B. immediately get the dial tone and continually dial the person who called you until you reach him
   C. signal the switchboard operator and ask her to re-establish the connection
   D. dial "O" for Operator and explain that you were disconnected

   2.____

3. The type of speech used by an office worker in telephone conversation greatly affects the communication.
   Of the following, the BEST way to express your ideas when telephoning is with a vocabulary that consists MAINLY of

   A. formal, intellectual sounding words
   B. often used colloquial words
   C. technical, emphatic words
   D. simple, descriptive words

   3.____

4. Suppose a clerk under your supervision has taken a personal phone call and is at the same time needed to answer a question regarding an assignment being handled by another member of your office. He appears confused as to what he should do. How should you instruct him later as to how to handle a similar situation?
   You should tell him to

   A. tell the caller to hold on while he answers the question
   B. tell the caller to call back a little later
   C. return the call during an assigned break
   D. finish the conversation quickly and answer the question

   4.____

5. You are asked to place a telephone call by your supervisor. When you place the call, you receive what appears to be a wrong number.
   Of the following, you should FIRST

   A. check the number with your supervisor to see if the number he gave you is correct
   B. ask the person on the other end what his number is and who he is
   C. check with the person on the other end to see if the number you dialed is the number you received
   D. apologize to the person on the other end for disturbing him and hang up

6. When you select someone to serve as supervisor of your unit during your absence on vacation and at other times, it would generally be BEST to choose the employee who is

   A. able to move the work along smoothly, without friction
   B. on staff longest
   C. liked best by the rest of the staff
   D. able to perform the work of each employee to be supervised

7. Successful supervision of handicapped persons employed in a department depends MOST on providing them with a work place and work climate

   A. which is safe and accident-free
   B. that requires close and direct supervision by others
   C. that requires the performance of routine, repetitive tasks under a minimum of pressure
   D. where they will be accepted by the other employees

8. Studies have indicated that when employees feel that their work is aimless and unchallenging, the allocation or payment of more money for this type of work is likely to

   A. contribute little to increased production
   B. bring more status to this work
   C. increase employees' feelings of security
   D. give employees greater motivation

9. An employee's performance has fallen below established minimum standards of quantity and quality.
   The threat of monetary or other disciplinary action as a device for improving this employee's performance would probably be acceptable and MOST effective

   A. only if applied as soon as the performance fell below standard
   B. only after more constructive techniques have failed
   C. at any time provided the employee understands that the punishment will be carried out
   D. at no time

10. A supervisor must, on short notice, ask his staff to work overtime.
    Of the following, a technique that is MOST likely to win their willing cooperation would be to

    A. explain that occasional overtime is part of the job requirement
    B. explain that they will be doing him a personal favor which he will appreciate very much

C. explain why the overtime is necessary
D. promise them that they can take the extra time off in the near future

11. On checking a completed work assignment of an employee, the supervisor finds that the work was not done correctly because the employee had not understood his instructions. Of the following, the BEST way to prevent repetition of this situation next time is for the supervisor to

   A. ask the employee whether he fully understood the instructions and tell him to ask questions in the future whenever anything is unclear
   B. ask the employee to repeat the instructions given and test his understanding with several key questions
   C. give the instructions a second time, emphasizing the more complicated aspects of the job
   D. give work instructions in writing

12. If, as a supervisor, you find yourself pressured for time to handle all of your job responsibilities, the one of the following tasks which it would be MOST appropriate for you to delegate to a subordinate is

   A. attending a staff conference of unit supervisors to discuss the implementation of a new departmental policy
   B. making staff work assignments
   C. interviewing a new employee
   D. checking work of certain employees for accuracy

13. Suppose you are unavoidably late for work one morning. When you arrive at 10 o'clock, you find there are several matters demanding your attention.
Which one of the following matters should you handle LAST?

   A. A visitor who had a 9:30 appointment with you has been waiting to see you since 9 o'clock.
   B. An employee on an assignment which should have been completed that morning is absent, and the work will have to be reassigned.
   C. Several letters which you dictated at the end of the previous day have been typed and are on your desk for signature and mailing.
   D. Your superior called asking you to get certain information for him when you come in and to call him back.

14. Suppose that you have assigned a typist to type a report containing considerable statistical and tabular material and have given her specific instructions as to how this material is to be laid out on each page. When she returns the completed report, you find that it was not prepared according to your instructions, but you may possibly be able to use it the way it was typed. When you question her, she states that she thought her layout was better but you were unavailable for consultation when she began the work.
Of the following, the BEST action for you to take is to

   A. criticize her for not doing the work according to your instructions
   B. have her retype the report
   C. praise her for her work but tell her she should have waited until she could consult you
   D. praise her for using initiative

4 (#3)

15. Of the following, the MOST effective way for a supervisor to correct poor work habits of an employee which result in low and poor quality output is to give the employee

   A. additional training
   B. less demanding assignments until his work improves
   C. continuous supervision
   D. more severe criticism

16. Of the following, the BEST way for a supervisor to teach an employee how to do a new and somewhat complicated job is to

   A. assign him to observe another employee who is already skilled in this work and instruct him to consult this employee if he has any questions
   B. explain to him how to do it, then demonstrate how it is done, then observe and correct the employee as he does it, then follow up
   C. give him a written, detailed, step-by-step explanation of how to do the job and instruct him to ask questions if anything is unclear when he does the work
   D. teach him the easiest part of the job first, then the other parts one at a time, in order of their difficulty, as the employee masters the easier parts

17. After an employee has completed telling his supervisor about a grievance against a co-worker, the supervisor tells the employee that he will take action to remove the cause of the grievance.
The action of the supervisor was

   A. *good,* because ill feeling between subordinates interferes with proper performance
   B. *poor,* because the supervisor should give both employees time to "cool off"
   C. *good,* because grievances that appear petty to the supervisor are important to subordinates
   D. *poor,* because the supervisor should tell the employee that he will investigate the matter before he comes to any conclusion

18. During work on an important project, one employee in a secretarial pool turns in several pages of typed copy, one page of which contains several errors.
Of these four comments which her supervisor might possibly make, which one would be MOST constructive?

   A. "You did such a poor job on this; I will have to have it done over."
   B. "You will have to do better, more consistently than this, if you want to be in charge of a secretarial pool yourself someday."
   C. "How come you made so many mistakes here? Your other pages were all right."
   D. "If my boss saw this, he would be very displeased with you."

19. A supervisor has general supervision over a large, complex project with many employees. The work is subdivided among small units of employees, each with a senior clerk or senior stenographer in charge. At a staff meeting, after all work assignments have been made, the supervisor tells all the employees that they are to take orders only from their immediate supervisor and instructs them to let him know if anyone else tries to give them orders.
This instruction by the supervising clerk is

A. *good,* because it may prevent the issuance of orders by unauthorized persons, which would interfere with the accomplishment of the assignment
B. *poor,* because employees should be instructed to take up such problems with their immediate supervisor
C. *good,* because orders issued by immediate supervisors would be precise and directly related to the tasks of the assignments while those issued by others would not be
D. *poor,* because it places upon all employees a responsibility which should not normally be theirs

20. A supervisor who is to direct a team of senior clerks and clerks in a complex project, calls them together beforehand to inform them of the tasks each employee will perform on this job.
Of the following, the CHIEF value of this action by the supervisor is that each member of this team will be able to

   A. work independently in the absence of the supervisor
   B. understand what he will do and how this will fit into the total picture
   C. share in the process of decision-making as an equal participant
   D. judge how well the plans for this assignment have been made

20.____

21. A supervisor who has both younger and older employees under his supervision may sometimes find that employee absenteeism seriously interferes with accomplishment of goals.
Studies of such employee absenteeism have shown that the absences of employees

   A. under 35 years of age are usually unexpected and the absences of employees over 45 years of age are usually unnecessary
   B. of all age groups show the same characteristics as to length of absence
   C. under 35 years of age are for frequent, short periods while the absences of employees over 45 years of age are less frequent but of longer duration
   D. under 35 years of age are for periods of long duration and the absences of employees over 45 years of age are for periods of short duration

21.____

22. Suppose you have a long-standing procedure for getting a certain job done by your subordinates that is apparently a good one. Changes in some steps of the procedure are made from time to time to handle special problems that come up.
For you to review this procedure periodically is desirable MAINLY because

   A. the system is working well
   B. checking routines periodically is a supervisor's chief responsibility
   C. subordinates may be confused as to how the procedure operates as a result of the changes made
   D. it is necessary to determine whether the procedure has become outdated or is in need of improvement

22.____

23. Suppose that a stranger enters the office you are in charge of and asks for the address and telephone number of one of your employees.
Of the following, it would be BEST for you to

   A. find out why he needs the information and release it if his reason is a good one
   B. explain that you are not permitted to release such information to unauthorized persons

23.____

C. give him the information but tell him it must be kept confidential
D. ask him to leave the office immediately

24. A member of the public approaches an employee who is at work at his desk. The employee cannot interrupt his work in order to take care of this person.
Of the following, the BEST and MOST courteous way of handling this situation is for the employee to

A. avoid looking up from his work until he is finished with what he is doing
B. tell this person that he will not be able to take care of him for quite a while
C. refer the individual to another employee who can take care of him right away
D. chat with the individual while he continues with his work

25. You answer a phone call from a citizen who urgently needs certain information you do not have, but you think you know who may have it. He is angry because he has already been switched to two different offices.
Of the following, it would be BEST for you to

A. give him the phone number of the person you think may have the information he wants, but explain you are not sure
B. tell him you regret you cannot help him because you are not sure who can give him the information
C. advise him that the best way he can be sure of getting the information he wants is to write a letter to the agency
D. get the phone number where he can be reached and tell him you will try to get the information he wants and will call him back later

KEY (CORRECT ANSWERS)

1.	B		11.	B
2.	A		12.	D
3.	D		13.	C
4.	C		14.	A
5.	C		15.	A
6.	A		16.	B
7.	D		17.	D
8.	A		18.	C
9.	B		19.	B
10.	C		20.	B

21. C
22. D
23. B
24. C
25. D

READING COMPREHENSION
UNDERSTANDING AND INTERPRETING WRITTEN MATERIAL
EXAMINATION SECTION
TEST 1

DIRECTIONS: Each question or incomplete statement is followed by several suggested answers or completions. Select the one that BEST answers the question or completes the statement. *PRINT THE LETTER OF THE CORRECT ANSWER IN THE SPACE AT THE RIGHT.*

1. Most managers make the mistake of using absolutes as signals of trouble or its absence. A quality problem emerges — that means trouble; a test is passed — we have no problems. Outside of routine organizations, there are always going to be such signals of trouble or success, but they are not very meaningful. Many times everything looks good, but the roof is about to cave in because something no one thought about and for which there is no rule, procedure, or test has been neglected. The specifics of such problems cannot be predicted, but they are often signaled in advance by changes in the organizational system: Managers spend less time on the project; minor problems proliferate; friction in the relationships between adjacent work groups or departments increases; verbal progress reports become overly glib, or overly reticent; changes occur in the rate at which certain events happen, not in whether or not they happen. And they are monitored by random probes into the organization — seeing how things are going. According to the above paragraph,

   A. managers do not spend enough time managing
   B. managers have a tendency to become overly glib when writing reports
   C. managers should be aware that problems that exist in the organization may not exhibit predictable signals of trouble
   D. managers should attempt to alleviate friction in the relationship between adjacent work groups by monitoring random probes into the organization's problems

1.____

2. *Lack of challenge* and *excessive zeal* are opposite villains. You cannot do your best on a problem unless you are motivated. Professional problem solvers learn to be motivated somewhat by money and future work that may come their way if they succeed. However, challenge must be present for at least some of the time, or the process ceases to be rewarding. On the other hand, an excessive motivation to succeed, especially to succeed quickly, can inhibit the creative process. The tortoise-and-the-hare phenomenon is often apparent in problem solving. The person who thinks up the simple elegant solution, although he or she may take longer in doing so, often wins. As in the race, the tortoise depends upon an inconsistent performance from the rabbit. And if the rabbit spends so little time on conceptualization that the rabbit merely chooses the first answers that occur, such inconsistency is almost guaranteed. According to the above paragraph,

   A. excessive motivation to succeed can be harmful in problem solving
   B. it is best to spend a long time on solving problems
   C. motivation is the most important component in problem solving
   D. choosing the first solution that occurs is a valid method of problem solving

2.____

3. Virginia Woolf's approach to the question of women and fiction, about which She wrote extensively, polemically, and in a profoundly feminist way, was grounded in a general theory of literature. She argued that the writer was the product of her or his historical circumstances and that material conditions were of crucial importance. Secondly, she claimed that these material circumstances had a profound effect on the psychological aspects of writing, and that they could be seen to influence the nature of the creative work itself. According to this paragraph,

   A. the material conditions and historical circumstances in which male and female writers find themselves greatly influence their work
   B. a woman must have an independent income to succeed as a writer
   C. Virginia Woolf preferred the writings of female authors, as their experiences more clearly reflected hers
   D. male writers are less likely than women writers to be influenced by material circumstances

4. A young person's first manager is likely to be the most influential person in his or her career. If this manager is unable or unwilling to develop the skills the young employee needs to perform effectively, the latter will set lower personal standards than he or she is capable of achieving, that person's self-image will be impaired, and he or she will develop negative attitudes toward the job, the employer, and—in all probability—his or her career. Since the chances of building a successful career with the employer will decline rapidly, he or she will leave, if that person has high aspirations, in hope of finding a better opportunity. If, on the other hand, the manager helps the employee to achieve maximum potential, he or she will build a foundation for a successful career. According to the above paragraph,

   A. if an employee has negative attitudes towards his or her job, the manager is to blame
   B. managers of young people often have a great influence upon their careers
   C. good employees will leave a job they like if they are not given a chance to develop their skills
   D. managers should develop the full potential of their young employees

5. The reason for these differences is not that the Greeks had a superior sense of form or an inferior imagination or joy in life, but that they thought differently. Perhaps an illustration will make this clear. With the historical plays of Shakespeare in mind, let the reader contemplate the only extant Greek play on a historical subject, the Persians of Aeschylus, a play written less than ten years after the event which it deals with, and performed before the Athenian people who had played so notable a part in the struggle—incidentally, immediately below the Acropolis which the Persians had sacked and defiled. Any Elizabethan dramatist would have given us a panorama of the whole war, its moments of despair, hope, and triumph; we should see on the stage the leaders who planned and some of the soldiers who won the victory. In the persians we see nothing of the sort. The scene is laid in the Persian capital, one action is seen only through Persian eyes, the course of the war is simplified so much that the naval battle of Artemisium is not mentioned, nor even the heroic defense of Thermopylae, and not a single Greek is mentioned by name. The contrast could hardly be more complete. Which sentence is BEST supported by the above paragraph?

   A. Greek plays are more interesting than Elizabethan plays.
   B. Elizabethan dramatists were more talented than Greek dramatists.

C. If early Greek dramatists had the same historical material as Shakespeare had, the final form the Greek work would take would be very different from the Elizabethan work.
D. Greeks were historically more inaccurate than Elizabethans.

6. The problem with present planning systems, public or private, is that accountability is weak. Private planning systems in the global corporations operate on a set of narrow incentives that frustrate sensible public policies such as full employment, environmental protection, and price stability. Public planning is Olympian and confused because there is neither a clear consensus on social values nor political priorities. To accomplish anything, explicit choices must be made, but these choices can be made effectively only with the active participation of the people most directly involved. This, not nostalgia for small-town times gone forever, is the reason that devolution of political power to local communities is a political necessity. The power to plan locally is a precondition for sensible integration of cities, regions, and countries into the world economy. According to the author, 6.____

   A. people most directly affected by issues should participate in deciding those issues
   B. private planning systems are preferable to public planning systems
   C. there is no good system of government
   D. county governments are more effective than state governments

Questions 7-11.

DIRECTIONS: Questions 7 through 11 are to be answered SOLELY on the basis of the following passage.

The ideal relationship for the interview is one of mutual confidence. To try to pretend, to put on a front of cordiality and friendship is extremely unwise for the interviewer because he will certainly convey, by subtle means, his real feelings. It is the interviewer's responsibility to take the lead in establishing a relationship of mutual confidence.

As the interviewer, you should help the interviewee to feel at ease and ready to talk. One of the best ways to do this is to be at ease yourself. If you are, it will probably be evident; if you are not, it will almost certainly be apparent to the interviewee. Begin the interview with topics for discussion which are easy to talk about and non-menacing. This interchange can be like the conversation of people when they are waiting for a bus, at the ballgame, or discussing the weather. However, do not prolong this warm-up too long since the interviewee knows as well as you do that these are not the things he came to discuss. Delaying too long in getting down to business may suggest to him that you are reluctant to deal with the topic.

Once you get onto the main topics, do all that you can to get the interviewee to talk freely with as little prodding from you as possible. This will probably require that you give him some idea of the area and of ways of looking at it. Avoid, however, prejudicing or coloring his remarks by what you say; especially, do not in any way indicate that there are certain things you want to hear, others which you do not want to hear. It is essential that he feel free to express his own ideas unhampered by your ideas, your values and preconceptions.

Do not appear to dominate the interview, nor have even the suggestion of a patronizing attitude. Ask some questions which will enable the interviewee to take pride in his knowledge. Take the attitude that the interviewee sincerely wants the interview to achieve its purpose. This creates a warm, permissive atmosphere that is most important in all interviews.

4 (#1)

7. Of the following, the BEST title for the above passage is 7.___

   A. PERMISSIVENESS IN INTERVIEWING
   B. INTERVIEWING TECHNIQUES
   C. THE FACTOR OF PRETENSE IN THE INTERVIEW
   D. THE CORDIAL INTERVIEW

8. Which of the following recommendations on the conduct of an interview is made by the above passage? 8.___

   A. Conduct the interview as if it were an interchange between people discussing the weather.
   B. The interview should be conducted in a highly impersonal manner.
   C. Allow enough time for the interview so that the interviewee does not feel rushed.
   D. Start the interview with topics which are not threatening to the interviewee.

9. The above passage indicates that the interviewer should 9.___

   A. feel free to express his opinions
   B. patronize the interviewee and display a permissive attitude
   C. permit the interviewee to give the needed information in his own fashion
   D. provide for privacy when conducting the interview

10. The meaning of the word *unhampered*, as it is used in the last sentence of the fourth paragraph of the above passage, is MOST NEARLY 10.___

    A. unheeded   B. unobstructed
    C. hindered   D. aided

11. It can be INFERRED from the above passage that 11.___

    A. interviewers, while generally mature, lack confidence
    B. certain methods in interviewing are more successful than others in obtaining information
    C. there is usually a reluctance on the part of interviewers to deal with unpleasant topics
    D. it is best for the interviewer not to waiver from the use of hard and fast rules when dealing with clients

Questions 12-19.

DIRECTIONS: Questions 12 through 19 are to be answered SOLELY on the basis of the following passage.

    Disabled cars pose a great danger to bridge traffic at any time, but during rush hours it is especially important that such vehicles be promptly detected and removed. The term *disabled car* is an all inclusive label referring to cars stalled due to a flat tire, mechanical failure, an accident, or locked bumpers. Flat tires are the most common reason why cars become disabled. The presence of disabled vehicles caused 68% of all traffic accidents last year. Of these, 75% were serious enough to require hospitalization of at least one of the vehicle's occupants.

The basic problem in the removal of disabled vehicles is detection of the car. Several methods have been proposed to aid detection. At a 1980 meeting of traffic experts and engineers, the idea of sinking electronic eyes into roadways was first suggested. Such *eyes* let officers know when traffic falls below normal speed and becomes congested. The basic argument against this approach is the high cost of installation of these *eyes*. One midwestern state has, since 1978, employed closed circuit television to detect the existence and locations of stalled vehicles. When stalled vehicles are seen on the closed circuit television screen, the information is immediately communicated by radio to units stationed along the roadway, thus enabling the prompt removal of these obstructions to traffic. However, many cities lack the necessary manpower and equipment to use this approach. For the past five years, several east-coast cities have used the method known as *safety chains*, consisting of mobile units which represent the links at the *safety chain*. Thses mobile units are stationed as posts one or two miles apart along roadways to detect disabled cars. Standard procedure is for the units in the *safety chain* to have roof blinker lights turned on to full rotation. The officer, upon spotting a disabled car, at once assumes a post that gives him the most control in directing traffic around the obstruction. Only after gaining such control does he investigate and decide what action should be taken.

12. From the above passage, the PERCENTAGE of accidents caused by disabled cars in which hospitalization was required by at least one of the occupants of a vehicle last year was

    A. 17%   B. 51%   C. 68%   D. 75%

13. According to the above passage, vehicles are MOST frequently disabled because of

    A. flat tires
    B. locked bumpers
    C. brake failure
    D. overheated motors

14. According to the above passage, in the electronic eye method of detection, the *eyes* are placed

    A. on lights along the roadway
    B. on patrol cars stationed along the roadway
    C. in booths spaced two miles apart
    D. into the roadway

15. According to the above passage, the factor COMMON to both the *safety chain* method and the *closed circuit television* method of detecting disabled vehicles is that both

    A. require the use of *electronic eyes*
    B. may be used where there is a shortage of officers
    C. employ units that are stationed along the highway
    D. require the use of trucks to move the heavy equipment used

16. The one of the following which is NOT discussed in the above passage as a method that may be used to detect disabled vehicles is

    A. closed circuit television
    B. radar
    C. electronic *eyes*
    D. safety chains

17. One DRAWBACK mentioned by the above passage to the use of the closed circuit television method for detection of disabled cars is that this technique

    A. cannot be used during bad weather
    B. does not provide for actual removal of the cars
    C. must be operated by a highly skilled staff of traffic engineers
    D. requires a large amount of manpower and equipment

18. The NEWEST of the methods discussed in the above passage for detection of disabled vehicles is

    A. electronic *eyes*   B. the mobile unit
    C. the safety chain   D. closed circuit television

19. When the *safety chain* method is being used, an officer who spots a disabled vehicle should FIRST

    A. turn off his roof blinker lights
    B. direct traffic around the disabled vehicle
    C. send a radio message to the nearest mobile unit
    D. conduct an investigation

20. The universe is 15 billion years old, and the geological underpinnings of the earth were formed long before the first sea creature slithered out of the slime. But it is only in the last 6,000 years or so that men have descended into mines to chop and scratch at the earth's crust. Human history is, as Carl Sagan has put it, the equivalent of a few seconds in the 15 billion year life of the earth. What alarms those who keep track of the earth's crust is that since 1950 human beings have managed to consume more minerals than were mined in all previous history, a splurge of a millisecond in geologic time that cannot be long repeated without using up the finite riches of the earth. Of the following, the MAIN idea of this paragraph is:

    A. There is true cause for concern at the escalating consumption of the earth's minerals in recent years
    B. Human history is the equivalent of a few seconds in the 15 billion year life of the earth
    C. The earth will soon run out of vital mineral resources
    D. The extraction of minerals from the earth's crust only began 6,000 years ago

21. The authors of the Economic Report of the President are collectively aware, despite their vision of the asset-rich household, of the real economy in which millions of Americans live. There are glimpses, throughout the Report, of the underworld in which about *23 million people* do not have public or private health insurance; in which *the number of people receiving unemployment compensation was 41 percent of the total unemployed,* in which the average dole for the compensated unemployed *is about one-half of take-home pay.* The authors understand, for example, that *a worker may become physically disabled and that individuals generally do not like the risk of losing their ability to earn income.* But such realities justify no more than the most limited interference in the (imperfect) market for disability insurance. There is only, as far as I can tell, one moment of genuine emotion in the entire Report when the authors' passions are stirred beyond market principles. They are discussing the leasing provisions of the 1981 Tax Act (conditions which so reduce tax revenues that they are apparently opposed in their present form by the Business Roundtable, the American Business Conference, and the National Association of Manufacturers).

In the dark days before the 1981 Act, according to the Report, *firms with temporary tax losses (a condition especially characteristic of new enterprises) were often unable to take advantage of investment tax incentives. The reason was that temporarily unprofitable companies had no taxable income against which to apply the investment tax deduction.* It was a piteous contingency for the truly needy entrepreneur. But all was made right with the Tax Act. Social security for the disabled incompetent corporation: the compassionate soul of Reagan's new economy. According to the above passage,

    A. the National Association of Manufacturers and those companies that are temporarily unprofitable oppose the leasing provisions of the 1981 Tax Act
    B. the authors of the Report are willing to ignore market principles in order to assist corporations unable to take advantage of tax incentives
    C. the authors of the Report feel the National Association of Manufacturers and the Business Roundtable are wrong in opposing the leasing provisions of the 1981 Tax Act
    D. the authors of the Report have more compassion for incompetent corporations than for disabled workers

22. Much of the lore of management in the West regards ambiguity as a symptom of a variety of organizational ills whose cure is larger doses of rationality, specificity, and decisiveness. But is ambiguity sometimes desirable? Ambiguity may be thought of as a shroud of the unknown surrounding certain events. The Japanese have a word for it, ma, for which there is no English translation. The word is valuable because it gives an explicit place to the unknowable aspect of things. In English, we may refer to an empty space between the chair and the table; the Japanese don't say the space is empty but *full of nothing*. However amusing the illustration, it goes to the core of the issue. Westerners speak of what is unknown primarily in reference to what is known (like the space between the chair and the table), while most Eastern languages give honor to the unknown in its own right.
Of course, there are many situations that a manager finds himself in where being explicit and decisive is not only helpful but necessary. There is considerable advantage, however, in having a dual frame of reference—recognizing the value of both the clear and the ambiguous. The point to bear in mind is that in certain situations, ambiguity may serve better than absolute clarity. Which sentence is BEST supported by the above passage?

    A. We should cultivate the art of being ambiguous.
    B. Ambiguity may sometimes be an effective managerial tool.
    C. Westerners do not have a dual frame of reference.
    D. It is important to recognize the ambiguous aspects of all situations.

23. Everyone ought to accustom himself to grasp in his thought at the same time facts that are at once so few and so simple, that he shall never believe that he has knowledge of anything which he does not mentally behold with a distinctiveness equal to that of the objects which he knows most distinctly of all. It is true that some people are born with a much greater aptitude for such discernment than others, but the mind can be made much more expert at such work by art and exercise. But there is one fact which I should here emphasize above all others; and that is everyone should firmly persuade himself that none of the sciences, however abstruse, is to be deduced from lofty and

obscure matters, but that they all proceed only from what is easy and more readily understood. According to the author,

   A. people should concentrate primarily on simple facts
   B. intellectually gifted people have a great advantage over others
   C. even difficult material and theories proceed from what is readily understood
   D. if a scientist cannot grasp a simple theory, he or she is destined to fail

24. Goethe's casual, observations about language contain a profound truth. Every word in every language is a part of a system of thinking unlike any other. Speakers of different languages live in different worlds; or rather, they live in the same world but can't help looking at it in different ways. Words stand for patterns of experience. As one generation hands its language down to the next, it also hands down a fixed pattern of thinking, seeing, and feeling. When we go from one language to another, nothing stays put; different peoples carry different nerve patterns in their brains, and there's no point where they fully match. According to the above passage,

   A. language differences and their ramifications are a major cause of tensions between nations
   B. it is not a good use of one's time to read novels that have been translated from another language because of the tremendous differences in interpretation
   C. differences in languages reflect the different experiences of people the world over
   D. language students should be especially careful to retain awareness of the subtleties of their native language

Questions 25-27.

DIRECTIONS: Questions 25 through 27 are to be answered SOLELY on the basis of the following passage.

The context of all education is twofold — individual and social. Its business is to make us more and more ourselves, to cultivate in each of us our own distinctive genius, however modest it may be, while showing us how this genius may be reconciled with the needs and claims of the society of which we are a part. Thought it is not education's aim to cultivate eccentrics, that society is richest, most flexible, and most humane that best uses and most tolerates eccentricity. Conformity beyond a point breeds sterile minds and, therefore, a sterile society.

The function of secondary — and still more of higher education is to affect the environment. Teachers are not, and should not be, social reformers. But they should be the catalytic agents by means of which young minds are influenced to desire and execute reform. To aspire to better things is a logical and desirable part of mental and spiritual growth.

25. Of the following, the MOST suitable title for the above passage is

   A. EDUCATION'S FUNCTION IN CREATING INDIVIDUAL DIFFERENCES
   B. THE NEED FOR EDUCATION TO ACQUAINT US WITH OUR SOCIAL ENVIRONMENT
   C. THE RESPONSIBILITY OF EDUCATION TOWARD THE INDIVIDUAL AND SOCIETY
   D. THE ROLE OF EDUCATION IN EXPLAINING THE NEEDS OF SOCIETY

26. On the basis of the above passage, it may be inferred that

    A. conformity is one of the forerunners of totalitarianism
    B. education should be designed to create at least a modest amount of genius in everyone
    C. tolerance of individual differences tends to give society opportunities for improvement
    D. reforms are usually initiated by people who are somewhat eccentric

26.____

27. On the basis of the above passage, it may be inferred that

    A. genius is likely to be accompanied by a desire for social reform
    B. nonconformity is an indication of the inquiring mind
    C. people who are not high school or college graduates are not able to affect the environment
    D. teachers may or may not be social reformers

27.____

Questions 28-30.

DIRECTIONS: Questions 28 through 30 are to be answered SOLELY on the basis of the following passage.

Disregard for odds and complete confidence in one's self have produced many of our great successes. But every young man who wants to go into business for himself should appraise himself as a candidate for the one percent to survive. What has he to offer that is new or better? Has he special talents, special know-how, a new invention or service, or more capital than the average competitor? Has he the most important qualification of all, a willingness to work harder than anyone else? A man who is working for himself without limitation of hours or personal sacrifice can run circles around any operation that relies on paid help. But he must forget the eight-hour day, the forty-hour week, and the annual vacation. When he stops work, his income stops unless he hires a substitute. Most small operations have their busiest day on Saturday, and the owner uses Sunday to catch up on his correspondence, bookkeeping, inventorying, and maintenance chores. The successful self-employed man invariably works harder and worries more than the man on a salary. His wife and children make corresponding sacrifices of family unity and continuity; they never know whether their man will be home or in a mood to enjoy family activities.

28. The title that BEST expresses the ideas of the above passage is

    A. OVERCOMING OBSTACLES
    B. RUNNING ONE'S OWN BUSINESS
    C. HOW TO BECOME A SUCCESS
    D. WHY SMALL BUSINESSES FAIL

28.____

29. The above passage suggests that

    A. small businesses are the ones that last
    B. salaried workers are untrustworthy
    C. a willingness to work will overcome loss of income
    D. working for one's self may lead to success

29.____

30. The author of the above passage would MOST likely believe in

    A. individual initiative
    B. socialism
    C. corporations
    D. government aid to small business

KEY (CORRECT ANSWERS)

1.	C	16.	B
2.	A	17.	D
3.	A	18.	A
4.	B	19.	B
5.	C	20.	A
6.	A	21.	D
7.	B	22.	B
8.	D	23.	C
9.	C	24.	C
10.	B	25.	C
11.	B	26.	C
12.	B	27.	D
13.	A	28.	B
14.	D	29.	D
15.	C	30.	A

WRITTEN ENGLISH EXPRESSION
EXAMINATION SECTION
TEST 1

DIRECTIONS: The following questions are designed to test your knowledge of grammar, sentence structure, correct usage, and punctuation. In each group there is one sentence that contains no errors. Select the letter of the CORRECT sentence. *PRINT THE LETTER OF THE CORRECT ANSWER IN THE SPACE AT THE RIGHT.*

1.
   A. A low ceiling is when the atmospheric conditions make flying inadvisable.
   B. They couldn't tell who the card was from.
   C. No one but you and I are to help him.
   D. What kind of a teacher would you like to be?
   E. To him fall the duties of foster parent.

   1.____

2.
   A. They couldn't tell whom the cable was from.
   B. We like these better than those kind.
   C. It is a test of you more than I.
   D. The person in charge being him, there can be no change in policy.
   E. Chicago is larger than any city in Illinois.

   2.____

3.
   A. Do as we do for the celebration.
   B. Do either of you care to join us?
   C. A child's food requirements differ from the adult.
   D. A large family including two uncles and four grandparents live at the hotel.
   E. Due to bad weather, the game was postponed.

   3.____

4.
   A. If they would have done that they might have succeeded.
   B. Neither the hot days or the humid nights annoy our Southern visitor.
   C. Some people do not gain favor because they are kind of tactless.
   D. No sooner had the turning point come than a new issue arose.
   E. I wish that I was in Florida now.

   4.____

5.
   A. We haven't hardly enough tine.
   B. Immigration is when people come into a foreign country to live.
   C. After each side gave their version, the affair was over with.
   D. Every one of the cars were tagged by the police.
   E. He either will fail in his attempt or will seek other employment.

   5.____

6.
   A. They can't seem to see it when I explain the theory.
   B. It is difficult to find the genuine signature between all those submitted.
   C. She can't understand why they don't remember who to give the letter to
   D. Every man and woman in America is interested in his tax bill.
   E. Honor as well as profit are to be gained by these studies.

   6.____

7.   A. He arrived safe.
     B. I do not have any faith in John running for office.
     C. The musicians began to play tunefully and keeping the proper tempo indicated for the selection.
     D. Mary's maid of honor bought the kind of an outfit suitable for an afternoon wedding.
     E. If you would have studied the problem carefully you would have found the solution more quickly.

8.   A. The new plant is to be electric lighted.
     B. The reason the speaker was offended was that the audience was inattentive.
     C. There appears to be conditions that govern his behavior.
     D. Either of the men are influential enough to control the situation.
     E. The gallery with all its pictures were destroyed.

9.   A. If you would have listened more carefully, you would have heard your name called.
     B. Did you inquire if your brother were returning soon?
     C. We are likely to have rain before nightfall.
     D. Let's you and I plan next summer's vacation together.
     E. The man whom I thought was my friend deceived me.

10. A. There's a man and his wife waiting for the doctor since early this morning.
     B. The owner of the market with his assistants is applying the most modern principles of merchandise display.
     C. Every one of the players on both of the competing teams were awarded a gold watch.
     D. The records of the trial indicated that, even before attaining manhood, the murderer's parents were both dead.
     E. We had no sooner entered the room when the bell rang.

11. A. Why don't you start the play like I told you?
     B. I didn't find the construction of the second house much different from that of the first one I saw.
     C. "When", inquired the child, "Will we begin celebrating my birthday?"
     D. There isn't nothing left to do but not to see him anymore.
     E. There goes the last piece of cake and the last spoonful of ice cream.

12. A. The child could find neither the shoe or the stocking.
     B. The musicians began to play tunefully and keeping the proper tempo indicated for the selection.
     C. The amount of curious people who turned out for Opening Night was beyond calculation.
     D. I fully expected that the children would be at their desks and to find them ready to begin work,
     E. "Indeed," mused the poll-taker, "the winning candidate is much happier than I."

13. A. Just as you said, I find myself gaining weight.
    B. A teacher should leave the capable pupils engage in creative activities.
    C. The teacher spoke continually during the entire lesson, which, of course, was poor procedure.
    D. We saw him steal into the room, pick up the letter, and tear it's contents to shreds.
    E. It is so dark that I can't hardly see.

    13.____

14. A. The new schedule of working hours and rates was satis factory to both employees and employer.
    B. Many common people feel keenly about the injustices of Power Politics.
    C. Mr. and Mrs. Burns felt that their grandchild was awfully cute when he waved good-bye.
    D. The tallest of the twins was also the most intelligent,
    E. Please come here and try and help me finish this piece of work.

    14.____

15. A. My younger brother insists that he is as tall as me.
    B. Suffering from a severe headache all day, one dose of the prescribed medicine relieved me,
    C. "Please let my brothers and I help you with your packages," said Frank to Mrs. Powers.
    D. Every one of the rooms we visited had displays of pupils' work in them.
    E. Do you intend bringing most of the refreshments yourself?

    15.____

16. A. The telephone linesmen, working steadily at their task during the severe storm, the telephones soon began to ring again.
    B. Meat, as well as fruits and vegetables, is considered essential to a proper diet.
    C. He looked like a real good boxer that night in the ring.
    D. The man has worked steadily for fifteen years before he decided to open his own business.
    E. The winters were hard and dreary, nothing could live without shelter.

    16.____

17. A. No one can foretell when I will have another opportunity like that one again.
    B. The last group of paintings shown appear really to have captured the most modern techniques,
    C. We searched high and low, both in the attic and cellar, but were unsuccessful in locating mementos.
    D. None of the guests was able to give the rules of the game accurately.
    E. When you go to the library tomorrow, please bring this book to the librarian in the reference room.

    17.____

18. A. After the debate, every one of the speakers realized that, given another chance, he could have done better.
    B. The reason given by the physician for the patient's trouble was because of his poor eating habits.
    C. The fog was so thick that the driver couldn't hardly see more than ten feet ahead.
    D. I suggest that you present the medal to who you think best.
    E. I don't approve of him going along.

    18.____

19. A. A decision made by a man without much deliberation is sometimes no different than a slow one.
    B. By the time Mr. Brown's son will graduate Dental School, he will be twenty-six years of age.
    C. Who did you predict would win the election?
    D. The auctioneer had less stamps to sell this year than last year.
    E. Being that he is occupied, I shall not disturb him.

20. A. Having pranced into the arena with little grace and unsteady hoof for the jumps ahead, the driver reined his horse.
    B. Once the dog wagged it's tail, you knew it was a friendly animal.
    C. Like a great many artists, his life was a tragedy.
    D. When asked to choose corn, cabbage, or potatoes, the diner selected the latter.
    E. The record of the winning team was among the most noteworthy of the season.

21. A. The maid wasn't so small that she couldn't reach the top window for cleaning.
    B. Many people feel that powdered coffee produces a really good flavor.
    C. Would you mind me trying that coat on for size?
    D. This chair looks much different than the chair we selected in the store.
    E. I wish that he would have talked to me about the lesson before he presented it.

22. A. After trying unsuccessfully to land a job in the city, Will located in the country on a farm.
    B. On the last attempt, the pole-vaulter came nearly to getting hurt.
    C. The observance of Armistice Day throughout the world offers an opportunity to reflect on the horrors of war.
    D. Outside of the mistakes in spelling, the child's letter was a very good one.
    E. The annual income of New York is far greater than Florida.

23. A. Scissors is always dangerous for a child to handle.
    B. I assure you that I will not yield to pressure to sell my interest.
    C. Ask him if he has recall of the incident which took place at our first meeting.
    D. The manager felt like as not to order his usher-captain to surrender his uniform.
    E. Everyone on the boat said their prayers when the storm grew worse.

24. A. The mother of the bride climaxed the occasion by exclaiming, "I want my children should be happy forever."
    B. We read in the papers where the prospects for peace are improving.
    C. "Can I share the cab with you?" was frequently heard during the period of gas rationing.
    D. The man was enamored with his friend"s sister.
    E. Had the police suspected the ruse, they would have taken proper precautions.

25. A. The teacher admonished the other students neither to speak to John, nor should they annoy him.
    B. Fortunately we had been told that there was but one service station in that area.
    C. An usher seldom rises above a theatre manager.
    D. The epic, "Gone With the Wind," is supposed to have taken place during the Civil War Era.
    E. Now that she has been graduated she should be encouraged to make her own choice as to the career she is to follow.

KEY (CORRECT ANSWERS)

1.	E	11.	B
2.	A	12.	E
3.	A	13.	A
4.	D	14.	A
5.	E	15.	E
6.	D	16.	B
7.	A	17.	D
8.	B	18.	A
9.	C	19.	C
10.	B	20.	E

21. B
22. C
23. B
24. E
25. B

TEST 2

DIRECTIONS: The following questions are designed to test your knowledge of grammar, sentence structure, correct usage, and punctuation. In each group, there is one sentence that contains no errors. Select the letter of the CORRECT sentence. *PRINT THE LETTER OF THE CORRECT ANSWER IN THE SPACE AT THE RIGHT.*

1. A. Shall you be at home, let us say, on Sunday at two o'clock?
   B. We see Mr. Lewis take his car out of the garage daily, newly polished always.
   C. We have no place to keep our rubbers, only in the hall closet.
   D. Isn't it true what you told me about the best way to prepare for an examination?
   E. Mathematics is among my favorite subjects.

   1.____

2. A. The host thought the guests were of the hungry kinds so he prepared much food.
   B. The museum is often visited by students who are fond of early inventions, and especially patent attorneys.
   C. I rose to nominate the man who most of us felt was the most diligent worker in the group.
   D. The child was sent to the store to purchase a bottle of milk, and brought home fresh rolls, too.
   E. Hidden away in the closet, I found the long-lost purse.

   2.____

3. A. The garden tool was sent to be sharpened, and a new handle to be put on.
   B. At the end of her vacation, Joan came home with little money, but which systematic thrift soon overcame.
   C. We people have opportunities to show the rest of the world how real democracy functions.
   D. The guide paddled along, then fell in a reverie which he related the history of the region.
   E. No sooner had the curtain dropped when the audience shouted its approval in chorus.

   3.____

4. A. The data you need is to be made available shortly.
   B. The first few strokes of the brush were enough to convince me that Tom could paint much better than me.
   C. We inquired if we could see the owner of the store, after we waited for one hour.
   D. The highly-strung parent was aggravated by the slightest noise that the baby made.
   E. We should have investigated the cause of the noise by bringing the car to a halt.

   4.____

5. A. The police, investigating the crime, were successful in discovering only one possibly valuable clue.
   B. Due to an unexpected change in plans, the violin soloist did not perform.
   C. Besides being awarded a Bachelor's degree at college, the scientist has since received many honorary degrees.
   D. The data offered in advance of the recent Presidential election seems to have possessed elements of inaccuracy.
   E. I don't believe your the only one who has been asked to come here.

   5.____

2 (#2)

6. A. I don't quite see that I will be able to completely finish the job in time. 6.____
    B. By my statement, I infer that you are guilty of the offense as charged.
    C. Wasn't it strange that they wouldn't let no one see the body?
    D. I hope that this is the kind of rolls you requested me to buy.
    E. The storekeeper distributed cigars as bonuses between his many customers.

7. A. He said he preferred the climate of Florida to California. 7.____
    B. Because of the excessive heat, a great amount of fruit juice was drunk by the guests.
    C. This week's dramatic presentation was neither as lively nor as entertaining as last week.
    D. The fashion expert believed that no one could develop new creations more successfully than him.
    E. A collection of Dicken's works is a "must" for every library.

8. A. There was such a large amount of books on the floor that I couldn't find a place for my rocking chair. 8.____
    B. Walking up the rickety stairs, the bottle slipped from his hands and smashed.
    C. The reason they granted his request was because he had a good record.
    D. Little Tommy was proud that the teacher always asked him to bring messages to the office.
    E. That kind of orange is grown only in Florida.

9. A. The new mayor is a resident of this city for thirty years. 9.____
    B. Do you mean to imply that had he not missed that shot he would have won?
    C. Next term I shall be studying French and history.
    D. I read in last night's paper where the sales tax is going to be abolished.
    E. In order to prevent breakage, she placed a sheet of paper between each of the plates when she packed them.

10. A. To have children vie against one another is psychologically unsound. 10.____
    B. Would anyone else care to discuss his baby?
    C. He was interested and aware of the problem.
    D. I sure would like to discover if he is motivating the lesson properly.
    E. The cloth was first lain on a flat surface; then it was pressed with a hot iron.

11. A. She graduated Barnard College twenty-five years ago. 11.____
    B. He studied the violin since he was seven.
    C. She is not so diligent a researcher as her classmate.
    D. He discovered that the new data corresponds with the facts disclosed by Werner.
    E. How could he enjoy the television program; the dog was barking and the baby was crying.

12. A. You have three alternatives: law, dentistry, or teaching. 12.____
    B. If I would have worked harder, I would have accomplished my purpose.
    C. He affected a rapid change of pace and his opponents were outdistanced.
    D. He looked prosperous, although he had been unemployed for a year.
    E. The engine not only furnishes power but light and heat as well.

13. A. The children shared one anothers toys and seemed quite happy.
     B. They lay in the sun for many hours, getting tanned.
     C. The reproduction arrived, and had been hung in the living room.
     D. First begin by calling the roll.
     E. Tell me where you hid it; no one shall ever find it.

14. A. Deliver these things to whomever arrives first.
     B. Everybody but she and me is going to the conference.
     C. If the number of patrons is small, we can serve them.
     D. When each of the contestants find their book, the debate may begin.
     E. Some people, farmers in particular, lament the substitution of butter by margarine.

15. A. After his illness, he stood in the country three weeks.
     B. If you wish to effect a change, submit your suggestions.
     C. It is silly to leave children play with knives.
     D. Play a trick on her by spilling water down her neck.
     E. There was such a crowd of people at the crossing we couldn't hardly get on the bus.

16. A. This is a time when all of us must show our faith and devotion to our country.
     B. Either you or I are certain to be elected president of the new club.
     C. The interpellation of the Minister of Finance forced him to explain his policies.
     D. After hoisting the anchor and removing the binnacle, the ship was ready to set sail.
     E. Please bring me a drink of cold water from the refrigerator.

17. A. Mistakes in English, when due to carelessness or haste, can easily be rectified.
     B. Mr. Jones is one of those persons who will try to keep a promise and usually does.
     C. Being very disturbed by what he had heard, Fred decided to postpone his decision.
     D. There is a telephone at the other end of the corridor which is constantly in use.
     E. In his teaching, he always kept the childrens' interests and needs in mind.

18. A. The lazy pupil, of course, will tend to write the minimum amount of words acceptable.
     B. His success as a political leader consisted mainly of his ability to utter platitudes in a firm and convincing manner.
     C. To be cognizant of current affairs, a person must not only read newspapers and magazines but also recent books by recognized authorities.
     D. Although we intended to have gone fishing, the sudden outbreak of a storm caused us to change our plans.
     E. It is the colleges that must take the responsibility for encouraging greater flexibility in the high-school curriculum.

19.
- A. "I am sorry," he said, "but John's answer was 'No'."
- B. A spirited argument followed between those who favored and opposed Marie's expulsion from the club.
- C. Whether a forward child should be humored or punished often depends upon the circumstances.
- D. Excessive alcoholism is certainly not conducive with efficient performance of one's work.
- E. Stroking his beard thoughtfully, an idea suddenly came to him.

19.____

20.
- A. "Take care, my children," he said sadly, "lest you not be deceived."
- B. Those continuous telephone calls are preventing Betty from completing her homework.
- C. They dug deep into the earth at the spot indicated on the map, but they found nothing.
- D. We petted and cozened the little girl until she finally stopped weeping.
- E. There was, in the mail, an inquiry for a house by a young couple with two or three bedrooms.

20.____

21.
- A. Please fill in the required information on the application form and return same by April 15.
- B. Tom was sitting there idly, watching the clouds scud across the sky.
- C. We started for home so that our parents would not suspect that anything out of the ordinary took place.
- D. The sudden abatement from the storm enabled the ladies to resume their journey.
- E. Each of the twelve members were agreed that the accused man was innocent.

21.____

22.
- A. The number of gifted students not continuing their education beyond secondary school present a nationwide problem.
- B. A man's animadversions against those he considers his enemies are usually reflections of his own inadequacies.
- C. The alembic of his fevered imagination produced some of the greatest romantic poetry of his era.
- D. The first case of smallpox dates back more than 3000 years and has gone unchecked until recently.
- E. He promised to go irregardless of the rain or snow.

22.____

23.
- A. The child picked up several of the coracles, which he had seen glittering in the sand, and brought them to his mother.
- B. He muttered in dejected tones – and no one contradicted him – "We have failed."
- C. A girl whom I believed to be she waved cheerily to me from a passing automobile.
- D. We discovered that she was a former resident of our own neighborhood who eloped some years ago with a milkman.
- E. It looks now like he will not be promoted after all.

23.____

24. A. Mary is the kind of a person on whom you can depend in any emergency.
    B. I am sure that either applicant can fill the job you offer competently and efficiently.
    C. Although we searched the entire room, the scissors was not to be found.
    D. Being that you are here, we can proceed with the discussion.
    E. In spite of our warning whistle, the huge ship continued to sail athwart our course.

24.___

25. A. The salaries earned by college graduates vary as much if not more than those earned by high school graduates.
    B. The apothegms that he felt to be so witty were all too often either trite or platitudinous.
    C. She read the letter carefully, took out one of the pages, and tore it into small pieces.
    D. A young man, who hopes to succeed, must be diligent in his work and alert to his opportunities.
    E. No one should plan a long journey for pleasure in these days.

25.___

KEY (CORRECT ANSWERS)

1.	A	11.	C
2.	C	12.	D
3.	C	13.	E
4.	E	14.	C
5.	A	15.	B
6.	D	16.	C
7.	B	17.	A
8.	E	18.	E
9.	B	19.	C
10.	B	20.	C
21.	B		
22.	C		
23.	B		
24.	E		
25.	B		

CLERICAL ABILITIES

EXAMINATION SECTION
TEST 1

DIRECTIONS: Each question or incomplete statement is followed by several suggested answers or completions. Select the one that BEST answers the question or completes the statement. *PRINT THE LETTER OF THE CORRECT ANSWER IN THE SPACE AT THE RIGHT.*

Questions 1 through 4 are to be answered on the basis of the information below:

The most commonly used filing system and the one that is easiest to learn is alphabetical filing. This involves putting records in an A to Z order, according to the letters of the alphabet. The name of a person is filed by using the following order: first, the surname or last name; second, the first name; third, the middle name or initial. For example, *Henry C. Young* is filed under Y and thereafter under *Young, Henry C.* The name of a company is filed in the same way. For example, *Long Cabinet Co.* is filed under *L*, while *John T. Long Cabinet Co.* is filed under *L* and thereafter under *Long, John T. Cabinet Co.*

1. The one of the following which lists the names of the persons in the CORRECT alphabetical order is 1.____

   A. Mary Carrie, Helen Carrol, James Carson, John Carter
   B. James Carson, Mary Carrie, John Carter, Helen Carrol
   C. Helen Carrol, James Carson, John Carter, Mary Carrie
   D. John Carter, Helen Carrol, Mary Carrie, James Carson

2. The one of the following which lists the names of the persons in the CORRECT alphabetical order is 2.____

   A. Jones, John C.; Jones, John A.; Jones, John P.; Jones, John K.
   B. Jones, John P.; Jones, John K.; Jones, John C.; Jones, John A.
   C. Jones, John A.; Jones, John C.; Jones, John K.; Jones, John P.
   D. Jones, John K.; Jones, John C.; Jones, John A.; Jones, John P.

3. The one of the following which lists the names of the companies in CORRECT alphabetical order is 3.____

   A. Blane Co., Blake Co., Block Co., Blear Co.
   B. Blake Co., Blane Co., Blear Co., Block Co.
   C. Block Co., Blear Co., Blane Co., Blake Co.
   D. Blear Co., Blake Co., Blane Co., Block Co.

4. You are to return to the file an index card on *Barry C. Wayne Materials and Supplies Co.* Of the following, the CORRECT alphabetical group that you should return the index card to is 4.____

   A. A to G   B. H to M   C. N to S   D. T to Z

Questions 5-10

DIRECTIONS: In each of questions 5 through 10, the names of four people are given. For each question, choose as your answer the one of the four names given which would be filed FIRST according to the usual system of alphabetical filing of names, as described in the following paragraph.

In filing names, you must start with the last name. Names are filed in order of the first letter of the last name, then the second letter, etc. Therefore, BAILY would be filed by BROWN, which would be filed before COLT. A name with fewer letters of the same type comes first; i.e., Smith before Smithe. If the last names are the same, the names are filed alphabetically by the first name. If the first name is an initial, a name with an initial would come before a first name that starts with the same letter as the initial. Therefore, I. BROWN would come before IRA BROWN. Finally, if both last name and first name are the same, the name would be filed alphabetically by the middle name, once again an initial coming before a middle name which starts with the same letter as the initial. If there is no middle name at all, the name would come before those with middle initials or names.

Sample Question:
- A. Lester Daniels
- B. William Dancer
- C. Nathan Danzig
- D. Dan Lester

The last names beginning with D are filed before the last name beginning with L. Since DANIELS, DANCER and DANZIG all begin with the same three letters, you must look at the fourth letter of the last name to determine which name should be filed first. C comes before I or Z, so DANCER is filed before DANIELS or DANZIG. Therefore, the answer to the question is B.

5. A. Scott Biala   B. Mary Byala
   C. Martin Baylor   D. Francis Bauer

6. A. Howard J. Black   B. Howard Black
   C. J. Howard Black   D. John H. Black

7. A. Theodora Garth Kingston   B. Theadore Barth Kingston
   C. Paulette Mary Huerta   D. Paul M. Huerta

8. A. Paulette Mary Huerta   B. Paul M. Huerta
   C. Paulette L. Huerta   D. Peter A. Huerta

9. A. Martha Hunt Morgan   B. Martin Hunt Morgan
   C. Mary H. Morgan   D. Martine H. Morgan

10. A. James T. Meerschaum   B. James M. Mershum
    C. James F. Mearshaum   D. James N. Meshum

Questions 11 through 14 are to be answered on the basis of the following information:

You are required to file various documents in file drawers which are labeled according to the following pattern:

DOCUMENTS

MEMOS
File	Subject
84PM1	(A-L)
84PM2	(M-Z)

REPORTS
File	Subject
84PR1	(A-L)
84PR2	(M-Z)

LETTERS
File	Subject
84PC1	(A-L)
84PC2	(M-Z)

INQUIRIES
File	Subject
84PQ1	(A-L)
84PQ2	(M-Z)

11. A letter dealing with a burglary should be filed in the drawer labeled
    A. 84PM1 B. 84PC1 C. 84PR1 D. 84PQ2

12. A report on Statistics should be found in the drawer labeled
    A. 84PM1 B. 84PC2 C. 84PR2 D. 84PQ2

13. An inquiry is received about parade permit procedures. It should be filed in the drawer labeled
    A. 84PM2 B. 84PC1 C. 84PR1 D. 84PQ2

14. A police officer has a question about a robbery report you filed. You should pull this file from the drawer labeled
    A. 84PM1 B. 84PM2 C. 84PR1 D. 84PR2

Questions 15-22

DIRECTIONS: Each of questions 15 through 22 consist of four or six numbered names. For each question, choose the option which indicates the order in which the names should be filed in accordance with the following filing instructions:
- File alphabetically according to last name, then first name, then middle initial
- File according to each successive letter within a name
- When comparing two names in which the letters in the longer name are identical to the corresponding letters in the shorter name, the shorter name is filed first
- When the last names are the same, initials are always filed before names beginning with the same letter

15. I. Ralph Robinson   II. Alfred Ross
    III. Luis Robles   IV. James Roberts

   The CORRECT filing sequence for the above names should be
   A. IV, II, I, III   B. I, IV, III, II
   C. III, IV, I, II   D. IV, I, III, II

16. I.   Irwin Goodwin   II. Inez Gonzalez
     III. Irene Goodman   IV. Ira S. Goodwin
     V.   Ruth I. Goldstein   VI. M.B. Goodman

    The CORRECT filing sequence for the above names should be
    A. V, II, I, IV, III, VI   B. V, II, VI, III, IV, I
    C. V, II, III, VI, IV, I   D. V, II, III, VI, I, IV

17. I.   George Allan   II. Gregory Allen
     III. Gary Allen   IV. George Allen

    The CORRECT filing sequence for the above names should be
    A. IV, III, I, II   B. I, IV, II, III
    C. III, IV, I, II   D. I, III, IV, II

18. I.   Simon Kauffman   II. Leo Kaufman
     III. Robert Kaufmann   IV. Paul Kauffman

    The CORRECT filing sequence for the above names should be
    A. I, IV, II, III   B. II, IV, III, I
    C. III, II, IV, I   D. I, II, III, IV

19. I.   Roberta Williams   II. Robin Wilson
     III. Roberta Wilson   IV. Robin Williams

    The CORRECT filing sequence for the above names should be
    A. III, II, IV, I   B. I, IV, III, II
    C. I, II, III, IV   D. III, I, II, IV

20. I.   Lawrence Shultz   II. Albert Schultz
     III. Theodore Schwartz   IV. Thomas Schwarz
     V.   Alvin Schultz   VI. Leonard Shultz

    The CORRECT filing sequence for the above names should be
    A. II, V, III, IV, I, VI   B. IV, III, V, I, II, VI
    C. II, V, I, VI, III, IV   D. I, VI, II, V, III, IV

21. I.   McArdle   II. Mayer
     III. Maletz   IV. McNiff
     V.   Meyer   VI. MacMahon

    The CORRECT filing sequence for the above names should be
    A. I, IV, VI, III, II, V   B. II, I, IV, VI, III, V
    C. VI, III, II, I, IV, V   D. VI, III, II, V, I, IV

22. I.   Jack E. Johnson   II. R.H. Jackson
     III. Bertha Jackson   IV. J.T. Johnson
     V.   Ann Johns   VI. John Jacobs

    The CORRECT filing sequence for the above names should be
    A. II, III, VI, V, IV, I   B. III, II, VI, V, IV, I
    C. VI, II, III, I, V, IV   D. III, II, VI, IV, V, I

Questions 23-30

DIRECTIONS: The code table below shows 10 letters with matching numbers. For each question, there are three sets of letters. Each set of letters is followed by a set of numbers which may or may not match their correct letter according to the code table. For each question, check all three sets of letters and numbers and mark your answer:

    A. if no pairs are correctly matched
    B. if only one pair is correctly matched
    C. if only two pairs are correctly matched
    D. if all three pairs are correctly matched

CODE TABLE

T	M	V	D	S	P	R	G	B	H
1	2	3	4	5	6	7	8	9	0

Sample Question: TMVDSP - 123456
                            RGBHTM-789011
                            DSPRGB-256789

In the sample question above, the first set of numbers correctly matches its set of letters. But the second and third pairs contain mistakes. In the second pair, M is incorrectly matched with number 1. According to the code table, letter M should be correctly matched with number 2. In the third pair, the letter D is incorrectly matched with number 2. According to the code table, letter D should be correctly matched with number 4. Since only one of the pairs is correctly matched, the answer is B.

23. RSBMRM   759262
    GDSRVH   845730
    VDBRTM   349713

24. TGVSDR   183247
    SMHRDP   520647
    TRMHSR   172057

25. DSPRGM   456782
    MVDBHT   234902
    HPMDBT   062491

26. BVPTRD   936184
    GDPHMB   807029
    GMRHMV   827032

23._____

24._____

25._____

26._____

27. MGVRSH   283750
    TRDMBS   174295
    SPRMGV   567283

28. SGBSDM   489542
    MGHPTM   290612
    MPBMHT   269301

29. TDPBHM   146902
    VPBMRS   369275
    GDMBHM   842902

30. MVPTBV   236194
    PDRTMB   647128
    BGTMSM   981232

27. ___
28. ___
29. ___
30. ___

KEY (CORRECT ANSWERS)

1.	A	11.	B	21.	C
2.	C	12.	C	22.	B
3.	B	13.	D	23.	B
4.	D	14.	D	24.	B
5.	D	15.	D	25.	C
6.	B	16.	C	26.	A
7.	B	17.	D	27.	D
8.	B	18.	A	28.	A
9.	A	19.	B	29.	D
10.	C	20.	A	30.	A

TEST 2

DIRECTIONS: Each question or incomplete statement is followed by several suggested answers or completions. Select the one that BEST answers the question or completes the statement. *PRINT THE LETTER OF THE CORRECT ANSWER IN THE SPACE AT THE RIGHT.*

Questions 1-10

DIRECTIONS: Questions 1 through 10 each consist of two columns, each containing four lines of names, numbers and/or addresses. For each question, compare the lines in Column I with the lines in Column II to see if they match exactly, and mark your answer according to the following instructions:
- A. all four lines match exactly
- B. only three lines match exactly
- C. only two lines match exactly
- D. only one line matches exactly

Column I	Column II	
1. Earl Hodgson 1409870 Shore Ave. Macon Rd	Earl Hodgson 1408970 Schore Ave. Macon Rd.	1._____
2. 9671485 470 Astor Court Halprin, Phillip Frank D. Poliseo	9671485 470 Astor Court Halperin, Phillip Frank D. Poliseo	2._____
3. Tandem Associates 144-17 Northern Blvd. Alberta Forchi Kings Park, NY 10751	Tandom Associates 144-17 Northern Blvd. Albert Forchi Kings Point, NY 10751	3._____
4. Bertha C. McCormack Clayton, MO 976-4242 New City, NY 10951	Bertha C. McCormack Clayton, MO 976-4242 New City, NY 10951	4._____
5. George C. Morill Columbia, SC 29201 Louis Ingham 3406 Forest Ave.	George C. Morrill Columbia, SD 29201 Louis Ingham 3406 Forest Ave.	5._____
6. 506 S. Elliott Pl. Herbert Hall 4712 Rockaway Pkway 169E. 7 St.	506 S. Elliott Pl. Hurbert Hall 4712 Rockaway Pkway 169E. 7 St.	6._____

7. 345 Park Ave.   345 Park Pl.   7.___
    Colman Oven Corp.   Coleman Oven Corp.
    Robert Conte   Robert Conti
    6179846   6179846

8. Grigori Schierber   Grigori Schierber   8.___
    Des Moines, Iowa   Des Moines, Iowa
    Gouverneur Hospital   Gouverneur Hospital
    91-35CresskillPl.   91-35Cresskill Pl.

9. Jeffery Janssen   Jeffrey Janssen   9.___
    8041071   8041071
    40 Rockefeller Plaza   40 Rockefeller Plaza
    407 6 St.   406 7 St.

10. 5971996   5871996   10.___
    3113 Knickerbocker Ave.   3113 Knickerbocker Ave.
    8434 Boston Post Rd.   8424 Boston Post Rd.
    Penn Station   Penn Station

Questions 11-14

DIRECTIONS: Questions 11 through 14 are to be answered by looking at the four groups of names and addresses listed below and then finding out the number of groups that have their corresponding numbered lines exactly the same.

	GROUP I	GROUP II
Line 1:	Richmond General Hospital	Richman General Hospital
Line 2:	Geriatric Clinic	Geriatric Clinic
Line 3:	3975 Paerdegat St.	3975 Peardegat St.
Line 4:	Loudonville, New York 11538	Londonville, New York 11538
	GROUP III	GROUP IV
Line 1:	Richmond General Hospital	Richmend General Hospital
Line 2:	Geriatric Clinic	Geriatric Clinic
Line 3:	3795 Paerdegat St.	3975 Paerdegat St.
Line 4:	Loudonville, New York 11358	Loudonville, New York 11538

11. In how many groups is line 1 exactly the same?   11.___

    A. 2   B. 3   C. 4   D. None

12. In how many groups is line 2 exactly the same?   12.___

    A. 2   B. 3   C. 4   D. None

13. In how many groups is line 3 exactly the same?   13.___

    A. 2   B. 3   C. 4   D. None

14. In how many groups is line 4 exactly the same?   14.___

    A. 2   B. 3   C. 4   D. None

Questions 15-18

DIRECTIONS: Each of questions 15 through 18 has two lists of names and addresses. Each list contains three sets of names and addresses. Check each of the three sets in the list on the right to see if they are the same as the corresponding set in the list on the left. Mark your answers as follows:
- A. if none of the sets are the same
- B. if only one of the sets is the same
- C. if only two of the sets are the same
- D. if all three of the sets are the same

15. Mary T. Berlinger
2351 Hampton St.
Monsey, NY 20117

    Eduardo Benes
    473 Kingston Avenue
    Central Islip, NY 11734

    Alan Carrington Fuchs
    17 Gnarled Hollow Road
    Los Angeles, CA 91635

    Mary T. Berlinger
    2351 Hampton St.
    Monsey, NY 20117

    Eduardo Benes
    473 Kingston Avenue
    Central Islip, NY 11734

    Alan Carrington Fuchs
    17 Gnarled Hollow Road
    Los Angeles, CA 91685

    15.____

16. David John Jacobson
178 35 St. Apt. 4C
New York, NY 00927

    Ann-Marie Calonella
    7243 South Ridge Blvd.
    Bakersfield, CA 96714

    Pauline M. Thompson
    872 Linden Ave.
    Houston, Texas 70321

    David John Jacobson
    178 53 St. Apt. 4C
    New York, NY 00927

    Ann-Marie Calonella
    7243 South Ridge Blvd.
    Bakersfield, CA 96714

    Pauline M. Thomson
    872 Linden Ave.
    Houston, Texas 70321

    16.____

17. Chester LeRoy Masterton
152 Lacy Rd.
Kankakee, Ill. 54532

    William Maloney
    S. LaCrosse Pla.
    Wausau, Wisconsin 52146

    Cynthia V. Barnes
    16 Pines Rd.
    Greenpoint, Miss. 20376

    Chester LeRoy Masterson
    152 Lacy Rd.
    Kankakee, Ill. 54532

    William Maloney
    S. LaCross Pla.
    Wausau, Wisconsin 52146

    Cynthia V. Barnes
    16 Pines Rd.
    Greenpoint, Miss. 20376

    17.____

18. Marcel Jean Frontenac
     8 Burton On The Water
     Calender, Me. 01471

     J. Scott Marsden
     174 S.Tipton St.
     Cleveland, Ohio

     Lawrence T. Haney
     171 McDonough St.
     Decatur, GA 31304

Marcel Jean Frontenac
6 Burton On The Water
Calender, Me. 01471

J. Scott Marsden
174 Tipton St.
Cleveland, Ohio

Lawrence T. Haney
171 McDonough St.
Decatur, GA 31304

18.____

Questions 19-26

DIRECTIONS: Each of questions 19 through 26 has two lists of numbers. Each list contains three sets of numbers. Check each of the three sets in the list on the right to see if they are the same as the corresponding set in the list on the left. Mark your answers as follows:

      A.   if none of the sets are the same
      B.   if only one of the sets is the same
      C.   if only two of the sets are the same
      D.   if all three of the sets are the same

19. 7354183476
     4474747744
     57914302311

7354983476
4474747774
57914902311

19.____

20. 7143592185
     8344517699
     9178531263

7143892185
8344518699
9178531263

20.____

21. 2572114731
     8806835476
     8255831246

257214731
8806835476
8255831246

21.____

22. 331476853821
     6976658532996
     3766042113715

331476858621
6976655832996
3766042113745

22.____

23. 8806663315
     74477138449
     211756663666

8806663315
74477138449
211756663666

23.____

24. 990006966996
     53022219743
     4171171117717

99000696996
53022219843
4171171177717

24.____

25. 24400222433004
     5300030055000355
     20000075532002022

24400222433004
5300030055500355
20000075532002022

25.____

26. 6111666406600011116   6111666406600111 6   26._____
     7111300117001100733   7111300117001100733
     26666446664476518   26666446664476518

Questions 27-30

DIRECTIONS: Questions 27 through 30 are to be answered by picking the answer which is in the correct numerical order, from the lowest to highest number, in each question.

27. A. 44533, 44518, 44516, 44547   27._____
    B. 44516, 44518, 44533, 44547
    C. 44547, 44533, 44518, 44516
    D. 44518, 44516, 44547, 44533

28. A. 95587, 95593, 95601, 95620   28._____
    B. 95601, 95620, 95587, 95593
    C. 95593, 95587, 95601, 95620
    D. 95620, 95601, 95593, 95587

29. A. 232212, 232208, 232232, 232223   29._____
    B. 232208, 232223, 232212, 232232
    C. 232208, 232212, 232223, 232232
    D. 232223, 232232, 232208, 232212

30. A. 113419, 113521, 113462, 113588   30._____
    B. 113588, 113462, 113521, 113419
    C. 113521, 113588, 113419, 113462
    D. 113419, 113462, 113521, 113588

KEY (CORRECT ANSWERS)

1.	C	11.	A	21.	C
2.	B	12.	C	22.	A
3.	D	13.	A	23.	D
4.	A	14.	A	24.	A
5.	C	15.	C	25.	C
6.	B	16.	B	26.	C
7.	D	17.	B	27.	B
8.	A	18.	B	28.	A
9.	D	19.	B	29.	C
10.	C	20.	B	30.	D

BASIC FUNDAMENTALS OF FILING SCIENCE

I. COMMENTARY

Filing is the systematic arrangement and storage of papers, cards, forms, catalogues, etc., so that they may be found easily and quickly. The importance of an efficient filing system cannot be emphasized too strongly. The filed materials form records which may be needed quickly to settle questions that may cause embarrassing situations if such evidence is not available. In addition to keeping papers in order so that they are readily available, the filing system must also be designed to keep papers in good condition. A filing system must be planned so that papers may be filed easily, withdrawn easily, and as quickly returned to their proper place. The cost of a filing system is also an important factor.

The need for a filing system arose when the business man began to carry on negotiations on a large scale. He could no longer be intimate with the details of his business. What was needed in the early era was a spindle or pigeon-hole desk. Filing in pigeon-hole desks is now almost completely extinct. It was an unsatisfactory practice since pigeon holes were not labeled, and the desk was an untidy mess.

II. BASIS OF FILING

The science of filing is an exact one and entails a thorough understanding of basic facts, materials, and methods. An overview of this important information now follows.

1. <u>Types of files</u>

   (1) SHANNON FILE

   This consists of a board, at one end of which are fastened two arches which may be opened laterally.

   (2) SPINDLE FILE

   This consists of a metal or wood base to which is attached a long, pointed spike. Papers are pushed down on the spike as received. This file is useful for temporary retention of papers.

   (3) BOX FILE

   This is a heavy cardboard or metal box, opening from the side like a book.

   (4) FLAT FILE

   This consists of a series of shallow drawers or trays, arranged like drawers in a cabinet.

   (5) BELLOWS FILE

   This is a heavy cardboard container with alphabetized or compartment sections, the ends of which are closed in such a manner that they resemble an accordion.

   (6) VERTICAL FILE

   This consists of one or more drawers in which the papers are stood on edge, usually in folders, and are indexed by guides. A series of two or more drawers in one unit is the usual file cabinet.

   (7) CLIP FILE

   This file has a large clip attached to a board and is very similar to the *SHANNON FILE.*

   (8) VISIBLE FILE

   Cards are filed flat in an overlapping arrangement which leaves a part of each card visible at all times.

   (9) ROTARY FILE

The *ROTARY FILE* has a number of visible card files attached to a post around which they can be revolved. The wheel file has visible cards which rotate around a horizontal axle.

    (10) TICKLER FILE

This consists of cards or folders marked with the days of the month, in which materials are filed and turned up on the appropriate day of the month.

2. <u>Aids in filing</u>

    (1) GUIDES

Guides are heavy cardboard, pasteboard, or bristol-board sheets the same size as folders. At the top is a tab on which is marked or printed the distinguishing letter, words, or numbers indicating the material filed in a section of the drawer.

    (2) SORTING TRAYS

Sorting trays are equipped with alphabetical guides to facilitate the sorting of papers preparatory to placing them in a file.

    (3) CODING

Once the classification or indexing caption has been determined, it must be indicated on the letter for filing purposes.

    (4) CROSS REFERENCE

Some letters or papers might easily be called for under two or more captions. For this purpose, a cross-reference card or sheet is placed in the folder or in the index.

3. <u>Variations of filing systems</u>

    (1) VARIADEX ALPHABETIC INDEX

Provides for more effective expansion of the alphabetic system.

    (2) TRIPLE-CHECK NUMERIC FILING

Entails a multiple cross-reference, as the name implies.

    (3) VARIADEX FILING

Makes use of color as an aid in filing.

    (4) DEWEY DECIMAL SYSTEM

The system is a numeric one used in libraries or for filing library materials in an office. This special type of filing system is used where material is grouped in finely divided categories, such as in libraries. With this method, all material to be filed is divided into ten major groups, from 000 to 900, and then subdivided into tens, units, and decimals.

4. <u>Centralized filing</u>

Centralized filing means keeping the files in one specific or central location. Decentralized filing means putting away papers in files of individual departments. The first step in the organization of a central filing department is to make a careful canvass of all desks in the offices. In this manner we can determine just what material needs to be filed, and what information each desk occupant requires from the central file. Only papers which may be used at some time by persons in the various offices should be placed in the central file. A paper that is to be used at some time by persons in the various offices should be placed in the central file. A paper that is to be used by one department only should never be filed in the central file.

5. <u>Methods of filing</u>

While there are various methods used for filing, actually there are only five basic systems: alphabetical, subject, numerical, geographic, and chronological. All other systems are derived from one of these or from a combination of two or more of them.

Since the purpose of a filing system is to store business records <u>systemically</u> so that any particular record can be found almost instantly when required, filing requires, in addition to the proper kinds of equipment and supplies, an effective method of indexing.

There are five basic systems of filing:

(1) ALPHABETIC FILING

Most filing is alphabetical. Other methods, as described below, require extensive alphabetization.

In alphabetic filing, lettered dividers or guides are arranged in alphabetic sequence. Material to be filed is placed behind the proper guide. All materials under each letter are also arranged alphabetically. Folders are used unless the file is a card index.

(2) SUBJECT FILING

This method is used when a single, complete file on a certain subject is desired. A subject file is often maintained to assemble all correspondence on a certain subject. Such files are valuable in connection with insurance claims, contract negotiations, personnel, and other investigations, special programs, and similar subjects.

(3) GEOGRAPHICAL FILE

Materials are filed according to location: states, cities, counties, or other subdivisions. Statistics and tax information are often filed in this manner.

(4) CHRONOLOGICAL FILE

Records are filed according to date. This method is used especially in "tickler" files that have guides numbered 1 to 31 for each day of the month. Each number indicates the day of the month when the filed item requires attention.

(5) NUMERICAL FILE

This method requires an alphabetic card index giving name and number. The card index is used to locate records numbered consecutively in the files according to date received or sequence in which issued, such as licenses, permits, etc.

6. <u>Indexing</u>

Determining the name or title under which an item is to be filed is known as <u>indexing</u>. For example, how would a letter from Robert E. Smith be filed? The name would be rearranged Smith,Robert E., so that the letter would be filed under the last name.

7. <u>Alphabetizing</u>

The arranging of names for filing is known as <u>alphabetizing</u>. For example, suppose you have four letters indexed under the names Johnson, Becker, Roe, and Stern. How should these letters be arranged in the files so that they may be found easily? You would arrange the four names alphabetically, thus, Becker, Johnson, Roe, and Stern.

III. RULES FOR INDEXING AND ALPHABETIZING
   1. The names of persons are to be transposed. Write the surname first, then the given name, and, finally, the middle name or initial. Then arrange the various names according to the alphabetic order of letters throughout the entire name. If there is a title, consider that after the middle name or initial.

NAMES	INDEXED AS
Arthur L.Bright	Bright, Arthur L.
Arthur S.Bright	Bright, Arthur S.
P.E. Cole	Cole, P.E.

Dr. John C. Fox   Fox, John C. (Dr.)

2. If a surname includes the same letters of another surname, with one or more additional letters added to the end, the shorter surname is placed first regardless of the given name or the initial of the given name.

NAMES	INDEXED AS
Robert E. Brown	Brown, Robert E.
Gerald A. Browne	Browne, Gerald A.
William O. Brownell	Brownell, William O.

3. Firm names are alphabetized under the surnames. Words like the, an, a, of, and for, are not considered.

NAMES	INDEXED AS
Bank of America	Bank of America
Bank Discount Dept.	Bank Discount Dept.
The Cranford Press	Cranford Press, The
Nelson Dwyer & Co.	Dwyer, Nelson, & Co.
Sears, Roebuck & Co.	Sears, Roebuck & Co.
Montgomery Ward & Co.	Ward, Montgomery, & Co.

4. The order of filing is determined first of all by the first letter of the names to be filed. If the first letters are the same, the order is determined by the second letters, and so on. In the following pairs of names, the order is determined by the letters underlined:

A_usten	H_a_yes	Ha_n_son	Har_v_ey	Heat_h_	Gree_n_	Schwa_rtz_
B_aker	H_e_ath	Har_p_er	Har_w_ood	Heat_on_	Gree_ne_	Schwa_rz_

5. When surnames are alike, those with initials only precede those with given names, unless the first initial comes alphabetically after the first letter of the name.

Gleason, S.   *but,*   Abbott, Mary
Gleason, S.W.   Abbott, W.B.
Gleason, Sidney

6. Hyphenated names are treated as if spelled without the hyphen.

Lloyd, Paul N.   Lloyd, Robert
Lloyd-Jones, James   Lloyd-Thomas, A.S.

7. Company names composed of single letters which are not used as abbreviations precede the other names beginning with the same letter.

B & S Garage   E Z Duplicator Co.
B X Cable Co.   Eagle Typewriter Co.
Babbitt, R.N.   Edison Company

8. The ampersand (&) and the apostrophe (') in firm names are disregarded in alphabetizing.

Nelson & Niller   M & C Amusement Corp.
Nelson, Walter J.   M C Art Assn.
Nelson's Bakery

9. Names beginning with Mac, Mc, or M' are usually placed in regular order as spelled. Some filing systems file separately names beginning with Mc.

MacDonald, R.J.   Mazza, Anthony
Macdonald, S.B.   McAdam, Wm.
Mace, Wm.   McAndrews, Jerry

10. Names beginning with St. are listed as if the name Saint were spelled in full. Numbered street names and all abbreviated names are treated as if spelled out in full.

Saginaw   Fifth Avenue Hotel   Hart Mfg. Co.
St. Louis   42nd Street Dress Shop Hart, Martin
St. Peter's Rectory   Hart, Chas.   Hart, Thos.

Sandford	Hart, Charlotte	Hart, Thomas A.
Smith, Wm.	Hart, Jas.	Hart, Thos. R.
Smith, Willis	Hart, Janice	

11. Federal, state, or city departments of government should be placed alphabetically under the governmental branch controlling them.

    Illinois, State of -- Departments and Commissions
      Banking Dept.
      Employment Bureau
    United States Government Departments
      Commerce
      Defense
      State
      Treasury

12. Alphabetic order

Each word in a name is an indexing unit. Arrange the names in alphabetic order by comparing similar units in each name. Consider the second units only when the first units are identical. Consider the third units only when both the first and second units are identical.

13. Single surnames or initials

A surname, when used alone, precedes the same surname with a first name or initial. A surname with a first initial only precedes a surname with a complete first name. This rule is sometimes stated, "nothing comes before something."

14. Surname prefixes

A surname prefix is not a separate indexing unit, but it is considered part of the surname. These prefixes include: d', D', Da, de, De, Del, Des, Di, Du, Fitz., La, Le, Mc, Mac, 'c, O', St., Van, Van der, Von, Von der, and others. The prefixes M', Mac, and Mc are indexed and filed exactly as they are spelled.

15. Names of firms

Names of firms and institutions are indexed and filed exactly as they are written when they do not contain the complete name of an individual.

16. Names of firms containing complete individual names

When the firm or institution name includes the complete name of an individual, the units are transposed for indexing in the same way as the name of an individual.

17. Article "The"

When the article the occurs at the beginning of a name, it is placed at the end in parentheses but it is not moved. In both cases, it is not an indexing unit and is disregarded in filing.

18. Hyphenated names

Hyphenated firm names are considered as separate indexing units. Hyphenated surnames of individuals are considered as one indexing unit; this applies also to hyphenated names of individuals whose complete names are part of a firm name.

19. Abbreviations

Abbreviations are considered as though the name were written in full; however, single letters other than abbreviations are considered as separate indexing units.

20. Conjunctions, prepositions and firm endings

Conjunctions and prepositions, such as and, for, in, of, are disregarded in indexing and filing but are not omitted or their order changed when writing names on cards and folders. Firm endings, such as Ltd., Inc., Co., Son, Bros., Mfg., and Corp., are treated as a unit in indexing and filing and are considered as though spelled in full, such as Brothers and Incorporated.

21. One or two words
    Names that may be spelled either as one or two words are indexed and filed as one word.
22. Compound geographic names
    Compound geographic names are considered as separate indexing and filing units, except when the first part of the name is not an English word, such as the Los in Los Angeles.
23. Titles or degrees of individuals, whether preceding or following the name, are not considered in indexing or filing. They are placed in parentheses after the given name or initial. Terms that designate seniority, such as Jr., Sr., 2d, are also placed in parentheses and are considered for indexing and filing only when the names to be indexed are otherwise identical.
    Exception A:
    When the name of an individual consists of a title and one name only, such as Queen Elizabeth, it is not transposed and the title is considered for indexing and filing.
    Exception B:
    When a title or foreign article is the initial word of a firm or association name, it is considered for indexing and filing.
24. Possessives
    When a word ends in apostrophe s, the s is not considered in indexing and filing. However, when a word ends in s apostrophe, because the s is part of the original word, it is considered. This rule is sometimes stated, "Consider everything up to the apostrophe."
25. United States and foreign government names
    Names pertaining to the federal government are indexed and filed under United States Government and then subdivided by title of the department, bureau, division, commission, or board. Names pertaining to foreign governments are indexed and filed under names of countries and then subdivided by title of the department, bureau, division, commission, or board. Phrases, such as department of, bureau of, division of, commission of, board of, when used in titles of governmental bodies, are placed in parentheses after the word they modify, but are disregarded in indexing and filing. Such phrases, however, are considered in indexing and filing nongovernmental names.
26. Other political subdivisions
    Names pertaining to other political subdivisions, such as states, counties, cities, or towns, are indexed and filed under the name of the political subdivision and then subdivided by the title of the department, bureau, division, commission, or board.
27. Addresses
    When the same name appears with different addresses, the names are indexed as usual and arranged alphabetically according to city or town. The State is considered only when there is duplication of both individual or company name and city name. If the same name is located at different addresses within the same city, then the names are arranged alphabetically by streets. If the same name is located at more than one address on the same street, then the names are arranged from the lower to the higher street number.
28. Numbers
    Any number in a name is considered as though it were written in words, and it is indexed and filed as one unit.

29. Bank names

Because the names of many banking institutions are alike in several respects, as first National Bank, Second National Bank, etc., banks are indexed and filed first by city location, then by bank name, with the state location written in parentheses and considered only if necessary

30. Married women

The legal name of a married woman is the one used for filing purposes. Legally, a man's surname is the only part of a man's name a woman assumes when she marries. Her legal name, therefore, could be either:

(1) Her own first and middle names together with her husband's surname, or
(2) Her own first name and maiden surname, together with her husband's surname.

Mrs. is placed in parentheses at the end of the name. Her husband's first and middle names are given in parentheses below her legal name.

31. An alphabetically arranged list of names illustrating many difficult points of alphabetizing follows.

COLUMN I	COLUMN II
Abbot , W.B.	54th St. Tailor Shop
Abbott, Alice	Forstall, W.J.
Allen, Alexander B.	44th St. Garage
Allen, Alexander B., Inc.	M A Delivery Co.
Andersen, Hans	M & C Amusement Corp.
Andersen, Hans E.	M C Art Assn.
Andersen, Hans E., Jr.	MacAdam, Wm.
Anderson, Andrew Andrews,	Macaulay, James
George Brown Motor Co., Boston	MacAulay, Wilson
Brown Motor Co., Chicago	MacDonald, R.J.
Brown Motor Co., Philadelphia	Macdonald, S.B.
Brown Motor Co., San Francisco	Mace, Wm.
Dean, Anna	Mazza, Anthony
Dean, Anna F.	McAdam, Wm.
Dean, Anna Frances	McAndrews, Jerry
Dean & Co.	Meade & Clark Co.
Deane-Arnold Apartments	Meade, S.T.
Deane's Pharmacy	Meade, Solomon
Deans, Felix A.	Sackett Publishing Co.
Dean's Studio	Sacks, Robert
Deans, Wm.	St.Andrew Hotel
Deans & Williams	St.John, Homer W.
East Randolph	Saks, Isaac B.
East St.Louis	Stephens, Ira
Easton, Pa.	Stevens, Delevan
Eastport, Me.	Stevens, Delila

IV. OFFICIAL EXAMINATION DIRECTIONS AND RULES

To preclude the possibility of conflicting or varying methods of filing, explicit directions and express rules are given to the candidate before he answers the filing questions on an examination.

The most recent official directions and rules for the filing questions are given immediately hereafter.

OFFICIAL DIRECTIONS

Each of questions ... to ... consists of four(five)names. For each question, select the one of the four(five)names that should be first (second)(third)(last) if the four(five)names were arranged in alphabetical order in accordance with the rules for alphabetical filing given below. Read these rules carefully. Then, for each question, indicate in the correspondingly numbered row on the answer sheet the letter preceding the name that should be first(second)(third)(last) in alphabetical order.

OFFICIAL RULES FOR ALPHABETICAL FILING

Names of Individuals

1. The names of individuals are filed in strict alphabetical order, first according to the last name, then according to first name or initial, and, finally, according to middle name or initial. For example: William Jones precedes George Kirk and Arthur S. Blake precedes Charles M. Blake.
2. When the last names are identical, the one with an initial instead of a first name precedes the one "with a first name beginning with the same initial. For example: J.Green precedes Joseph Green.
3. When identical last names also have identical first names, the one without a middle name or initial precedes the one with a middle name or initial. For example:Robert Jackson precedes both Robert C.Jackson and Robert Chester Jackson.
4. When last names are identical and the first names are also identical, the one with a middle initial precedes the one with a middle name beginning with the same initial. For example: Peter A. Brown precedes Peter Alvin Brown.
5. Prefixes such as De, El, La, and Van are considered parts of the names they precede. For example:Wilfred DeWald precedes Alexander Duval.
6. Last names beginning with "Mac" or "Mc" are filed as spelled.
7. Abbreviated names are treated as if they were spelled out. For example: Jos. is filed as Joseph and Robt. is filed as Robert.
8. Titles and designations such as Dr. ,Mrs., Prof. are disregarded in filing.

Names of Business Organizations

1. The names of business organizations are filed exactly as written, except that an organization bearing the name of an individual is filed alphabetically according to the name of the individual in accordance with the rules for filing names of individuals given above. For example: Thomas Allison Machine Company precedes Northern Baking Company.
2. When numerals occur in a name, they are treated as if they were spelled out. For example: 6 stands for six and 4th stands for fourth.
3. When the following words occur in names, they are disregarded: the, of, and Sample: Choose the name that should be filed *third*.

    (A) Fred Town   (2)   (C) D. Town   (1)
    (B) Jack Towne (3)   (D) Jack S.Towne (4)

The numbers in parentheses indicate the proper alphabetical order in which these names should be filed. Since the name that should be filed <u>third</u> is Jack Towne, the answer is (B).

FILING

EXAMINATION SECTION
TEST 1

DIRECTIONS: Each of the following questions contains four names. For each question, choose the name that should be FIRST if the four names are to be arranged in alphabetical order in accordance with the Rules for Alphabetical Filing given before. Read these rules carefully. Then, for each question, indicate in the space at the right the letter before the name that should be FIRST in alphabetical order.

SAMPLE QUESTION
- A. Jane Earl (2)
- B. James A. Earle (4)
- C. James Earl (1)
- D. J. Earle (3)

The numbers in parentheses show the proper alphabetical order in which these names should be filed. Since the name that should be filed FIRST is James Earl, the answer to the Sample Question is C.

1. A. Majorca Leather Goods
   B. Robert Maiorca and Sons
   C. Maintenance Management Corp.
   D. Majestic Carpet Mills

   1.____

2. A. Municipal Telephone Service
   B. Municipal Reference Library
   C. Municipal Credit Union
   D. Municipal Broadcasting System

   2.____

3. A. Robert B. Pierce   B. R. Bruce Pierce
   C. Ronald Pierce   D. Robert Bruce Pierce

   3.____

4. A. Four Seasons Sports Club
   B. 14 Street Shopping Center
   C. Forty Thieves Restaurant
   D. 42nd St. Theaters

   4.____

5. A. Franco Franceschini   B. Amos Franchini
   C. Sandra Franceschia   D. Lilie Franchinesca

   5.____

KEY (CORRECT ANSWERS)

1. C
2. D
3. B
4. D
5. C

———

TEST 2

DIRECTIONS: Same as for Test 1.

1.
   A. Alan Carson, M. D.
   B. The Andrew Carlton Nursing Home
   C. Prof., Alfred P. Carlton
   D. Mr. A. Peter Carlton

   1.____

2.
   A. Chas. A. Denner
   C. Charles Denner
   B. H. Jeffrey Dener
   D. Harold Dener

   2.____

3.
   A. James C. Maziola
   C. James Maziola
   B. Joseph A. Mazzola
   D. J. Alfred Mazzola

   3.____

4.
   A. Bureau of Family Affairs
   B. Office of the Comptroller
   C. Department of Gas & Electricity
   D. Board of Estimate

   4.____

5.
   A. Robert Alan Pearson
   C. Robert Allen Pearson
   B. John Charles Pierson
   D. John Chester Pierson

   5.____

6.
   A. The Johnson Manufacturing Co.
   B. C. J. Johnston
   C. Bernard Johnsen
   D. Prof. Corey Johnstone

   6.____

7.
   A. Ninteenth Century Book Shop
   B. Ninth Federal Bank
   C. 19th Hole Coffee Shop
   D. 92nd St. Station

   7.____

8.
   A. George S. McNeely
   C. Mr. G. Stephen McNeally
   B. Hugh J. Macintosh
   D. Mr. H. James Macintosh

   8.____

KEY (CORRECT ANSWERS)

1. D
2. B
3. C
4. B
5. A

6. C
7. A
8. D

TEST 3

DIRECTIONS: Each of the following questions consists of four names. For each question, choose the one of the four names that should be *LAST* if the four names were arranged in alphabetical order in accordance with the Rules for Alphabetical Filing given before. Read these rules carefully. Then, for each question, indicate in the space at the right the letter before the name that should be *LAST* in alphabetical order.

SAMPLE QUESTION.
- A. Jane Earl (2)
- B. James A. Earle (4)
- C. James Earl (1)
- D. J. Earle (3)

The numbers in parentheses show the proper alphabetical order in which these names should be filed. Since the name that should be filed *LAST* is James A. Earle, the answer to the Sample Question is B.

1. A. Steiner, Michael B. Steinblau, Dr. Walter   1.___
   C. Steinet, Gary D. Stein, Prof. Edward

2. A. The Paper Goods Warehouse   2.___
   B. T. Pane and Sons Inc.
   C. Paley, Wallace
   D. Painting Supplies Inc.

3. A. D'Angelo, F. B. De Nove, C.   3.___
   C. Daniels, Frank D. Dovarre, Carl

4. A. Berene, Arnold B. Berene, Arnold L.   4.___
   C. Beren, Arnold Lee D. Berene, A.

5. A. Kallinski, Liza B. Kalinsky, L.   5.___
   C. Kallinky, E. D. Kallinsky, Elizabeth

6. A. Morgeno, Salvatore   6.___
   B. Megan, J.
   C. J. Morgenthal Consultant Services
   D. Morgan, Janet

7. A. Ritter, G. B. Ritter, George   7.___
   C. Riter, George H. D. Ritter, G. H.

8. A. Wheeler, Adele N. B. Wieler, Ada   8.___
   C. Weiler, Adelaide D. Wheiler, Adele

9. A. Macan, Toby B. Maccini, T.   9.___
   C. MacAvoy, Thomas D. Mackel, Theodore

10. A. Loomus, Kenneth
    B. Lomis Paper Supplies
    C. Loo, N.
    D. Loomis Machine Repair Company

10.____

KEY (CORRECT ANSWERS)

1. C
2. A
3. D
4. B
5. D

6. C
7. B
8. B
9. D
10. A

TEST 4

DIRECTIONS: In the following questions there are five notations numbered 1 through 5 shown in Column I. Each notation is made up of a supplier's name, a contract number, and a date and is to be filed according to the following rules:

First: File in alphabetical order.

Second: When two or more notations have the same supplier, file according to the contract number in numerical order beginning with the lowest number.

Third: When two or more notations have the same supplier and contract number, file according to the date beginning with the earliest date.

In Column II the lumbers 1 through 5 are arranged in four ways to show different possible orders in which the merchandise information might be filed. Pick the answer (A, B, C, or D) in Column II in which the notations are arranged according to the above filing rules.

SAMPLE QUESTION

Column I

1. Cluney   (4865)   6/17/72
2. Roster   (2466)   5/10/71
3. Altool   (7114)   10/15/72
4. Cluney   (5276)   12/18/71
5. Cluney   (4865)   4/8/72

Column II

A. 2, 3, 4, 1, 5
B. 2, 5, 1, 3, 4
C. 3, 2, 1, 4, 5
D. 3, 5, 1, 4, 2

The *correct* way to file the notations is:
3. Altool   (7114)   10/15/72
5. Cluney   (4865)   4/8/72
1. Cluney   (4865)   6/17/72
4. Cluney   (5276)   12/18/71
2. Roster   (2466)   5/10/71

The correct filing order is shown by the numbers in front of each name (3, 5, 1, 4, 2). The answer to the Sample Question is the letter in Column II in front of the numbers 3, 5, 1, 4, 2. This answer is D.

Column I

1. 1. Fenten (38511) 1/4/73
   2. Meadowlane (5020) 11/1/72
   3. Whitehall (36142) 6/22/72
   4. Clinton (4141) 5/26/71
   5. Mester (8006) 4/20/71

2. 1. Harvard (2286) 2/19/70
   2. Parker (1781) 4/12/72
   3. Lenson (9044) 6/6/72
   4. Brothers (38380) 10/11/72
   5. Parker (41400) 12/20/70

Column II

A. 3, 5, 2, 1, 4
B. 4, 1, 2, 5, 3
C. 4, 2, 5, 3, 1
D. 5, 4, 3, 1, 2

A. 2, 4, 3, 1, 5
B. 2, 1, 3, 4, 5
C. 4, 1, 3, 2, 5
D. 5, 2, 3, 1, 4

1.____

2.____

2 (#4)

3.
   1. Newtone (3197) 8/22/70
   2. Merritt (4071) 8/8/72
   3. Writebest (60666) 4/7/71
   4. Maltons (34380) 3/30/72
   5. Merrit (4071) 7/16/71

   A. 1, 4, 2, 5, 3
   B. 4, 2, 1, 5, 3
   C. 4, 5, 2, 1, 3
   D. 5, 2, 4, 3, 1

   3.____

4.
   1. Weinburt (45514) 6/4/71
   2. Owntye (35860) 10/4/72
   3. Weinburt (45514) 2/1/72
   4. Fasttex (7677) 11/10/71
   5. Owntye (4574) 7/17/72

   A. 4, 5, 2, 1, 3
   B. 4, 2, 5, 3, 1
   C. 4, 2, 5, 1, 3
   D. 4, 5, 2, 3, 1

   4.____

5.
   1. Premier (1003) 7/29/70
   2. Phylson (0031) 5/5/72
   3. Lathen (3328) 10/3/71
   4. Harper (8046) 8/18/72
   5. Lathen (3328) 12/1/72

   A. 2, 1, 4, 3, 5
   B. 3, 5, 4, 1, 2
   C. 4, 1, 2, 3, 5
   D. 4, 3, 5, 2, 1

   5.____

6.
   1. Repper (46071) 10/14/72
   2. Destex (77271) 8/27/72
   3. Clawson (30736) 7/28/71
   4. Destex (27207) 8/17/71
   5. Destex (77271) 4/14/71

   A. 3, 2, 4, 5, 1
   B. 3, 4, 2, 5, 1
   C. 3, 4, 5, 2, 1
   D. 3, 5, 4, 2, 1

   6.____

KEY (CORRECT ANSWERS)

1. B
2. C
3. C
4. A
5. D
6. C

TEST 5

DIRECTIONS: Each of the following questions repre-sents five cards to be filed, numbered 1 through 5 shown in Column I. Each card is made up of the employee's name, a work assignment code number shown in parentheses, and the date of this assignment. The cards are to be filed according to the following rules:

    First: File in alphabetical order.

    Second: When two or more cards have the same employee's name, file according to the work assignment number beginning with the lowest number.

    Third: When two or more cards have the same employee's name and same assignment number, file according to the as-signment date beginning with the earliest date.

Column II shows the cards arranged in four different orders. Pick the answer (A, B, C, or D) in Column II which shows the cards arranged correctly according to the above filing rules.

SAMPLE QUESTION: See Sample Question (with answer) for Test 4.

Now answer the following questions according to these rules.

Column I   Column II

1.
1. Prichard (013469) 4/6/71
2. Parks (678941) 2/7/71
3. Williams (551467) 3/6/70
4. Wilson (551466) 8/9/67
5. Stanhope (300014) 8/9/67

A. 5, 4, 3, 2, 1
B. 1, 2, 5, 3, 4
C. 2, 1, 5, 3, 4
D. 1, 5, 4, 3, 2

2.
1. Ridgeway (623809) 8/11/71
2. Travers (305439) 4/5/67
3. Tayler (818134) 7/5/68
4. Travers (305349) 5/6/70
5. Ridgeway (623089) 10/9/71

A. 5, 1, 3, 4, 2
B. 5, 1, 3, 2, 4
C. 1, 5, 3, 2, 4
D. 1, 5, 4, 2, 3

3.
1. Jaffe (384737) 2/19/71
2. Inez (859176) 8/8/72
3. Ingrahm (946460) 8/6/69
4. Karp (256146) 5/5/70
5. Ingrahm (946460) 6/4/70

A. 3, 5, 2, 4, 1
B. 3, 5, 2, 1, 4
C. 2, 3, 5, 1, 4
D. 2, 3, 5, 4, 1

4.
1. Marrano (369421) 7/24/69
2. Marks (652910) 2/23/71
3. Netto (556772) 3/10/72
4. Marks (652901) 2/17/72
5. Netto (556772) 6/17/70

A. 1, 5, 3, 4, 2
B. 3, 5, 4, 2, 1
C. 2, 4, 1, 5, 3
D. 4, 2, 1, 5, 3

5. 1. Abernathy (712467) 6/23/70   A. 5, 3, 1, 2, 4   5.____
    2. Acevedo   (680262) 6/23/68   B. 5, 4, 2, 3, 1
    3. Aaron   (967647) 1/17/69   C. 1, 3, 5, 2, 4
    4. Acevedo   (680622) 5/14/67   D. 2, 4, 1, 5, 3
    5. Aaron   (967647) 4/1/65

6. 1. Simon   (645219) 8/19/70   A. 4, 1, 2, 5, 3   6.____
    2. Simon   (645219) 9/2/68   B. 4, 5, 2, 1, 3
    3. Simons   (645218) 7/7/70   C. 3, 5, 2, 1, 4
    4. Simms   (646439) 10/12/71   D. 5, 1, 2, 3, 4
    5. Simon   (645219) 10/16/67

7. 1. Rappaport (312230) 6/11/71   A. 4, 3, 1, 2, 5   7.____
    2. Rascio   (777510) 2/9/70   B. 4, 3, 1, 5, 2
    3. Rappaport (312230) 7/3/67   C. 3, 4, 1, 5, 2
    4. Rapaport   (312330) 9/6/70   D. 5, 2, 4, 3, 1
    5. Rascio   (777501) 7/7/70

8. 1. Johnson   (843250) 6/8/67   A. 1, 3, 2, 4, 5   8.____
    2. Johnson   (843205) 4/3/70   B. 1, 3, 2, 5, 4
    3. Johnson   (843205) 8/6/67   C. 3, 2, 1, 4, 5
    4. Johnson   (843602) 3/8/71   D. 3, 2, 1, 5, 4
    5. Johnson   (843602) 8/3/70

KEY (CORRECT ANSWERS)

1. C
2. A
3. C
4. D
5. A

6. B
7. B
8. D

TEST 6

DIRECTIONS: In each of the following questions there are four groups of names. One of the groups in each question is *NOT* in correct alphabetic order. Mark the letter of that group next to the number that corresponds to the number of the question.

1. A. Ace Advertising Agency; Acel, Erwin; Ad Graphics; Ade, E. J. & Co.
   B. Advertising Bureau, Inc.; Advertising Guild, Inc.; Advertising Ideas, Inc.; Advertising Sales Co.
   C. Allan Associates; Allen-Wayne, Inc.; Alley & Richards, Inc.; Allum, Ralph
   D. Anderson & Cairnes; Amos Parrish & Co.; Anderson Merrill Co.; Anderson, Milton

   1.____

2. A. Bach, Henry; Badillo, John; Baer, Budd; Bair, Albert
   B. Baker, Lynn; Bakers, Albert; Bailin, Henry; Bakers Franchise Corp.
   C. Bernhardt, Manfred; Bernstein, Jerome; Best, Frank; Benton Associates
   D. Brandford, Edward; Branstatter Associates; Brown, Martel; Browne, Bert

   2.____

3. A. Cone, Robert; Contempo, Bernard; Conti Advertising; Cooper, James
   B. Cramer, Zed; Creative Sales; Crofton, Ada; Cromwell, Samuel
   C. Cheever, Fred; Chernow Advertising; Chenault Associates; Chesler, Arthur
   D. Chain Store Advertising; Chair Lawrence & Co.; Chaite, Alexander E.; Chase, Luis

   3.____

4. A. Delahanty, Francis; Dela McCarthy Associates; Dele- hanty, Kurnit; Delroy, Stewart
   B. Doerfler, B. R.; Doherty, Clifford; Dorchester Apartments; Dorchester, Monroe
   C. Drayer, Stella; Dreher, Norton; Dreyer, Harvey; Dryer, Lester
   D. Duble, Normal; Duevell, William C.; Du Fine, August; Dugan, Harold

   4.____

5. A. Esmond, Walter; Esty, Willia; Ettinger, Carl; Everett, Austin
   B. Enlos, Cartez; Entertainment, Inc.; Englemore, Irwin; Equity Associates
   C. Einhorn, Anna Mrs.; Einhorn, Arlene; Eisele, Mary; Eisele, Minnie Mrs.
   D. Eagen, Roy; Egale, George; Egan, Barrett; Eisen, Henry

   5.____

6. A. Funt-Rand Inc.; Furman, Fainer & Co.; Furman Roth & Co.; Fusco, Frank A.
   B. Friedan, Phillip; Friedman, Mitchell; Friend, Harvey; Friend, Herbert
   C. Folkart Greeting Cards; Food Service; Foote, Cornelius; Foreign Advertising
   D. Finkels, Eliot; Finnerman, John; Finneran, Joseph; Fire-stone, Albert

   6.____

7. A. Gubitz, Jay; Guild, Dorothy; Gumbiner, B.; Gussow, Leonard
    B. Gore, Smith; Gotham Art, Inc.; Gotham Editors Service; Gotham-Vladimir, Inc.
    C. Georgian, Wolf; Gerdts, H. J.; German News Co.; Germaine, Werner
    D. Gardner, Fred; Gardner, Roy; Garner, Roy; Gaynor & Ducal, Inc.

7.____

8. A. Howard, E. T.; Howard, Francis; Howson, Allen; Hoyt, Charles
    B. Houston, Byron; House of Graphics; Rowland, Lynne; Hoyle, Mortimer
    C. Hi-Lite Art Service; Hickerson, J. M.; Hickey, Murphy Hicks, Gilbert
    D. Hyman, Bram; Hyman, Charles B.; Hyman, Claire; Hyman, Claude

8.____

9. A. Idone, Leopold; Ingraham, Evelyn; Ianuzzi, Frank; Itkin, Simon
    B. Ideas, Inc.; Inter-Racial Press, Inc.; International Association; Iverson, Ford
    C. Il Trionofo; Inwood Bake Shop; Iridor, Rose; Italian Pastry
    D. Ionadi, Anthony; Irena, Louise; Iris, Ysabella; Isabelle, Arlia

9.____

10. A. Jonas, Myron; Johnstone, John; Jones, Julius; Joptha, Meyer
    B. Jeanne's Beauty Shoppe; Jeger, Jans; Jem, H.; Jim's Grill
    C. Jacobs, Abraham & Co.; Jacobs, Harold A.; Jacobs, Joseph; Jacobs, M. J.
    D. Japan Air Lines; Jensen, Arne; Judson, P.; Juliano, Jeremiah

10.____

KEY (CORRECT ANSWERS)

1. D
2. B
3. C
4. A
5. B

6. D
7. C
8. B
9. A
10. A

TEST 7

DIRECTIONS: Below are ten groups of names, numbered 1 through 10. For each group, three different filing arrangements of the names in the group are given. In only *ONE* of these arrangements are the names in correct filing order according to standard rules for filing. For each group, select the *ONE* arrangement, lettered A, B, C, that is CORRECT.

1. *Arrangement A*
Nichols, C. Arnold
Nichols, Bruce
Nicholson, Arthur

   Arrangement C
Nicholson, Arthur
Nichols, Bruce
Nichols, C. Arnold

   Arrangement B
Nichols, Bruce
Nichols, C. Arnold
Nicholson, Arthur

   1.____

2. *Arrangement A*
Schaefer's Drug Store
Schaefer, Harry T.
Schaefer Bros.

   Arrangement C
Schaefer Bros;
Schaefer's Drug Store
Schaefer, Harry T.

   Arrangement B
Schaefer Bros.
Schaefer, Harry T.
Schaefer's Drug Store

   2.____

3. *Arrangement A*
Adams' Dime Store
Adami, David
Adams, Donald

   Arrangement B
Adami, David
Adams' Dime Store
Adams, Donald

   Arrangement C
Adami, David
Adams, Donald
Adams' Dime Store

   3.____

4. *Arrangement A*
Newton, Jas. F.
Newton, Janet
Newton-Jarvis Law Firm

   Arrangement C
Newton, Janet
Newton-Jarvis Law Firm
Newton, Jas. F.

   Arrangement B
Newton-Jarvis Law Firm
Newton, Jas. F.
Newton, Janet

   4.____

5. *Arrangement A*
Radford and Bigelow
Radford Transfer Co.
Radford-Smith, Albert

   Arrangement C
Radford Transfer Co.
Radford and Bigelow
Radford-Smith, Albert

   Arrangement B
Radford and Bigelow
Radford-Smith, Albert
Radford Transfer Co.

   5.____

6. *Arrangement A*
Trent, Inc.
Trent Farm Products
20th Century Film Corp.

Arrangement C
Trent Farm Products
Trent, Inc.
20th Century Film Corp.

Arrangement B
20th Century Film Corp.
Trent Farm Products
Trent, Inc.

6._____

7. *Arrangement A*
Morrell, Ralph
M.R.B. Paper Co.
Mt.Ranier Hospital

Arrangement B
Morrell, Ralph
Mt.Ranier Hospital
M.R.B. Paper Co.

Arrangement C
M.R.B. Paper Co.
Morrell, Ralph
Mt.Ranier Hospital

7._____

8. *Arrangement A*
Vanity Faire Shop
Van Loon, Charles
The Williams Magazine Corp.

Arrangement C
Van Loon, Charles
Vanity Faire Shop
The Williams Magazine Corp.

Arrangement B
The Williams Magazine Corp.
Van Loon, Charles
Vanity Faire Shop

8._____

9. *Arrangement A*
Crane and Jones Ins. Co.
Little Folks Shop
L. J. Coughtry Mfg. Co.

Arrangement C
Little Folks Shop
L. J. Coughtry Mfg. Co.
Crane and Jones Ins. Co.

Arrangement B
L. J. Coughtry Mfg. Co.
Crane and Jones Ins. Co.
Little Folks Shop

9._____

10. *Arrangement A*
South Arlington Garage
N. Y. State Dept. of Audit and Control
State Antique Shop

Arrangement C
State Antique Shop
South Arlington Garage
N. Y. State Dept. of Audit and Control

Arrangement B
N. Y. State Dept. of Audit and Control
South Arlington Garage
State Antique Shop

10._____

KEY (CORRECT ANSWERS)

1. B
2. C
3. B
4. A
5. B

6. C
7. A
8. A
9. B
10. B

TEST 8

DIRECTIONS: Same as for Test 7.

1. *Arrangement A* *Arrangement B* *Arrangement C* 1.____
   Gillilan, William Gililane, Ethel Gillihane, Harry
   Gililane, Ethel Gillihane, Harry Gillilan, William
   Gillihane, Harry Gillilan, William Gililane, Ethel

2. Stevens, J.Donald Stevenson, David Stevens, J.Donald 2.____
   Stevenson, David Stevens, J.Donald Stevens, James
   Stevens, James Stevens, James Stevenson, David

3. Brooks, Arthur E. Brooks, H.T. Brooks, H.Albert 3.____
   Brooks, H.Albert Brooks. H.Albert Brooks, Arthur E.
   Brooks, H.T. Brooks. Arthur E. Brooks, H.T.

4. *Arrangement A* *Arrangement B* 4.____
   Lafayette, Earl Le Grange, Wm. J.
   Le Grange, Wm. J. La Roux Haberdashery
   La Roux Haberdashery Lafayette, Earl

   Arrangement C
   Lafayette, Earl
   La Roux Haberdashery
   Le Grange, Wm. J.

5. *Arrangement A* *Arrangement B* 5.____
   Mosher Bros. Mosher's Auto Repair
   Mosher's Auto Repair Mosher Bros.
   Mosher, Dorothy Mosher, Dorothy

   Arrangement C
   Mosher Bros.
   Mosher, Dorothy
   Mosher's Auto Repair

6. *Arrangement A* *Arrangement B* *Arrangement C* 6.____
   Ainsworth, Inc. Ainsworth, George Air-O-Pad Co.
   Ainsworth,George Ainsworth, Inc. Ainsworth, George
   Air-O-Pad Co. Air-O-Pad Co. Ainsworth, Inc.

7. *Arrangement A* *Arrangement B* 7.____
   Peters' Printing Co. Peterbridge, Alfred
   Peterbridge, Alfred Peters, Paul
   Peters, Paul Peters' Printing Co.

   Arrangement C
   Peters, Paul
   Peters' Printing Co.
   Peterbridge, Alfred

2 (#8)

8. *Arrangement A*
   Sprague-Miller, Ella
   Sprague (and) Reed
   Sprague Insurance Co.

   Arrangement B
   Sprague (and) Reed
   Sprague Insurance Co.
   Sprague-Miller, Ella

   8.____

   Arrangement C
   Sprague Insurance Co.
   Sprague (and) Reed
   Sprague-Miller, Ella

9. *Arrangement A*
   Ellis, Chalmers Adv. Agency
   Ellis, Chas.
   Ellis, Charlotte

   Arrangement B
   Ellis, Chas.
   Ellis, Charlotte
   Ellis, Chalmers Adv. Agency

   9.____

   Arrangement C
   Ellis, Charlotte
   Ellis, Chas.
   Ellis, Chalmers Adv. Agency

10. *Arrangement A*
    Adams, Paul
    Five Acres Coffee Shop
    Fielding Adjust. Co.

    Arrangement B
    Five Acres Coffee Shop
    Adams, Paul
    Fielding Adjust. Co.

    10.____

    Arrangement C
    Adams, Paul
    Fielding Adjust. Co.
    Five Acres Coffee Chop

KEY (CORRECT ANSWERS)

1. B
2. C
3. A
4. C
5. B

6. B
7. B
8. C
9. A
10. C

TEST 9

DIRECTIONS: Below in Section A is a diagram representing 40 divisional drawers in alphabetic file, numbered 1 through 40. Below in Section B is a list of 30 names to be filed, numbered 1 through 30, with a drawer number opposite each name, representing the drawer in which it is assumed a file clerk has filed the name.

Determine which are filed *CORRECTLY* and which are filed *INCORRECTLY* based on standard rules for indexing and filing. If the name is filed *CORRECTLY,* print in the space at the right the letter C. If the name is filed *INCORRECTLY,* print in the space at the right the letter I.

SECTION A

1 Aa-Al	6 Bs-Bz	11 Ea-Er	16 Gp-Gz	21 Kp-Kz	26 Mo-Mz	31 Qa-Qz	36 Ta-Ti
2 Am-Au	7 Ca-Ch	12 Es-Ez	17 Ha-Hz	22 La-Le	27 Na-Nz	32 Ra-Rz	37 Tj-Tz
3 Av-Az	8 Ci-Co	13 Fa-Fr	18 Ia-Iz	23 Lf-Lz	28 Oa-Oz	33 Sa-Si	38 U-V
4 Ba-Bi	9 Cp-Cz	14 Fa-Fz	19 Ja-Jz	24 Ma-Mi	29 Pa-Pr	34 Sj-St	39 Wa-Wz
5 Bj-Br	10 Da-Dz	15 Ga-Go	20 Ka-Ko	25 Mj-Mo	30 Ps-Pz	35 Su-Sz	40 X-Y-Z

SECTION B

	Name or Title	Drawer No.	
1.	William O'Dea	28	1._____
2.	J. Arthur Crawford	8	2._____
3.	DuPont Chemical Co.	10	3._____
4.	Arnold Bros. Mfg. Co.	2	4._____
5.	Dr. Charles Ellis	10	5._____
6.	Gray and Doyle Adv. Agency	16	6._____
7.	Tom's Smoke Shop	37	7._____
8.	Wm. E. Jarrett Motor Corp.	39	8._____
9.	Penn-York Air Service	29	9._____
10.	Corinne La Fleur	13	10._____
11.	Cartright, Incorporated	7	11._____
12.	7th Ave. Market	24	12._____
13.	Ft.Schuyler Apts.	13	13._____
14.	Madame Louise	23	14._____

15.	Commerce Dept., U. S. Govt.	38	15.____
16.	Norman Bulwer-Lytton	6	16.____
17.	Hilton Memorial Library	17	17.____
18.	The Linen Chest Gift Shop	36	18.____
19.	Ready Mix Supply Co.	32	19.____
20.	City Service Taxi	8	20.____
21.	A.R.C. Transportation Co.	37	21.____
22.	New Jersey Insurance Co.	19	22.____
23.	Capt. Larry Keith	20	23.____
24.	Girl Scouts Council	15	24.____
25.	University of Michigan	24	25.____
26.	Sister Ursula	38	26.____
27.	Am. Legion Post #9	22	27.____
28.	Board of Hudson River Reg. Dist.	17	28.____
29.	Mid West Bus Lines	39	29.____
30.	South West Tours, Inc.	34	30.____

KEY (CORRECT ANSWERS)

1.	C	16.	C
2.	I	17.	C
3.	C	18.	I
4.	C	19.	C
5.	I	20.	C
6.	C	21.	I
7.	C	22.	I
8.	I	23.	C
9.	C	24.	C
10.	I	25.	I
11.	C	26.	I
12.	I	27.	I
13.	C	28.	C
14.	I	29.	I
15.	C	30.	C

TEST 10

DIRECTIONS: Each question or incomplete statement is followed by several suggested answers or completions. Select the one that BEST answers the question or completes the statement. *PRINT THE LETTER OF THE CORRECT ANSWER IN THE SPACE AT THE RIGHT.*

1. Of the following statements about the numeric system of filing, the one which is CORRECT is that it

   A. is the least accurate of all methods of filing
   B. eliminates the need for cross-referencing
   C. allows for very limited expansion
   D. requires a separate index

2. When more than one name or subject is involved in a piece of correspondence to be filed, the office assistant should, *generally,*

   A. prepare a cross-reference sheet
   B. establish a geographical filing system
   C. prepare out-guides
   D. establish a separate index card file for noting such correspondence

3. A tickler file is MOST generally used for

   A. identification of material contained in a numeric file
   B. maintenance of a current listing of telephone numbers
   C. follow-up of matters requiring future attention
   D. control of records borrowed or otherwise removed from the file

4. In filing, the name Ms. "Ann Catalana-Moss" should *generally* be indexed as

   A. Moss, Catalana, Ann (Ms.)
   B. Catalana-Moss, Ann (Ms.)
   C. Ann Catalana-Moss (Ms.)
   D. Moss-Catalana, Ann (Ms.)

5. An office assistant has a set of four cards, each of which contains one of the following names. In alphabetic filing, the FIRST of the cards to be filed is

   A. (Ms.)Alma John
   B. Mrs. John (Patricia) Edwards
   C. John-Edward School Supplies, Inc.
   D. John H. Edwards

6. *Generally,* of the following, the name to be filed FIRST in an alphabetical filing system is

   A. Diane Maestro
   B. Diana McElroy
   C. James Mackell
   D. James McKell

7. According to *generally* recognized rules of filing in an alphabetic filing system, the one of the following names which normally should be filed LAST is

   A. Department of Education, New York State
   B. F. B. I.
   C. Police Department of New York City
   D. P. S. 81 of New York City

KEY (CORRECT ANSWERS)

1. D
2. A
3. C
4. B
5. D
6. C
7. B

RECORD KEEPING
EXAMINATION SECTION
TEST 1

DIRECTIONS: Each question or incomplete statement is followed by several suggested answers or completions. Select the one that BEST answers the question or completes the statement. *PRINT THE LETTER OF THE CORRECT ANSWER IN THE SPACE AT THE RIGHT.*

Questions 1-15.

DIRECTIONS: Questions 1 through 15 are to be answered on the basis of the following list of company names below. Arrange a file alphabetically, word-by-word, disregarding punctuation, conjunctions, and apostrophes. Then answer the questions.
A Bee C Reading Materials
ABCO Parts
A Better Course for Test Preparation
AAA Auto Parts Co.
A-Z Auto Parts, Inc.
Aabar Books
Abbey, Joanne
Boman-Sylvan Law Firm
BMW Autowerks
C Q Service Company
Chappell-Murray, Inc.
E&E Life Insurance
Emcrisco
Gigi Arts
Gordon, Jon & Associates
SOS Plumbing
Schmidt, J.B. Co.

1. Which of these files should appear FIRST?   1.____

   A. ABCO Parts
   B. A Bee C Reading Materials
   C. A Better Course for Test Preparation
   D. AAA Auto Parts Co.

2. Which of these files should appear SECOND?   2.____

   A. A-Z Auto Parts, Inc.
   B. A Bee C Reading Materials
   C. A Better Course for Test Preparation
   D. AAA Auto Parts Co.

3. Which of these files should appear THIRD?   3.____

   A. ABCO Parts
   B. A Bee C Reading Materials
   C. Aabar Books
   D. AAA Auto Parts Co.

4. Which of these files should appear FOURTH?

   A. Aabar Books
   B. ABCO Parts
   C. Abbey, Joanne
   D. AAA Auto Parts Co.

5. Which of these files should appear LAST?

   A. Gordon, Jon & Associates
   B. Gigi Arts
   C. Schmidt, J.B. Co.
   D. SOS Plumbing

6. Which of these files should appear between A-Z Auto Parts, Inc. and Abbey, Joanne?

   A. A Bee C Reading Materials
   B. AAA Auto Parts Co.
   C. ABCO Parts
   D. A Better Course for Test Preparation

7. Which of these files should appear between ABCO Parts and Aabar Books?

   A. A Bee C Reading Materials
   B. Abbey, Joanne
   C. Aabar Books
   D. A-Z Auto Parts

8. Which of these files should appear between Abbey, Joanne and Boman-Sylvan Law Firm?

   A. A Better Course for Test Preparation
   B. BMW Autowerks
   C. Chappell-Murray, Inc.
   D. Aabar Books

9. Which of these files should appear between Abbey, Joanne and C Q Service?

   A. A-Z Auto Parts, Inc.
   B. BMW Autowerks
   C. Choices A and B
   D. Chappell-Murray, Inc.

10. Which of these files should appear between C Q Service Company and Emcrisco?

    A. Chappell-Murray, Inc.
    B. E&E Life Insurance
    C. Gigi Arts
    D. Choices A and B

11. Which of these files should NOT appear between C Q Service Company and E&E Life Insurance?

    A. Gordon, Jon & Associates
    B. Emcrisco
    C. Gigi Arts
    D. All of the above

3 (#1)

12. Which of these files should appear between Chappell-Murray Inc., and Gigi Arts? 12.____

   A. CQ Service Inc. E&E Life Insurance, and Emcrisco
   B. Emcrisco, E&E Life Insurance, and Gordon, Jon & Associates
   C. E&E Life Insurance and Emcrisco
   D. Emcrisco and Gordon, Jon & Associates

13. Which of these files should appear between Gordon, Jon & Associates and SOS Plumbing? 13.____

   A. Gigi Arts   B. Schmidt, J.B. Co.
   C. Choices A and B   D. None of the above

14. Each of the choices lists the four files in their proper alphabetical order except 14.____

   A. E&E Life Insurance; Gigi Arts; Gordon, Jon & Associates; SOS Plumbing
   B. E&E Life Insurance; Emcrisco; Gigi Arts; SOS Plumbing
   C. Emcrisco; Gordon, Jon & Associates; SOS Plumbing; Schmidt, J.B. Co.
   D. Emcrisco; Gigi Arts; Gordon, Jon & Associates; SOS Plumbing

15. Which of the choices lists the four files in their proper alphabetical order? 15.____

   A. Gigi Arts; Gordon, Jon & Associates; SOS Plumbing; Schmidt, J.B. Co.
   B. Gordon, Jon & Associates; Gigi Arts; Schmidt, J.B. Co.; SOS Plumbing
   C. Gordon, Jon & Associates; Gigi Arts; SOS Plumbing; Schmidt, J.B. Co.
   D. Gigi Arts; Gordon, Jon & Associates; Schmidt, J.B. Co.; SOS Plumbing

16. The alphabetical filing order of two businesses with identical names is determined by the 16.____

   A. length of time each business has been operating
   B. addresses of the businesses
   C. last name of the company president
   D. none of the above

17. In an alphabetical filing system, if a business name includes a number, it should be 17.____

   A. disregarded
   B. considered a number and placed at the end of an alphabetical section
   C. treated as though it were written in words and alphabetized accordingly
   D. considered a number and placed at the beginning of an alphabetical section

18. If a business name includes a contraction (such as *don't* or *it's*), how should that word be treated in an alphabetical filing system? 18.____

   A. Divide the word into its separate parts and treat it as two words.
   B. Ignore the letters that come after the apostrophe.
   C. Ignore the word that contains the contraction.
   D. Ignore the apostrophe and consider all letters in the contraction.

19. In what order should the parts of an address be considered when using an alphabetical filing system? 19.____

   A. City or town; state; street name; house or building number
   B. State; city or town; street name; house or building number
   C. House or building number; street name; city or town; state
   D. Street name; city or town; state

4 (#1)

20. A business record should be cross-referenced when a(n) 20.___

   A. organization is known by an abbreviated name
   B. business has a name change because of a sale, incorporation, or other reason
   C. business is known by a *coined* or common name which differs from a dictionary spelling
   D. all of the above

21. A geographical filing system is MOST effective when 21.___

   A. location is more important than name
   B. many names or titles sound alike
   C. dealing with companies who have offices all over the world
   D. filing personal and business files

Questions 22-25.

DIRECTIONS: Questions 22 through 25 are to be answered on the basis of the list of items below, which are to be filed geographically. Organize the items geographically and then answer the questions.

   1. University Press at Berkeley, U.S.
   2. Maria Sanchez, Mexico City, Mexico
   3. Great Expectations Ltd. in London, England
   4. Justice League, Cape Town, South Africa, Africa
   5. Crown Pearls Ltd. in London, England
   6. Joseph Prasad in London, England

22. Which of the following arrangements of the items is composed according to the policy of: *Continent, Country, City, Firm or Individual Name?* 22.___

   A. 5, 3, 4, 6, 2, 1   B. 4, 5, 3, 6, 2, 1
   C. 1, 4, 5, 3, 6, 2 .   D. 4, 5, 3, 6, 1, 2

23. Which of the following files is arranged according to the policy of: *Continent, Country, City, Firm or Individual Name?* 23.___

   A. South Africa. Africa. Cape Town. Justice League
   B. Mexico. Mexico City, Maria Sanchez
   C. North America. United States. Berkeley. University Press
   D. England. Europe. London. Prasad, Joseph

24. Which of the following arrangements of the items is composed according to the policy of: *Country, City, Firm or Individual Name?* 24.___

   A. 5, 6, 3, 2, 4, 1   B. 1, 5, 6, 3, 2, 4
   C. 6, 5, 3, 2, 4, 1   D. 5, 3, 6, 2, 4, 1

25. Which of the following files is arranged according to a policy of: *Country, City, Firm or Individual Name?* 25.___

   A. England. London. Crown Pearls Ltd.
   B. North America. United States. Berkeley. University Press
   C. Africa. Cape Town. Justice League
   D. Mexico City. Mexico. Maria Sanchez

26. Under which of the following circumstances would a phonetic filing system be MOST effective? 26.____

    A. When the person in charge of filing can't spell very well
    B. With large files with names that sound alike
    C. With large files with names that are spelled alike
    D. All of the above

Questions 27-29.

DIRECTIONS: Questions 27 through 29 are to be answered on the basis of the following list of numerical files.
   1. 391-023-100
   2. 361-132-170
   3. 385-732-200
   4. 381-432-150
   5. 391-632-387
   6. 361-423-303
   7. 391-123-271

27. Which of the following arrangements of the files follows a consecutive-digit system? 27.____

    A. 2, 3, 4, 1   B. 1, 5, 7, 3
    C. 2, 4, 3, 1   D. 3, 1, 5, 7

28. Which of the following arrangements follows a terminal-digit system? 28.____

    A. 1, 7, 2, 4, 3   B. 2, 1, 4, 5, 7
    C. 7, 6, 5, 4, 3   D. 1, 4, 2, 3, 7

29. Which of the following lists follows a middle-digit system? 29.____

    A. 1, 7, 2, 6, 4, 5, 3   B. 1, 2, 7, 4, 6, 5, 3
    C. 7, 2, 1, 3, 5, 6, 4   D. 7, 1, 2, 4, 6, 5, 3

Questions 30-31.

DIRECTIONS: Questions 30 and 31 are to be answered on the basis of the following information.
   1. Reconfirm Laura Bates appointment with James Caldecort on December 12 at 9:30 A.M.
   2. Laurence Kinder contact Julia Lucas on August 3 and set up a meeting for week of September 23 at 4 P.M.
   3. John Lutz contact Larry Waverly on August 3 and set up appointment for September 23 at 9:30 A.M.
   4. Call for tickets for Gerry Stanton August 21 for New Jersey on September 23, flight 143 at 4:43 P.M.

30. A chronological file for the above information would be   30.___

    A. 4, 3, 2, 1   B. 3, 2, 4, 1
    C. 4, 2, 3, 1   D. 3, 1, 2, 4

31. Using the above information, a chronological file for the date of September 23 would be   31.___

    A. 2, 3, 4   B. 3, 1, 4   C. 3, 2, 4   D. 4, 3, 2

Questions 32-34.

DIRECTIONS: Questions 32 through 34 are to be answered on the basis of the following information.
1. Call Roger Epstein, Ashoke Naipaul, Jon Anderson, and Sarah Washington on April 19 at 1:00 P.M. to set up meeting with Alika D'Ornay for June 6 in New York.
2. Call Martin Ames before noon on April 19 to confirm afternoon meeting with Bob Greenwood on April 20th
3. Set up meeting room at noon for 2:30 P.M. meeting on April 19th;
4. Ashley Stanton contact Bob Greenwood at 9:00 A.M. on April 20 and set up meeting for June 6 at 8:30 A.M.
5. Carol Guiland contact Shelby Van Ness during afternoon of April 20 and set up meeting for June 6 at 10:00 A.M.
6. Call airline and reserve tickets on June 6 for Roger Epstein trip *to* Denver on July 8
7. Meeting at 2:30 P.M. on April 19th

32. A chronological file for all of the above information would be   32.___

    A. 2, 1, 3, 7, 5, 4, 6   B. 3, 7, 2, 1, 4, 5, 6
    C. 3, 7, 1, 2, 5, 4, 6   D. 2, 3, 1, 7, 4, 5, 6

33. A chronological file for the date of April 19th would be   33.___

    A. 2, 3, 7, 1   B. 2, 3, 1, 7
    C. 7, 1, 3, 2   D. 3, 7, 1, 2

34. Add the following information to the file, and then create a chronological file for April 20th: 34.___
    8. April 20: 3:00 P.M. meeting between Bob Greenwood and Martin Ames.

    A. 4, 5, 8   B. 4, 8, 5   C. 8, 5, 4   D. 5, 4, 8

35. The PRIMARY advantage of computer records filing over a manual system is   35.___

    A. speed of retrieval   B. accuracy
    C. cost   D. potential file loss

KEY (CORRECT ANSWERS)

1.	B		16.	B
2.	C		17.	C
3.	D		18.	D
4.	A		19.	A
5.	D		20.	D
6.	C		21.	A
7.	B		22.	B
8.	B		23.	C
9.	C		24.	D
10.	D		25.	A
11.	D		26.	B
12.	C		27.	C
13.	B		28.	D
14.	C		29.	A
15.	D		30.	B

31. C
32. D
33. B
34. A
35. A

———

PHILOSOPHY, PRINCIPLES, PRACTICES AND TECHNICS
OF
SUPERVISION, ADMINISTRATION, MANAGEMENT AND ORGANIZATION

TABLE OF CONTENTS

		Page
I.	MEANING OF SUPERVISION	1
II.	THE OLD AND THE NEW SUPERVISION	1
III.	THE EIGHT (8) BASIC PRINCIPLES OF THE NEW SUPERVISION	1
	1. Principle of Responsibility	1
	2. Principle of Authority	2
	3. Principle of Self-Growth	2
	4. Principle of Individual Worth	2
	5. Principle of Creative Leadership	2
	6. Principle of Success and Failure	2
	7. Principle of Science	3
	8. Principle of Cooperation	3
IV.	WHAT IS ADMINISTRATION?	3
	1. Practices commonly classed as "Supervisory"	3
	2. Practices commonly classed as "Administrative"	3
	3. Practices classified as both "Supervisory" and "Administrative"	4
V.	RESPONSIBILITIES OF THE SUPERVISOR	4
VI.	COMPETENCIES OF THE SUPERVISOR	4
VII.	THE PROFESSIONAL SUPERVISOR—EMPLOYEE RELATIONSHIP	4
VIII.	MINI-TEXT IN SUPERVISION, ADMINISTRATION, MANAGEMENT AND ORGANIZATION	5
	A. Brief Highlights	5
	1. Levels of Management	5
	2. What the Supervisor Must Learn	6
	3. A Definition of Supervision	6
	4. Elements of the Team Concept	6
	5. Principles of Organization	6
	6. The Four Important Parts of Every Job	6
	7. Principles of Delegation	6
	8. Principles of Effective Communications	7
	9. Principles of Work Improvement	7

TABLE OF CONTENTS (CONTINUED)

10. Areas of Job Improvement	7
11. Seven Key Points in Making Improvements	7
12. Corrective Techniques for Job Improvement	7
13. A Planning Checklist	8
14. Five Characteristics of Good Directions	8
15. Types of Directions	8
16. Controls	8
17. Orienting the New Employee	8
18. Checklist for Orienting New Employees	8
19. Principles of Learning	9
20. Causes of Poor Performance	9
21. Four Major Steps in On-The-Job Instructions	9
22. Employees Want Five Things	9
23. Some Don'ts in Regard to Praise	9
24. How to Gain Your Workers' Confidence	9
25. Sources of Employee Problems	9
26. The Supervisor's Key to Discipline	10
27. Five Important Processes of Management	10
28. When the Supervisor Fails to Plan	10
29. Fourteen General Principles of Management	10
30. Change	10

B. Brief Topical Summaries — 11
    I. Who/What is the Supervisor? — 11
    II. The Sociology of Work — 11
    III. Principles and Practices of Supervision — 12
    IV. Dynamic Leadership — 12
    V. Processes for Solving Problems — 12
    VI. Training for Results — 13
    VII. Health, Safety and Accident Prevention — 13
    VIII. Equal Employment Opportunity — 13
    IX. Improving Communications — 14
    X. Self-Development — 14
    XI. Teaching and Training — 14
        A. The Teaching Process — 14
            1. Preparation — 14
            2. Presentation — 15
            3. Summary — 15
            4. Application — 15
            5. Evaluation — 15
        B. Teaching Methods — 15
            1. Lecture — 15
            2. Discussion — 15
            3. Demonstration — 16
            4. Performance — 16
            5. Which Method to Use — 16

PHILOSOPHY, PRINCIPLES, PRACTICES, AND TECHNICS
OF
SUPERVISION, ADMINISTRATION, MANAGEMENT AND ORGANIZATION

I. MEANING OF SUPERVISION

The extension of the democratic philosophy has been accompanied by an extension in the scope of supervision. Modern leaders and supervisors no longer think of supervision in the narrow sense of being confined chiefly to visiting employees, supplying materials, or rating the staff. They regard supervision as being intimately related to all the concerned agencies of society, they speak of the supervisor's function in terms of "growth", rather than the "improvement," of employees.

This modern concept of supervision may be defined as follows:

Supervision is leadership and the development of leadership within groups which are cooperatively engaged in inspection, research, training, guidance and evaluation.

II. THE OLD AND THE NEW SUPERVISION

TRADITIONAL
1. Inspection
2. Focused on the employee
3. Visitation
4. Random and haphazard
5. Imposed and authoritarian
6. One person usually

MODERN
1. Study and analysis
2. Focused on aims, materials, methods, supervisors, employees, environment
3. Demonstrations, intervisitation, workshops, directed reading, bulletins, etc.
4. Definitely organized and planned (scientific)
5. Cooperative and democratic
6. Many persons involved (creative)

III THE EIGHT (8) BASIC PRINCIPLES OF THE NEW SUPERVISION

1. *PRINCIPLE OF RESPONSIBILITY*
   Authority to act and responsibility for acting must be joined.
   a. If you give responsibility, give authority.
   b. Define employee duties clearly.
   c. Protect employees from criticism by others.
   d. Recognize the rights as well as obligations of employees.
   e. Achieve the aims of a democratic society insofar as it is possible within the area of your work.
   f. Establish a situation favorable to training and learning.
   g. Accept ultimate responsibility for everything done in your section, unit, office, division, department.
   h. Good administration and good supervision are inseparable.

2. PRINCIPLE OF AUTHORITY
The success of the supervisor is measured by the extent to which the power of authority is not used.
- a. Exercise simplicity and informality in supervision.
- b. Use the simplest machinery of supervision.
- c. If it is good for the organization as a whole, it is probably justified.
- d. Seldom be arbitrary or authoritative.
- e. Do not base your work on the power of position or of personality.
- f. Permit and encourage the free expression of opinions.

3. PRINCIPLE OF SELF-GROWTH
The success of the supervisor is measured by the extent to which, and the speed with which, he is no longer needed.
- a. Base criticism on principles, not on specifics.
- b. Point out higher activities to employees.
- c. Train for self-thinking by employees, to meet new situations.
- d. Stimulate initiative, self-reliance and individual responsibility.
- e. Concentrate on stimulating the growth of employees rather than on removing defects.

4. PRINCIPLE OF INDIVIDUAL WORTH
Respect for the individual is a paramount consideration in supervision.
- a. Be human and sympathetic in dealing with employees.
- b. Don't nag about things to be done.
- c. Recognize the individual differences among employees and seek opportunities to permit best expression of each personality.

5. PRINCIPLE OF CREATIVE LEADERSHIP
The best supervision is that which is not apparent to the employee.
- a. Stimulate, don't drive employees to creative action.
- b. Emphasize doing good things.
- c. Encourage employees to do what they do best.
- d. Do not be too greatly concerned with details of subject or method.
- e. Do not be concerned exclusively with immediate problems and activities.
- f. Reveal higher activities and make them both desired and maximally possible.
- g. Determine procedures in the light of each situation but see that these are derived from a sound basic philosophy.
- h. Aid, inspire and lead so as to liberate the creative spirit latent in all good employees.

6. PRINCIPLE OF SUCCESS AND FAILURE
There are no unsuccessful employees, only unsuccessful supervisors who have failed to give proper leadership.
- a. Adapt suggestions to the capacities, attitudes, and prejudices of employees.
- b. Be gradual, be progressive, be persistent.
- c. Help the employee find the general principle; have the employee apply his own problem to the general principle.
- d. Give adequate appreciation for good work and honest effort.
- e. Anticipate employee difficulties and help to prevent them.
- f. Encourage employees to do the desirable things they will do anyway.
- g. Judge your supervision by the results it secures.

7. PRINCIPLE OF SCIENCE
Successful supervision is scientific, objective, and experimental. It is based on facts, not on prejudices.
       a. Be cumulative in results.
       b. Never divorce your suggestions from the goals of training.
       c. Don't be impatient of results.
       d. Keep all matters on a professional, not a personal level.
       e. Do not be concerned exclusively with immediate problems and activities.
       f. Use objective means of determining achievement and rating where possible.

8. PRINCIPLE OF COOPERATION
Supervision is a cooperative enterprise between supervisor and employee.
       a. Begin with conditions as they are.
       b. Ask opinions of all involved when formulating policies.
       c. Organization is as good as its weakest link.
       d. Let employees help to determine policies and department programs.
       e. Be approachable and accessible - physically and mentally.
       f. Develop pleasant social relationships.

IV. WHAT IS ADMINISTRATION?

Administration is concerned with providing the environment, the material facilities, and the operational procedures that will promote the maximum growth and development of supervisors and employees. (Organization is an aspect, and a concomitant, of administration.)

There is no sharp line of demarcation between supervision and administration; these functions are intimately interrelated and, often, overlapping. They are complementary activities.

1. PRACTICES COMMONLY CLASSED AS "SUPERVISORY"
       a. Conducting employees conferences
       b. Visiting sections, units, offices, divisions, departments
       c. Arranging for demonstrations
       d. Examining plans
       e. Suggesting professional reading
       f. Interpreting bulletins
       g. Recommending in-service training courses
       h. Encouraging experimentation
       i. Appraising employee morale
       j. Providing for intervisitation

2. PRACTICES COMMONLY CLASSIFIED AS "ADMINISTRATIVE"
       a. Management of the office
       b. Arrangement of schedules for extra duties
       c. Assignment of rooms or areas
       d. Distribution of supplies
       e. Keeping records and reports
       f. Care of audio-visual materials
       g. Keeping inventory records
       h. Checking record cards and books
       i. Programming special activities
       j. Checking on the attendance and punctuality of employees

3. PRACTICES COMMONLY CLASSIFIED AS BOTH "SUPERVISORY" AND "ADMINISTRATIVE"
   a. Program construction
   b. Testing or evaluating outcomes
   c. Personnel accounting
   d. Ordering instructional materials

V. RESPONSIBILITIES OF THE SUPERVISOR

A person employed in a supervisory capacity must constantly be able to improve his own efficiency and ability. He represents the employer to the employees and only continuous self-examination can make him a capable supervisor.

Leadership and training are the supervisor's responsibility. An efficient working unit is one in which the employees work with the supervisor. It is his job to bring out the best in his employees. He must always be relaxed, courteous and calm in his association with his employees. Their feelings are important, and a harsh attitude does not develop the most efficient employees.

VI. COMPETENCIES OF THE SUPERVISOR

1. Complete knowledge of the duties and responsibilities of his position.
2. To be able to organize a job, plan ahead and carry through.
3. To have self-confidence and initiative.
4. To be able to handle the unexpected situation and make quick decisions.
5. To be able to properly train subordinates in the positions they are best suited for.
6. To be able to keep good human relations among his subordinates.
7. To be able to keep good human relations between his subordinates and himself and to earn their respect and trust.

VII. THE PROFESSIONAL SUPERVISOR-EMPLOYEE RELATIONSHIP

There are two kinds of efficiency: one kind is only apparent and is produced in organizations through the exercise of mere discipline; this is but a simulation of the second, or true, efficiency which springs from spontaneous cooperation. If you are a manager, no matter how great or small your responsibility, it is your job, in the final analysis, to create and develop this involuntary cooperation among the people whom you supervise. For, no matter how powerful a combination of money, machines, and materials a company may have, this is a dead and sterile thing without a team of willing, thinking and articulate people to guide it.

The following 21 points are presented as indicative of the exemplary basic relationship that should exist between supervisor and employee:

1. Each person wants to be liked and respected by his fellow employee and wants to be treated with consideration and respect by his superior.
2. The most competent employee will make an error. However, in a unit where good relations exist between the supervisor and his employees, tenseness and fear do not exist. Thus, errors are not hidden or covered up and the efficiency of a unit is not impaired.
3. Subordinates resent rules, regulations, or orders that are unreasonable or unexplained.
4. Subordinates are quick to resent unfairness, harshness, injustices and favoritism.
5. An employee will accept responsibility if he knows that he will be complimented for a job well done, and not too harshly chastised for failure; that his supervisor will check the cause of the failure, and, if it was the supervisor's fault, he will assume the blame therefore. If it was the employee's fault, his supervisor will explain the correct method or means of handling the responsibility.

6. An employee wants to receive credit for a suggestion he has made, that is used. If a suggestion cannot be used, the employee is entitled to an explanation. The supervisor should not say "no" and close the subject.
7. Fear and worry slow up a worker's ability. Poor working environment can impair his physical and mental health. A good supervisor avoids forceful methods, threats and arguments to get a job done.
8. A forceful supervisor is able to train his employees individually and as a team, and is able to motivate them in the proper channels.
9. A mature supervisor is able to properly evaluate his subordinates and to keep them happy and satisfied.
10. A sensitive supervisor will never patronize his subordinates.
11. A worthy supervisor will respect his employees' confidences.
12. Definite and clear-cut responsibilities should be assigned to each executive.
13. Responsibility should always be coupled with corresponding authority.
14. No change should be made in the scope or responsibilities of a position without a definite understanding to that effect on the part of all persons concerned.
15. No executive or employee, occupying a single position in the organization, should be subject to definite orders from more than one source.
16. Orders should never be given to subordinates over the head of a responsible executive. Rather than do this, the officer in question should be supplanted.
17. Criticisms of subordinates should, whoever possible, be made privately, and in no case should a subordinate be criticized in the presence of executives or employees of equal or lower rank.
18. No dispute or difference between executives or employees as to authority or responsibilities should be considered too trivial for prompt and careful adjudication.
19. Promotions, wage changes, and disciplinary action should always be approved by the executive immediately superior to the one directly responsible.
20. No executive or employee should ever be required, or expected, to be at the same time an assistant to, and critic of, another.
21. Any executive whose work is subject to regular inspection should, whever practicable, be given the assistance and facilities necessary to enable him to maintain an independent check of the quality of his work.

VIII. MINI-TEXT IN SUPERVISION, ADMINISTRATION, MANAGEMENT, AND ORGANIZATION

A. BRIEF HIGHLIGHTS

Listed concisely and sequentially are major headings and important data in the field for quick recall and review.

1. *LEVELS OF MANAGEMENT*

    Any organization of some size has several levels of management. In terms of a ladder the levels are:

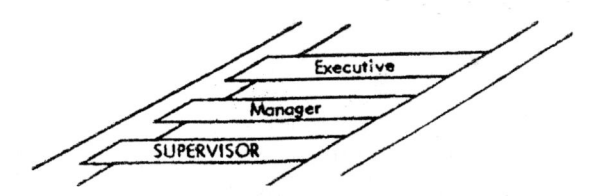

    ```
    Executive
    Manager
    SUPERVISOR
    ```

The first level is very important because it is the beginning point of management leadership.

2. WHAT THE SUPERVISOR MUST LEARN
A supervisor must learn to:
(1) Deal with people and their differences
(2) Get the job done through people
(3) Recognize the problems when they exist
(4) Overcome obstacles to good performance
(5) Evaluate the performance of people
(6) Check his own performance in terms of accomplishment

3. A DEFINITION OF SUPERVISOR
The term supervisor means any individual having authority, in the interests of the employer, to hire, transfer, suspend, lay-off, recall, promote, discharge, assign, reward, or discipline other employees or responsibility to direct them, or to adjust their grievances, or effectively to recommend such action, if, in connection with the foregoing, exercise of such authority is not of a merely routine or clerical nature but requires the use of independent judgment.

4. ELEMENTS OF THE TEAM CONCEPT
What is involved in teamwork? The component parts are:
(1) Members   (3) Goals   (5) Cooperation
(2) A leader   (4) Plans   (6) Spirit

5. PRINCIPLES OF ORGANIZATION
(1) A team member must know what his job is.
(2) Be sure that the nature and scope of a job are understood.
(3) Authority and responsibility should be carefully spelled out.
(4) A supervisor should be permitted to make the maximum number of decisions affecting his employees.
(5) Employees should report to only one supervisor.
(6) A supervisor should direct only as many employees as he can handle effectively.
(7) An organization plan should be flexible.
(8) Inspection and performance of work should be separate.
(9) Organizational problems should receive immediate attention.
(10) Assign work in line with ability and experience.

6. THE FOUR IMPORTANT PARTS OF EVERY JOB
(1) Inherent in every job is the *accountability* for results.
(2) A second set of factors in every job is *responsibilities*.
(3) Along with duties and responsibilities one must have the *authority* to act within certain limits without obtaining permission to proceed.
(4) No job exists in a vacuum. The supervisor is surrounded by key *relationships*.

7. PRINCIPLES OF DELEGATION
Where work is delegated for the first time, the supervisor should think in terms of these questions:
(1) Who is best qualified to do this?
(2) Can an employee improve his abilities by doing this?
(3) How long should an employee spend on this?
(4) Are there any special problems for which he will need guidance?
(5) How broad a delegation can I make?

8. PRINCIPLES OF EFFECTIVE COMMUNICATIONS
   (1) Determine the media
   (2) To whom directed?
   (3) Identification and source authority
   (4) Is communication understood?

9. PRINCIPLES OF WORK IMPROVEMENT
   (1) Most people usually do only the work which is assigned to them
   (2) Workers are likely to fit assigned work into the time available to perform it
   (3) A good workload usually stimulates output
   (4) People usually do their best work when they know that results will be reviewed or inspected
   (5) Employees usually feel that someone else is responsible for conditions of work, workplace layout, job methods, type of tools/equipment, and other such factors
   (6) Employees are usually defensive about their job security
   (7) Employees have natural resistance to change
   (8) Employees can support or destroy a supervisor
   (9) A supervisor usually earns the respect of his people through his personal example of diligence and efficiency

10. AREAS OF JOB IMPROVEMENT
The areas of job improvement are quite numerous, but the most common ones which a supervisor can identify and utilize are:
   (1) Departmental layout
   (2) Flow of work
   (3) Workplace layout
   (4) Utilization of manpower
   (5) Work methods
   (6) Materials handling
   (7) Utilization
   (8) Motion economy

11. SEVEN KEY POINTS IN MAKING IMPROVEMENTS
   (1) Select the job to be improved
   (2) Study how it is being done now
   (3) Question the present method
   (4) Determine actions to be taken
   (5) Chart proposed method
   (6) Get approval and apply
   (7) Solicit worker participation

12. CORRECTIVE TECHNIQUES OF JOB IMPROVEMENT

Specific Problems	General Improvement	Corrective Techniques
(1) Size of workload	(1) Departmental layout	(1) Study with scale model
(2) Inability to meet schedules	(2) Flow of work	(2) Flow chart study
(3) Strain and fatigue	(3) Work plan layout	(3) Motion analysis
(4) Improper use of men and skills	(4) Utilization of manpower	(4) Comparison of units produced to standard allowance
(5) Waste, poor quality, unsafe conditions	(5) Work methods	(5) Methods analysis
(6) Bottleneck conditions that hinder output	(6) Materials handling	(6) Flow chart & equipment study
(7) Poor utilization of equipment and machine	(7) Utilization of equipment	(7) Down time vs. running time
(8) Efficiency and productivity of labor	(8) Motion economy	(8) Motion analysis

13. *A PLANNING CHECKLIST*

(1) Objectives	(6) Resources	(11) Safety
(2) Controls	(7) Manpower	(12) Money
(3) Delegations	(8) Equipment	(13) Work
(4) Communications	(9) Supplies and materials	(14) Timing of improvements
(5) Resources	(10) Utilization of time	

14. *FIVE CHARACTERISTICS OF GOOD DIRECTIONS*

In order to get results, directions must be:

(1) Possible of accomplishment
(2) Agreeable with worker interests
(3) Related to mission
(4) Planned and complete
(5) Unmistakably clear

15. *TYPES OF DIRECTIONS*

(1) Demands or direct orders
(2) Requests
(3) Suggestion or implication
(4) Volunteering

16. *CONTROLS*

A typical listing of the overall areas in which the supervisor should establish controls might be:

(1) Manpower
(2) Materials
(3) Quality of work
(4) Quantity of work
(5) Time
(6) Space
(7) Money
(8) Methods

17. *ORIENTING THE NEW EMPLOYEE*

(1) Prepare for him
(2) Welcome the new employee
(3) Orientation for the job
(4) Follow-up

18. *CHECKLIST FOR ORIENTING NEW EMPLOYEES*   Yes   No

(1) Do your appreciate the feelings of new employees when they first report for work?   ____ ____
(2) Are you aware of the fact that the new employee must make a big adjustment to his job?   ____ ____
(3) Have you given him good reasons for liking the job and the organization?   ____ ____
(4) Have you prepared for his first day on the job?
(5) Did you welcome him cordially and make him feel needed?
(6) Did you establish rapport with him so that he feels free to talk and discuss matters with you?
(7) Did you explain his job to him and his relationship to you?   ____ ____
(8) Does he know that his work will be evaluated periodically on a basis that is fair and objective?   ____ ____
(9) Did you introduce him to his fellow workers in such a way that they are likely to accept him?   ____ ____
(10) Does he know what employee benefits he will receive?
(11) Does he understand the importance of being on the job and what to do if he must leave his duty station?   ____ ____
(12) Has he been impressed with the importance of accident prevention and safe practice?   ____ ____
(13) Does he generally know his way around the department?   ____ ____
(14) Is he under the guidance of a sponsor who will teach the right ways of doing things?   ____ ____
(15) Do you plan to follow-up so that he will continue to adjust successfully to his job?   ____ ____

19. PRINCIPLES OF LEARNING
(1) Motivation   (2) Demonstration or explanation   (3) Practice

20. CAUSES OF POOR PERFORMANCE
(1) Improper training for job
(2) Wrong tools
(3) Inadequate directions
(4) Lack of supervisory follow-up
(5) Poor communications
(6) Lack of standards of performance
(7) Wrong work habits
(8) Low morale
(9) Other

21. FOUR MAJOR STEPS IN ON-THE-JOB INSTRUCTION
(1) Prepare the worker
(2) Present the operation
(3) Tryout performance
(4) Follow-up

22. EMPLOYEES WANT FIVE THINGS
(1) Security   (2) Opportunity   (3) Recognition   (4) Inclusion   (5) Expression

23. SOME DON'TS IN REGARD TO PRAISE
(1) Don't praise a person for something he hasn't done
(2) Don't praise a person unless you can be sincere
(3) Don't be sparing in praise just because your superior withholds it from you
(4) Don't let too much time elapse between good performance and recognition of it

24. HOW TO GAIN YOUR WORKERS' CONFIDENCE
Methods of developing confidence include such things as:
(1) Knowing the interests, habits, hobbies of employees
(2) Admitting your own inadequacies
(3) Sharing and telling of confidence in others
(4) Supporting people when they are in trouble
(5) Delegating matters that can be well handled
(6) Being frank and straightforward about problems and working conditions
(7) Encouraging others to bring their problems to you
(8) Taking action on problems which impede worker progress

25. SOURCES OF EMPLOYEE PROBLEMS
On-the-job causes might be such things as:
(1) A feeling that favoritism is exercised in assignments
(2) Assignment of overtime
(3) An undue amount of supervision
(4) Changing methods or systems
(5) Stealing of ideas or trade secrets
(6) Lack of interest in job
(7) Threat of reduction in force
(8) Ignorance or lack of communications
(9) Poor equipment
(10) Lack of knowing how supervisor feels toward employee
(11) Shift assignments

Off-the-job problems might have to do with:
(1) Health   (2) Finances   (3) Housing   (4) Family

26. THE SUPERVISOR'S KEY TO DISCIPLINE
There are several key points about discipline which the supervisor should keep in mind:
  (1) Job discipline is one of the disciplines of life and is directed by the supervisor.
  (2) It is more important to correct an employee fault than to fix blame for it.
  (3) Employee performance is affected by problems both on the job and off.
  (4) Sudden or abrupt changes in behavior can be indications of important employee problems.
  (5) Problems should be dealt with as soon as possible after they are identified.
  (6) The attitude of the supervisor may have more to do with solving problems than the techniques of problem solving.
  (7) Correction of employee behavior should be resorted to only after the supervisor is sure that training or counseling will not be helpful.
  (8) Be sure to document your disciplinary actions.
  (9) Make sure that you are disciplining on the basis of facts rather than personal feelings.
  (10) Take each disciplinary step in order, being careful not to make snap judgments, or decisions based on impatience.

27. FIVE IMPORTANT PROCESSES OF MANAGEMENT
  (1) Planning   (2) Organizing   (3) Scheduling
  (4) Controlling   (5) Motivating

28. WHEN THE SUPERVISOR FAILS TO PLAN
  (1) Supervisor creates impression of not knowing his job
  (2) May lead to excessive overtime
  (3) Job runs itself -- supervisor lacks control
  (4) Deadlines and appointments missed
  (5) Parts of the work go undone
  (6) Work interrupted by emergencies
  (7) Sets a bad example
  (8) Uneven workload creates peaks and valleys
  (9) Too much time on minor details at expense of more important tasks

29. FOURTEEN GENERAL PRINCIPLES OF MANAGEMENT
  (1) Division of work
  (2) Authority and responsibility
  (3) Discipline
  (4) Unity of command
  (5) Unity of direction
  (6) Subordination of individual interest to general interest
  (7) Remuneration of personnel
  (8) Centralization
  (9) Scalar chain
  (10) Order
  (11) Equity
  (12) Stability of tenure of personnel
  (13) Initiative
  (14) Esprit de corps

30. CHANGE
Bringing about change is perhaps attempted more often, and yet less well understood, than anything else the supervisor does. How do people generally react to change? (People tend to resist change that is imposed upon them by other individuals or circumstances.

Change is characteristic of every situation. It is a part of every real endeavor where the efforts of people are concerned.

A. Why do people resist change?
   People may resist change because of:
   (1) Fear of the unknown
   (2) Implied criticism
   (3) Unpleasant experiences in the past
   (4) Fear of loss of status
   (5) Threat to the ego
   (6) Fear of loss of economic stability

B. How can we best overcome the resistance to change?
   In initiating change, take these steps:
   (1) Get ready to sell
   (2) Identify sources of help
   (3) Anticipate objections
   (4) Sell benefits
   (5) Listen in depth
   (6) Follow up

B. BRIEF TOPICAL SUMMARIES

I. WHO/WHAT IS THE SUPERVISOR?
1. The supervisor is often called the "highest level employee and the lowest level manager."
2. A supervisor is a member of both management and the work group. He acts as a bridge between the two.
3. Most problems in supervision are in the area of human relations, or people problems.
4. Employees expect: Respect, opportunity to learn and to advance, and a sense of belonging, and so forth.
5. Supervisors are responsible for directing people and organizing work. Planning is of paramount importance.
6. A position description is a set of duties and responsibilities inherent to a given position.
7. It is important to keep the position description up-to-date and to provide each employee with his own copy.

II. THE SOCIOLOGY OF WORK
1. People are alike in many ways; however, each individual is unique.
2. The supervisor is challenged in getting to know employee differences. Acquiring skills in evaluating individuals is an asset.
3. Maintaining meaningful working relationships in the organization is of great importance.
4. The supervisor has an obligation to help individuals to develop to their fullest potential.
5. Job rotation on a planned basis helps to build versatility and to maintain interest and enthusiasm in work groups.
6. Cross training (job rotation) provides backup skills.
7. The supervisor can help reduce tension by maintaining a sense of humor, providing guidance to employees, and by making reasonable and timely decisions. Employees respond favorably to working under reasonably predictable circumstances.
8. Change is characteristic of all managerial behavior. The supervisor must adjust to changes in procedures, new methods, technological changes, and to a number of new and sometimes challenging situations.
9. To overcome the natural tendency for people to resist change, the supervisor should become more skillful in initiating change.

III. PRINCIPLES AND PRACTICES OF SUPERVISION
1. Employees should be required to answer to only one superior.
2. A supervisor can effectively direct only a limited number of employees, depending upon the complexity, variety, and proximity of the jobs involved.
3. The organizational chart presents the organization in graphic form. It reflects lines of authority and responsibility as well as interrelationships of units within the organization.
4. Distribution of work can be improved through an analysis using the "Work Distribution Chart."
5. The "Work Distribution Chart" reflects the division of work within a unit in understandable form.
6. When related tasks are given to an employee, he has a better chance of increasing his skills through training.
7. The individual who is given the responsibility for tasks must also be given the appropriate authority to insure adequate results.
8. The supervisor should delegate repetitive, routine work. Preparation of recurring reports, maintaining leave and attendance records are some examples.
9. Good discipline is essential to good task performance. Discipline is reflected in the actions of employees on the job in the absence of supervision.
10. Disciplinary action may have to be taken when the positive aspects of discipline have failed. Reprimand, warning, and suspension are examples of disciplinary action.
11. If a situation calls for a reprimand, be sure it is deserved and remember it is to be done in private.

IV. DYNAMIC LEADERSHIP
1. A style is a personal method or manner of exerting influence.
2. Authoritarian leaders often see themselves as the source of power and authority.
3. The democratic leader often perceives the group as the source of authority and power.
4. Supervisors tend to do better when using the pattern of leadership that is most natural for them.
5. Social scientists suggest that the effective supervisor use the leadership style that best fits the problem or circumstances involved.
6. All four styles -- telling, selling, consulting, joining -- have their place. Using one does not preclude using the other at another time.
7. The theory X point of view assumes that the average person dislikes work, will avoid it whenever possible, and must be coerced to achieve organizational objectives.
8. The theory Y point of view assumes that the average person considers work to be as natural as play, and, when the individual is committed, he requires little supervision or direction to accomplish desired objectives.
9. The leader's basic assumptions concerning human behavior and human nature affect his actions, decisions, and other managerial practices.
10. Dissatisfaction among employees is often present, but difficult to isolate. The supervisor should seek to weaken dissatisfaction by keeping promises, being sincere and considerate, keeping employees informed, and so forth.
11. Constructive suggestions should be encouraged during the natural progress of the work.

V. PROCESSES FOR SOLVING PROBLEMS
1. People find their daily tasks more meaningful and satisfying when they can improve them.
2. The causes of problems, or the key factors, are often hidden in the background. Ability to solve problems often involves the ability to isolate them from their backgrounds. There is some substance to the cliché that some persons "can't see the forest for the trees."
3. New procedures are often developed from old ones. Problems should be broken down into manageable parts. New ideas can be adapted from old ones.

4. People think differently in problem-solving situations. Using a logical, patterned approach is often useful. One approach found to be useful includes these steps:
    (a) Define the problem
    (b) Establish objectives
    (c) Get the facts
    (d) Weigh and decide
    (e) Take action
    (f) Evaluate action

VI. TRAINING FOR RESULTS

1. Participants respond best when they feel training is important to them.
2. The supervisor has responsibility for the training and development of those who report to him.
3. When training is delegated to others, great care must be exercised to insure the trainer has knowledge, aptitude, and interest for his work as a trainer.
4. Training (learning) of some type goes on continually. The most successful supervisor makes certain the learning contributes in a productive manner to operational goals.
5. New employees are particularly susceptible to training. Older employees facing new job situations require specific training, as well as having need for development and growth opportunities.
6. Training needs require continuous monitoring.
7. The training officer of an agency is a professional with a responsibility to assist supervisors in solving training problems.
8. Many of the self-development steps important to the supervisor's own growth are equally important to the development of peers and subordinates. Knowledge of these is important when the supervisor consults with others on development and growth opportunities.

VII. HEALTH, SAFETY, AND ACCIDENT PREVENTION

1. Management-minded supervisors take appropriate measures to assist employees in maintaining health and in assuring safe practices in the work environment.
2. Effective safety training and practices help to avoid injury and accidents.
3. Safety should be a management goal. All infractions of safety which are observed should be corrected without exception.
4. Employees' safety attitude, training and instruction, provision of safe tools and equipment, supervision, and leadership are considered highly important factors which contribute to safety and which can be influenced directly by supervisors.
5. When accidents do occur they should be investigated promptly for very important reasons, including the fact that information which is gained can be used to prevent accidents in the future.

VIII. EQUAL EMPLOYMENT OPPORTUNITY

1. The supervisor should endeavor to treat all employees fairly, without regard to religion, race, sex, or national origin.
2. Groups tend to reflect the attitude of the leader. Prejudice can be detected even in very subtle form. Supervisors must strive to create a feeling of mutual respect and confidence in every employee.
3. Complete utilization of all human resources is a national goal. Equitable consideration should be accorded women in the work force, minority-group members, the physically and mentally handicapped, and the older employee. The important question is: "Who can do the job?"
4. Training opportunities, recognition for performance, overtime assignments, promotional opportunities, and all other personnel actions are to be handled on an equitable basis.

IX. IMPROVING COMMUNICATIONS

1. Communications is achieving understanding between the sender and the receiver of a message. It also means sharing information -- the creation of understanding.
2. Communication is basic to all human activity. Words are means of conveying meanings; however, real meanings are in people.
3. There are very practical differences in the effectiveness of one-way, impersonal, and two-way communications. Words spoken face-to-face are better understood. Telephone conversations are effective, but lack the rapport of person-to-person exchanges. The whole person communicates.
4. Cooperation and communication in an organization go hand in hand. When there is a mutual respect between people, spelling out rules and procedures for communicating is unnecessary.
5. There are several barriers to effective communications. These include failure to listen with respect and understanding, lack of skill in feedback, and misinterpreting the meanings of words used by the speaker. It is also common practice to listen to what we want to hear, and tune out things we do not want to hear.
6. Communication is management's chief problem. The supervisor should accept the challenge to communicate more effectively and to improve interagency and intra-agency communications.
7. The supervisor may often plan for and conduct meetings. The planning phase is critical and may determine the success or the failure of a meeting.
8. Speaking before groups usually requires extra effort. Stage fright may never disappear completely, but it can be controlled.

X. SELF-DEVELOPMENT

1. Every employee is responsible for his own self-development.
2. Toastmaster and toastmistress clubs offer opportunities to improve skills in oral communications.
3. Planning for one's own self-development is of vital importance. Supervisors know their own strengths and limitations better than anyone else.
4. Many opportunities are open to aid the supervisor in his developmental efforts, including job assignments; training opportunities, both governmental and non-governmental -- to include universities and professional conferences and seminars.
5. Programmed instruction offers a means of studying at one's own rate.
6. Where difficulties may arise from a supervisor's being away from his work for training, he may participate in televised home study or correspondence courses to meet his self-develop- ment needs.

XI. TEACHING AND TRAINING

A. The Teaching Process

Teaching is encouraging and guiding the learning activities of students toward established goals. In most cases this process consists in five steps: preparation, presentation, summarization, evaluation, and application.

1. Preparation

Preparation is twofold in nature; that of the supervisor and the employee.
Preparation by the supervisor is absolutely essential to success. He must know what, when, where, how, and whom he will teach. Some of the factors that should be considered are:

(1) The objectives
(2) The materials needed
(3) The methods to be used
(4) Employee participation
(5) Employee interest
(6) Training aids
(7) Evaluation
(8) Summarization

Employee preparation consists in preparing the employee to receive the material. Probably the most important single factor in the preparation of the employee is arousing and maintaining his interest. He must know the objectives of the training, why he is there, how the material can be used, and its importance to him.

2. Presentation

In presentation, have a carefully designed plan and follow it.
The plan should be accurate and complete, yet flexible enough to meet situations as they arise. The method of presentation will be determined by the particular situation and objectives.

3. Summary

A summary should be made at the end of every training unit and program. In addition, there may be internal summaries depending on the nature of the material being taught. The important thing is that the trainee must always be able to understand how each part of the new material relates to the whole.

4. Application

The supervisor must arrange work so the employee will be given a chance to apply new knowledge or skills while the material is still clear in his mind and interest is high. The trainee does not really know whether he has learned the material until he has been given a chance to apply it. If the material is not applied, it loses most of its value.

5. Evaluation

The purpose of all training is to promote learning. To determine whether the training has been a success or failure, the supervisor must evaluate this learning.
In the broadest sense evaluation includes all the devices, methods, skills, and techniques used by the supervisor to keep him self and the employees informed as to their progress toward the objectives they are pursuing. The extent to which the employee has mastered the knowledge, skills, and abilities, or changed his attitudes, as determined by the program objectives, is the extent to which instruction has succeeded or failed.
Evaluation should not be confined to the end of the lesson, day, or program but should be used continuously. We shall note later the way this relates to the rest of the teaching process.

B. Teaching Methods

A teaching method is a pattern of identifiable student and instructor activity used in presenting training material.
All supervisors are faced with the problem of deciding which method should be used at a given time.
As with all methods, there are certain advantages and disadvantages to each method.

1. Lecture

The lecture is direct oral presentation of material by the supervisor. The present trend is to place less emphasis on the trainer's activity and more on that of the trainee.

2. Discussion

Teaching by discussion or conference involves using questions and other techniques to arouse interest and focus attention upon certain areas, and by doing so creating a learning situation. This can be one of the most valuable methods because it gives the employees 'an opportunity to express their ideas and pool their knowledge.

3. Demonstration

The demonstration is used to teach how something works or how to do something. It can be used to show a principle or what the results of a series of actions will be. A well-staged demonstration is particularly effective because it shows proper methods of performance in a realistic manner.

4. Performance

Performance is one of the most fundamental of all learning techniques or teaching methods. The trainee may be able to tell how a specific operation should be performed but he cannot be sure he knows how to perform the operation until he has done so.

5. Which Method to Use

Moreover, there are other methods and techniques of teaching. It is difficult to use any method without other methods entering into it. In any learning situation a combination of methods is usually more effective than anyone method alone.

Finally, evaluation must be integrated into the other aspects of the teaching-learning process.

It must be used in the motivation of the trainees; it must be used to assist in developing understanding during the training; and it must be related to employee application of the results of training.

This is distinctly the role of the supervisor.

BASIC FUNDAMENTALS OF LIBRARY SCIENCE

TABLE OF CONTENTS

	Page
DEWEY DECIMAL SYSTEM	1
PREPARING TO USE THE LIBRARY	1
THREE TYPES OF BOOK CARDS	2
Author Card	2
Title Card	2
Subject Card	3
Call Number	3
PERIODICALS	3
PERIODICALS FILE	3
PERIODICAL INDEXES	3
TEST IN LIBRARY SCIENCE	4
I. Using a Card Catalog	4
II. Understanding Entries in a Periodical Index	5
III. Identifying Library Terms	7
IV. Finding a Book by its Call Number	7
V. General	9
KEY (CORRECT ANSWERS)	10

BASIC FUNDAMENTALS OF LIBRARY SCIENCE

The problem of classifying' all human knowledge has produced a branch of learning called "library science." A lasting contribution to a simple and understandable method of locating a book on any topic was designed by Melvil Dewey in 1876. His plan divided all knowledge into ten large classes and then dubdivided each class according to related groups.

DEWEY DECIMAL SYSTEM

1. Subject Classification

The Dewey Decimal Classification System is the accepted and most widely used subject classification system in libraries throughout the world.

2. Classification by Three (3) Groups

There are three groups of classification in the system. A basic group of ten (10) classifications arranges all knowledge as represented by books within groups by classifications numbered 000-900.

The second group is the "100 division"; each group of the basic "10 divisions" is again divided into 9 sub-sctions allowing for more detailed and specialized subjects not identified in the 10 basic divisions.

3. There is a third, still further specialized "One thousand" group where each of the "100" classifications are further divided by decimalized, more specified, subject classifications. The "1,000" group is mainly used by highly specialized scientific and much diversified libraries.

These are the subject classes of the Dewey System:

000-099   General works (included bibliography, encyclopedias, collections, periodicals, newspapers,etc.)

100-199   Philosophy (includes psychology, logic, ethics, conduct, etc.) 200-299 Religion (includes mythology, natural theology, Bible, church history, etc.)

300-399   Social Science (includes economics, government, law, education, commerce, etc.)

400-499   Language (includes dictionaries, grammars, philology, etc.) 500-599 Science (includes mathematics, chemistry, physics, astronomy, geology, etc.) 600-699 Useful Arts (includes agriculture, engineering, aviation, medicine, manufactures, etc.) 700-799 Fine Arts (includes sculpture, painting, music, photography, gardening, etc.)

800-899   Literature (includes poetry, plays, orations, etc.) 900-999 History (includes geoegraphy, travel, biography, ancient and modern history, etc.)

PREPARING TO USE THE LIBRARY

Your ability to use the library and its resources is an important factor in determining your success. Skill and efficiency in finding the library materials you need for assignments and research papers will increase the amount of time you have to devote to reading or organizing information.

These are some of the preparations you can make now.
1. Develop skill in using your local library. You can increase your familiarity with the card catalog and the periodical indexes, such as the *Readers' Guide to Periodical Literature,* in any library.
2. Take the *Test in Library Science* to see how you can improve your knowledge of the library.
3. Read in such books as *Books, Libraries and You* by Jessie Edna Boyd, *The Library Key* by Margaret G.Cook, and *Making Books Work, a Guide to the Use of Libraries* by Jennie Maas Flexner.

You can find other titles by looking under the subject heading LIBRARIES AND READERS in the card catalog of your library. THREE TYPES OF BOOK CARDS

Here are the three general types of cards which are used to represent a book in the main catalog.

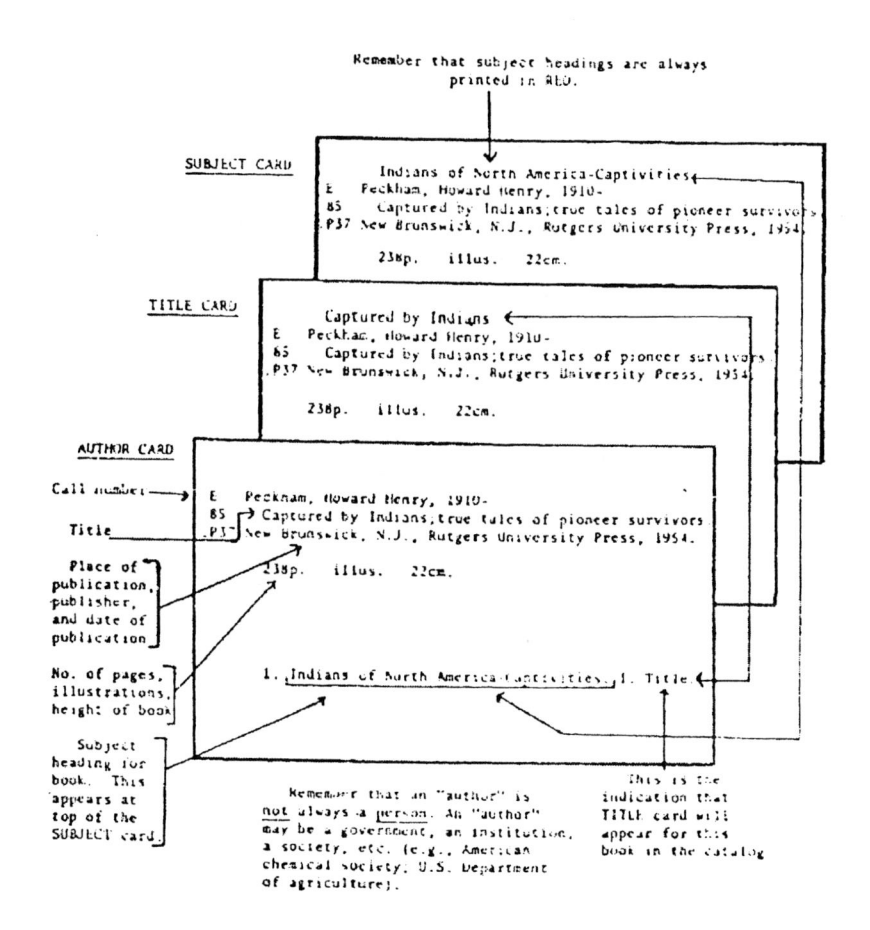

CARD CATALOG

The Card Catalog lists all books in the library by author. The majority of books also have title and subject cards.

Author card

If the author is known, look in the catalog under the author's name. The "author" for some works may be a society, an institution, or a government department.

Title card

Books with distinctive titles, anonymous works and periodicals will have a title card.

Subject card
To find books on a specific subject, look in the catalog under that subject heading. (Subject headings are printed in red on the Catalog Card.)

Call number
The letters and numbers in the upper left-hand corner of the Catalog Card are the book's call number. Copy this call number accurately, for it will determine the shelf location of the book. The word "Reference" marked in red in the upper right-hand corner of the catalog card indicates that the item is shelved in the Reference Section, and "Periodical" marked in yellow on the Catalog Card indicates that the item is shelved in the Periodicals Section. PERIODICALS

All magazines are arranged in alphabetical order by title. PERIODICALS FILE
To determine whether the Library has a specific magazine, consult the Periodicals File. Check the title of the magazine needed, and note that there are two cards for each title.

The bottom card lists the current issues available. The top card lists back bound volumes.

Those marked "Ask at Ref.Desk" may be obtained from the Reference Librarian. PERIODICAL INDEXES

Material in magazines is more up-to-date than books and is a valuable source of information. To find articles on a chosen subject, use the periodical indexes.

The Readers' Guide to Periodical Literature is the most familiar of these indexes. In the front of each volume is a list of the periodicals indexed and a key to abbreviations. Similar aids appear in the front of other periodical indexes.

Sample entry: WEASELS

     WONDERFUL WHITE WEASEL. R.Beck. il OUTDOOR LIFE 135:48-9+
  Ja '65

Explanation :   An illustrated article on the subject WEASELS entitled WONDERFUL WHITE WEASEL, by R.Beck, will be found in volume 135 of OUTDOOR LIFE, pages 48-9 (continued on later pages of the same issue), the January 1965 number.

Major libraries subscribe to the following indexes:
- Art Index
- Biography Index
- Book Review Index
- British Humanities Index
- Essay and General Literature Index
    This is helpful for locating criticism of works of literature.
- An Index to Book Reviews in the Humanities
- International Index ceased publications June, 1965 and continued as Social Science and Humanities Index
- The Music Index The New York
- Times Index Nineteenth Century Readers' Guide
- Poole's Index
- Poverty and Human Resources Abstracts
- Psychological Abstracts
- Public Affairs Information Service.Bulletin of the (PAIS) is a subject index to current books, pamphlets, periodical articles, government documents, and other library materials in economics and public affairs.

<u>Readers' Guide to Periodical Literature</u>
<u>Social Science and Humanities Index a continuation of the International Index</u>
<u>Sociological Abstracts</u>

Do you have the basic skills for using a library efficiently? You should be able to answer AT LEAST 33 of the following questions correctly. *CHECK YOUR ANSWERS BY TURNING TO THE ANSWER KEY AT THE BACK OF THIS SECTION.*
USING A CARD CATALOG
Questions 1-9.

DIRECTIONS: An author card (or "main entry" card) is shown below. Identify each item on the card by selecting the CORRECT letters for them. *PRINT THE LETTER OF THE CORRECT ANSWER IN THE SPACE AT THE RIGHT.*

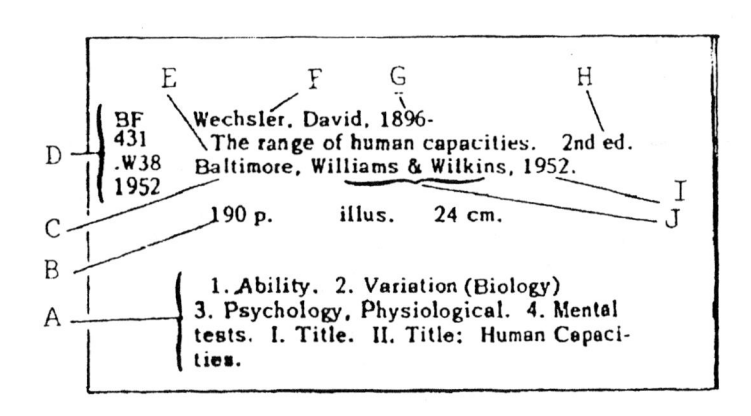

```
           E        F       G              H
        BF    \Wechsler, David, 1896-
        431    \The range of human capacities.  2nd ed.
    D ─┤.W38    Baltimore, Williams & Wilkins, 1952.
        1952                                             I
                                                         
    C ──────  190 p.     illus.    24 cm.         ─── J
                                                         
    B ──────
              1. Ability.  2. Variation (Biology)
    A ──────  3. Psychology, Physiological.  4. Mental
              tests.  I. Title.  II. Title: Human Capaci-
              ties.
```

Sample Answer:

0. <u>F</u>

1. Date book was published.   1.____

2. Number of pages in book.   2.____

3. Title.   3.____

4. Place of publication.   4.____

5. Call number.   5.____

6. Year author was born   6.____

7. Edition.   7.____

8. Publisher.   8.____

9. Other headings under which cards for this book may be found.   9.____

Questions 10-13.

DIRECTIONS: Select the letter preceding the word or phrase which completes each of the following statements correctly.

10. The library's title card for the book THE LATE GEORGE APLEY can be found by looking in the card catalog under

    A. Apley, George   B. The   C. Late   D. George   E. Apley

11. A catalog card for a book by John F. Kennedy would be found in the drawer labelled

    A. JEFFERSON-JOHNSON,ROY
    B. PRESCOTT-PRICELESS
    C. KIERNAN-KLAY
    D. U.S.PRESIDENT-U.S.SOCIAL SECURITY
    E. KENNEBEC-KIERKEGAARD

12. The title cards for these three periodicals would be found in the card catalog arranged in which of the following orders:

    A. NEW YORKER, NEWSWEEK, NEW YORK TIMES MAGAZINE
    B. NEWSWEEK, NEW YORKER, NEW YORK TIMES MAGAZINE
    C. NEW YORK TIMES MAGAZINE, NEW YORKER, NEWSWEEK
    D. NEW YORKER, NEW YORK TIMES MAGAZINE, NEWSWEEK
    E. NEWSWEEK, NEW YORK TIMES MAGAZINE, NEW YORKER

13. A card for a copy of the U.N.Charter would be found in the catalog drawer marked

    A. TWENTIETH-UNAMUNO
    B. UNITED MINE WORKERS-UNITED SHOE MACHINERY
    C. U.S.BUREAU-U.S. CONGRESS
    D. U.S.SOCIAL POLICY-UNIVERSITAS
    E. CHANCEL-CIARDI

II. UNDERSTANDING ENTRIES IN A PERIODICAL INDEX

Questions 14-25.

DIRECTIONS: The following items are excerpts from THE READERS' GUIDE TO PERIODICAL LITERATURE. Identify each lettered section of the entries by placing the correct letters in the spaces.(There are more letters than spaces, so some of the letters will not be used.)

```
A ─── UNITED NATIONS                V                     H ─────── Security Council
         Ambassador Goldberg holds news conference at            Security Council urged to respond to
         New York; transcript of conference.                     challenge in southeast Asia; letter,
   B ──── July 28, 1965; with questions and answers.  ── U   M ── July 30, 1965. A. J. Goldberg. Dept
         A. J. Goldberg. Dept. State Bul 53:272+                 State Bul 53:278-80+  Ag 16, '65
   C ─────  Ag 16 '65                            ─────── T          │    │    │  │
         U.N. out of its teens. I.D. Talmadge. il Sr Schol ── S      L     •I   J   K
   E ──── 87:16-17+  S 16 '65
   D ──── Whatever became of the United Nations? ──────── Q
         America 113:235│ S 4 '65
         F    R
                         Charter ─────────────────────── P
         Up-dating the pre-atomic United Nations; address,
         June 20, 1965. C.P. Romulo. Vital Speeches
         31:658-61 Ag 15 '65; Excerpts. Sat R 48:34-5+
         Jl 24 '65. ──────── N                        ── O
                                     G
```

14. Title of magazine containing a transcript of a news con-conference held by U.N. Ambassador Arthur Goldberg. 14._____

15. Magazine in which the full text of C.P. Romulo's address on the U.N. appears. 15._____

16. Author of an article titled U.N. OUT OF ITS TEENS. 16._____

17. Date on which Ambassador Goldberg wrote a letter urging the Security Council to respond to the challenge of southeast Asia. 17._____

18. Title of an article for which no author is listed. 18._____

19. Date of the SATURDAY REVIEW issue which contains excerptsl of a speech called "Up-Dating the Pre-Atomic United Nations." 19._____

20. Pages in the DEPARTMENT OF STATE BULLETIN on which Ambassador Goldberg's letter appears. 20._____

21. Symbol indicating that the letter is continued on a later page. 21._____

22. Volume number of the magazine in which the article by I.D. Talmadge is printed. 22._____

23. Symbols meaning September 16, 1965. 23._____

24. The general subject heading under which all five articles are listed. 24._____

25. A subject heading subdivision. 25._____

Questions 26-27.

DIRECTIONS: Select the letter preceding the phrase which completes each of the following statements correctly.

26. To determine whether or not the library has THE MAGAZINE OF AMERICAN HISTORY, check in 26._____

   A. the list of magazine titles in the front of THE READERS' GUIDE TO PERIODICAL LITERATURE
   B. the library's card catalog

C. Ulrich's GUIDE TO PERIODICALS
D. SATURDAY REVIEW
E. THE LIBRARY JOURNAL

27. THE READERS' GUIDE is a good place to look for material on the Job Corps because it 27.___

    A. indexes only the best books and magazines in each field
    B. is a guide to articles on many subjects appearing in all of the library's periodicals
    C. indexes recent discussions on the subject in many magazines
    D. specializes in official government information
    E. does all of the above

III. IDENTIFYING LIBRARY TERMS

Questions 28-32.

DIRECTIONS: Match the correct definitions with these terms by placing the correct letters in the blanks. (Some of the letters will not be used.)

28. Bibliography

    A. Word or phrase printed in A. Word or phrase printed in log to indicate the major log to indicate the major   28.___

29. Anthology

    B. Brief written summary of the major ideas presented in an article or book   29.___

30. Index

    C. List of books and/or articles on one subject or by one author   30.___

31. Abstract

    D. Collection of selections from the writings of one or several authors   31.___

32. Subject heading

    E. Written account of a person's life   32.___

    F. Alphabetical list of subjects with the pages on which they are to be found in a book or periodical

    G. Subordinate, usually explanatory title, additional to the main title and usually printed below it

IV. FINDING A BOOK BY ITS CALL NUMBER

Questions 33-38.

DIRECTIONS: The Library of Congress classification system call numbers shown below are arranged in order, just as the books bearing those call numbers would be arranged on the shelves. To show where other call numbers would be located, select the letter of the CORRECT ANSWER.

A.	B.	C.	D.	E.	F.	G.	H.	I.	J.	K.
PS 201 .L67 1961	PS 201 .M44	PS 208 .B87 1944	PS 351 .D7	PS 351 .D77	PS 3513 .A2	PS 3515 .D72	PS 3515.3 A66	PS 3526 .N21	PS 3526.17 P2	PS 3526.37 A10

	L.	M.	N.
	PS 3526.37 C20	PS 3526.37 C37	PT 1 .R2

33. A book with the call number PS
     201
     .L67
 would be shelved

 A. Before A   B. Between A & B   C. Between B & C
 D. Between C & D E. Between D & E

34. A book with the call number PS
     208
     .B87
     1944a
 would be shelved

 A. Between A & B B. Between C & D C. Between B & C
 D. Between C & D E. Between D & E

35. A book with the call number PS
     351
     D8
 would be shelved

 A. Between C & D B. Between D & E C. Between E & F
 D. Between F & G E. Between G & H

36. A book with the call number PS
     3526.3
     M53
 would be shelved

 A. Between L & M B. Between J & K C. Between K & L
 D. Between M & 0 E. Between 0 & P

37. A book with the call number PS
     3526.37
     C205
 would be shelved

 A. Between L & M B. Between N & 0 C. Between M & N
 D. Between 0 & P E. Between P & Q

38. A book with the call number PS
     3526.37
     C3
 would be shelved

 A. Between M & N B. Between L & M C. Between N & 0
 D. Between *0 & P* E. Between P & Q

V. General

Questions 39-40.

DIRECTIONS: Each question or incomplete statement is followed by several suggested answers or completions. Select the one that BEST answers the question or completes the statement. *PRINT THE LETTER OF THE CORRECT ANSWER IN TEE SPACE AT THE RIGHT.*

39. When it is finished (in 610 volumes), the _____ will be the MOST monumental national bibliography in the world.   39.___

    A. UNION LIST OF SERIALS IN LIBRARIES OF THE UNITED STATES AND CANADA
    B. UNITED STATES CATALOG
    C. READERS' GUIDE TO PERIODICAL LITERATURE
    D. NATIONAL UNION CATALOG

40. For those who wish to investigate the publishing companies and the people who control them, to locate the date a company was founded, who owned it, when it changed hands, what firm succeeded it, and other information of a similar nature, the periodical _____ is clearly invaluable.   40.___

    A. PUBLISHERS' TRADE LIST ANNUAL (PTLA)
    B. CUMULATIVE BOOK INDEX
    C. AMERICAN BOOKTRADE DIRECTORY
    D. PUBLISHERS WEEKLY

KEY (CORRECT ANSWERS)

1. I
2. B
3. E
4. C
5. D
6. G
7. H
8. J
9. A
10. C - The first word of the title which is not an article.
11. E - Every book in the library is listed in the card catalog under the author's name. (Warning: The "author" may be a society, a university, or some other institution.)
12. C - A title is alphabetized word-by-word; therefore, "New" comes before "Newsweek," "New York" before "New Yorker."
13. B - The United Nations, not an individual, is the author of this work.
14. T 16. Q 18. D 20. J 22. E 24. A 26. B 28. C 30. F 32. A
15. O 17. M 19. N 21. K 23. R 25. P/H 27. C 29. D 31. B
33. A - When two call numbers are identical except that one has a year or some other figure added at its end, the shorter call numbers comes first.
34. B
35. C - The numbers which follow a. are regarded as decimals; therefore, .D77 precedes .D8.
36. B - 3526.3 precedes 3526.37
37. A - .C20 precedes .C205
38. B - .C3 precedes .C37 (Read the call number line-by-line, and put a J before a P, before a PB, etc. Put a lower number before a greater one.)
39. D
40. D

ANSWER SHEET

TEST NO. _____ PART _____ TITLE OF POSITION _____
(AS GIVEN IN EXAMINATION ANNOUNCEMENT - INCLUDE OPTION, IF ANY)

PLACE OF EXAMINATION _____ _____ DATE _____
(CITY OR TOWN) (STATE)

RATING

USE THE SPECIAL PENCIL. MAKE GLOSSY BLACK MARKS.

Make only ONE mark for each answer. Additional and stray marks may be counted as mistakes. In making corrections, erase errors COMPLETELY.

ANSWER SHEET

TEST NO. _____ PART _____ TITLE OF POSITION _____
(AS GIVEN IN EXAMINATION ANNOUNCEMENT - INCLUDE OPTION, IF ANY)

PLACE OF EXAMINATION _____ DATE _____
(CITY OR TOWN)   (STATE)

RATING

USE THE SPECIAL PENCIL. MAKE GLOSSY BLACK MARKS.

Make only ONE mark for each answer. Additional and stray marks may be counted as mistakes. In making corrections, erase errors COMPLETELY.

TWO WEEK LOAN
CLIFTON PARK-HALFMOON PUBLIC LIBRARY, NY
0 00 06 04289694